TROUBLED PLEASURES:
THE FICTION OF J.G. FARRELL

Troubled Pleasures

THE FICTION OF
J.G. FARRELL

Ralph J. Crane & Jennifer Livett

FOUR COURTS PRESS

Set in 10 on 13 point Janson Text for
FOUR COURTS PRESS
Fumbally Lane, Dublin 8, Ireland
Email: info@four-courts-press.ie
and in North America for
FOUR COURTS PRESS
c/o ISBS, 5804 N.E. Hassalo Street, Portland, OR 97213.

A catalogue record for this title
is available from the British Library.

ISBN 1–85182–310–7

This book is printed on an acid-free and a wood-free paper.

Printed in Great Britain
by Hartnolls Ltd, Bodmin, Cornwall

For our families
Joy, Callum, and Rhiannon
Brian, Kate, and David

Contents

Preface

Ralph Crane would like to thank the University of Waikato for support in the form of a UWRC grant, and for a period of study leave in 1996 which enabled him to spend three months as a Visiting Research Fellow at the University of Tasmania and later to consult the Farrell manuscript collection held in the Trinity College Library, Dublin.

Jennifer Livett would like to thank the Australian Research Council for a grant in 1995 which enabled her to consult the Farrell holdings at Trinity College Dublin.

Both authors would like to thank Mrs Prudence Farrell and the Board of Trinity College Dublin for permission to quote from the Papers of James Gordon Farrell (1935–79), Trinity College Dublin.

I am deeply interested in trying to write universal as opposed to regional novels, the sort of books in which people trying to adjust themselves to abrupt changes in their civilization whether it be in Ireland or Japan may be able to recognise themselves.

J.G. Farrell

Introduction

By a general concensus of readers and critics the novels which represent J.G. Farrell's best writing are *Troubles* (1970), *The Siege of Krishnapur* (1973), and *The Singapore Grip* (1978), the so-called 'Empire Trilogy'. These fictions, the last three of six novels Farrell published during his lifetime, are linked by their subject matter, though not directly by plot: they present three different aspects of the decline and fall of the British Empire. In *Troubles* Farrell deals with the period of Irish history from 1919 to 1920; in *The Siege of Krishnapur* with the so-called Indian Mutiny of 1857; and in *The Singapore Grip* with the fall of Singapore to the Japanese during the Second World War. This historical subject matter and Farrell's extraordinary style of ironic black comedy won him several major literary prizes and an enthusiastic general readership in the first years of pub-lication. Paradoxically, both subject-matter and style, although they continued to be admired by 'common readers', became a source of unease for academic commentators during the decade of the 1980s and led to a devaluing of his work.

Critics writing immediately after Farrell's untimely death in 1979 spoke with confidence about his standing among his own generation. Their hesitancy was only about whether he had reached the height of his powers or written enough to gain permanent literary status. In his obituary for the *Sunday Telegraph* Francis King claimed that '[a]t a time when a panorama of the modern English novel resembles a plateau, he promised to be a mountain'.[1] Derek Mahon, in the *New Statesman*, wrote in a similar vein: 'marvellous as the "Empire Trilogy" is, it was only the beginning of something. ... He measured himself, I suspect, against the giants of modern literature; and, given the time, he might have joined them'.[2] John Spurling was less inclined to equivocate: 'I believe he was one of the two or three best English novelists of his generation'.[3] Yet there followed a critical eclipse for Farrell which is indicated by the references to his work in several excellent surveys of the twentieth-century English novel, and the absence of any references in others. Although Farrell is mentioned in three of the eight essays collected in Malcolm Bradbury's and David Palmer's *The Contemporary English Novel* (1979) the comments are either brief, or, as in Bernard Bergonzi's longer and more interested treatment, there is a sense of puzzlement about Farrell's intentions and achievement.[4] Martin Green in his two-volume study *Dreams of Adventure, Deeds of Empire* (1980) and *The English Novel in the Twentieth Century: The Doom of Empire* (1984) makes no mention of Farrell even in the section 'Ex-Imperial England'. Patrick Swinden in *The*

English Novel of History and Society, 1940–80 (1984) deals with Farrell in two sentences (and only then via Richard Hughes),[5] while Randall Stevenson, in his impressive study *The British Novel since the Thirties* (1986) places him in the company of three 'popular' writers: Ian Fleming, Paul Scott, and Julian Mitchell. It is only in more recent surveys that the obscuration finally passes. Malcolm Bradbury in *The Modern British Novel* (1993) acknowledges the interest of Farrell's three novels published in the 1960s, and refers to the novels which comprise the later trilogy as 'works of contemporary consciousness as well as large-scale historical re-creation ... , works of elaborate form and complex metaphor as well as descriptive writing'.[6]

Farrell's reputation was largely kept alive in this period by Ronald Binns's excellent book *J.G. Farrell* (1986). Binns puts a persuasive case for Farrell, comprehensive and full of critical insight, thus making it inevitable that any new account of Farrell must be indebted to him; but Binns and the authors of a handful of book chapters and journal articles on Farrell remained fairly lonely voices until the early 1990s. Neil McEwan is notable among these for the substantial chapter on the Empire trilogy in his study of the historical novel, *Perspective in British Historical Fiction Today* (1987). Linda Hutcheon's *A Poetics of Postmodernism: History, Theory, Fiction* (1988), specifically oriented towards professional academic readers, assesses a plethora of novels from the 1960s to the late 1980s, but does not mention Farrell.

Hutcheon's omission is particularly interesting because her searching discussion of postmodern fiction pays detailed attention to the large number of postmodern novels she terms 'historiographic metafictions', a group to which Farrell's novels would surely belong. Her examination of the differences between nineteenth-century historical fiction and postmodern historical fiction clearly reveals (by implication) some of the reasons why Farrell's work seemed by some critical judgement to belong to the earlier rather than the later category. Using Georg Lukács's theory of character 'types' from his study *The Historical Novel* (1962), a book much admired by Farrell, Hutcheon's first point is that

> the protagonists of historiographic metafiction are anything but proper types: they are the ex-centrics, the marginalized, the peripheral figures of fictional history – the Coalhouse Walkers (in *Ragtime*), the Saleem Sinais (in *Midnight's Children*), the Fevvers (in *Nights at the Circus*). ... The narrative form enacts the fact that [the protagonist] is not a type of anything, no matter how much he may try to see himself as representing the New Left or his parents' cause.[7]

Certainly this is a point at which Farrell might be thought to belong to the older school of historical writing. As several critics have noted, his central characters are all types of very English upper-middle-class males, embodying certain kinds of muddled, tolerant, liberal-humanism. This can, though, be misleading in at least two ways. It can lead to a spurious correlation between Farrell's views and those of his protagonists, and it can obscure the fact that Farrell's presentation of these 'heroes' is never simple. He is always deeply concerned with ideas of the heroic and their larger ideological consequences in Western society. He foregrounds the discursive nature of heroism in ways that, we shall argue, are very postmodern: he constructs cumulative assemblies of fictional scenes which convey dissatisfaction with social and literary ideas of the heroic as these are constructed in language and genre, while at the same time illustrating the almost irresistible temptation for individuals to think about life as narrative, using these very heroic models provided by the culture.

The second point at which Farrell appears to be 'unpostmodern', is that his incorporation of documentary reference material into the trilogy appears to make reference to 'the world', and to textual records of the world, without sufficiently recognising the problematic relations between the two, and without acknowledging that 'history' is a socially constructed discourse situated somewhere between 'world' and 'text'. The foregrounding of these complex relations became crucial to poststructuralist critical thinking and to postmodern fictional practice during the very decade in which the trilogy appeared. The reforming zeal attending the early coming of 'theory' into literary criticism during the 1970s contributed markedly to the view of Farrell as an old-fashioned 'historical novelist' with an unfashionable, humanist stance. Recent poststructuralist readings are beginning to find this view unjust.[8]

It is certainly true that, as one of his friends commented, Farrell was addicted to information.[9] One can only be staggered by the prodigious amount of primary and secondary reading he managed to cover as preliminary to writing about each of the periods he chose to deal with. Visits to the Farrell manuscript holdings at Trinity College Library in Dublin illustrate vividly Farrell's pursuit of 'the facts' of the times and places in which the trilogy is set.[10] His research covered newspapers, diaries, letters, academic and popular histories of every pursuasion, art and literature of the time, and even oral accounts. Though much admired by some,[11] his careful research (often called 'meticulous'), and his concern for 'accuracy' and 'verisimilitude', become suspect under the gaze of various kinds of poststructuralism. 'Accuracy' to what?, becomes the question. To whose version of history?, since history, while not in itself 'merely' text, can only be textually transmitted.

Farrell unquestionably does have respect for certain kinds of 'facts'. One of the reasons why he uses fictional rather than real sites in the first two novels of the trilogy – Kilnalough as a fictional promontory in County Wicklow, Krishnapur for Lucknow – is to free himself from the necessities of actual geography and 'real' history. In writing *The Singapore Grip* he was doing something 'more ambitious and more difficult':

> It is not just that Singapore cannot fall on the wrong date. I cannot, for example, even arrange the weather to suit myself although sometimes even the historians disagree. There were other dilemmas. I would have preferred, for the shape of the book, to order the Japanese into the attack a few months earlier and have delayed their advance down the peninsula. But if the book is to have any historical basis you can't do that sort of thing. Nobody would put up with it.[12]

He refuses the licence which some later postmodern novelists take to deal more subversively with history. His novels cannot be numbered among those cited by Linda Hutcheon,

> like *Foe*, *Burning Water*, or *Famous Last Words*, [in which] certain known historical details are deliberately falsified in order to foreground the possible mnemonic failures of recorded history and the constant potential for both deliberate and inadvertent error.[13]

Hutcheon defends this postmodern play 'upon the truth and lies of the historical record', though she does concede that some of the results are 'disturbing' and even 'unnerving'.[14] This is in fact, a highly contentious issue with fiercely debated implications about the ethics and politics of postmodernism. Those who distort history to show its proneness to distortion may open the way to those who wish to distort history from less altruistic motives. David Irving's denial of the holocaust, and the furore in Australia over Helen Darville-Demidenko's book about the Second World War, *The Hand that Signed the Paper* (1994), indicate that this is a point where poststructuralist theory is at its most contentious. 'Facts' are always debatable, and indeed may be as culturally constructed as their subsequent interpretation, but few poststructuralists would want to deny that there are such things as brute events which did or did not take place on a certain day under certain conditions of weather.

Whatever the external referent is in Farrell, it is not treated as an unproblematical 'given', a coherent entity called 'the world', or 'history'; but this is sometimes obscured by his irony, a notoriously unstable element. *The Siege of Krishnapur's* parodic/ironic relation to nineteenth-century 'Mutiny' novels and to a line of other English-Indian (or Indian-English) novels went unnoticed by its early critics who treated it as an old-fashioned example of those very imperialist genres it was satirising. As we shall argue, Farrell shows at times an almost New Historicist awareness that history is a continual process of interchange between events, texts, and the general culture of any period, a process in which all these elements are mutually influential.

Even more importantly, Farrell's novels are not, in Mikhail Bakhtin's terms, 'monologic'. The documentary voices Farrell quotes are certainly, in one sense, used to build up 'an impression of the period', but the 'sense of the period' so achieved is not monologic (essentially, forming a monologue, a single author-directed view of the period) but dialogic (forming a dialogue) in the way Bakhtin describes in his assessment of the differences between Tolstoy (monologic), and Dostoevsky (dialogic).[15] The orts, scraps and fragments of other writing that Farrell suggests, quotes, or interweaves by a multitude of means, form an assemblage, a polyphony of voices, a 'heteroglossia', which speak into and against each other to reveal the past as always an irresolvable network of contradictions, not as a single monolothic referent, say, 'the Victorian period'.

If Farrell's writing is ruled out of postmodernism by the limitations he puts on his licence to play, it is also on similar grounds judged to be 'realist', a word which in the 1970s, and still to some extent now, implies old-fashioned or reactionary unless it is given some respectable prefix: 'magic-', 'neo-', 'dirty-'. Realist art seems to propose itself duplicitously as an imitation of 'life', or 'society', always concealing the modifying effects of the medium, language, and the artificiality of genre. In doing this it naturalises one (bourgeois, Western, white, male) version of reality as the only unarguable reality. As John McLeod admits along the way to a persuasive defence of Farrell in 'Exhibiting Empire in *The Siege of Krishnapur*':

> It might seem that [Farrell's documentary] references add a sense of referential certainty to the text, implicating the text with an existing archive and thus adding weight to the familiar view that the novel is '[r]ealist in method'.[16]

Malcolm Bradbury, writing on Farrell in 1989, invokes the view of Farrell as realist when he judges that Farrell's writing of historical novels is an indication that he was apparently unable to move past 'that gravitational tug of realism which so much great modern writing had already tested'.[17] What is overlooked here is the fact that Farrell's methods of using his documents are anything but realist. Even in his simplest techniques, as for example, the use of the newspaper extracts in *Troubles*, Farrell's usage is far more reminiscent of modernist experimentation than realist writing: it bears a strong similarity to the way in which John Dos Passos uses newspapers in the *U.S.A.* trilogy (1930–36), for instance.

By contrast with 'realist' art, modernist art, as Linda Hutcheon says, 'be it visual or verbal – tends to declare its status as art first'.[18] Postmodern art goes further: it foregrounds the tensions between art and life, and between the world and textual versions of the world, thus giving rise to 'metafictions' and 'meta-histories'. Our contention is that the subtleties of Farrell's irony and the concentration on only certain aspects of his documentary reference have obscured the extent to which he engages in a metahistorical, metafictional project which is centrally postmodern.

If one looks to postmodern theorizing outside the specifically literary, Farrell's practice becomes more understandable in terms of exactly these changes in attitudes to history. Donna Landry and Gerald MacLean (writing, significantly, from a Marxist perspective similar to, but later than, Farrell's own), identify as postmodern the '[c]oncern with history writing as knowledge production, as production of knowledge in which the historian is always interested', and see it as leading to reflection 'on the politics of the historical enterprise itself, and on the question of whose agency and interests are being represented'.[19] Regarded in the light of these comments, Farrell's painstaking use of documentary material points to a postmodernity that lies in his attempts to examine the human subject positioned in relation to the public discourses of a liberal humanist ideology which his characters can neither continue to believe in, nor yet reject. In a frequently-quoted comment Farrell said that in *Troubles*, the first volume of the trilogy, he had tried, 'to show people "undergoing" history, to use an expression of Sartre's',[20] but he also shows history continuously in the process of turning from experience into text, and in *The Singapore Grip*, into the filmic representation of reality.

In *Troubles* the newspaper extracts (discussed in Chapter 4) unsettle any 'centred' focus. The words of the *Irish Times*, controlled by British liberal humanist ideology, often stand in the novel as direct illustration of the gap between the discourses of imperial control and the actual situation in Ireland, a dramatisation of part of the process by which historical discourses are formed. Farrell's technique here actually fulfills Hutcheon's condition for postmodern historiography, since it 'implies an anti-idealist distinction between the real past and the past as object of knowledge'.[21]

The potential for misunderstanding Farrell's achievements is indicated by Mary Sullivan's review of *The Singapore Grip* when it was published in 1978. This was a moment when what Doris Lessing called 'a great whirlwind of change'[22] in literature and criticism was probably at its most confusing. Sullivan rather wearily praises the novel's 'mountain of detailed reconstruction', and 'assiduous bibliography' before going on to say:

> The history is all just so; the songs are perfectly period; the most evocative films are adroitly dropped into the narrative. But the motives and the natures of the people, constantly asserted, are not shown to us, so that they remain remote, and the changing, complex, tumultuous background remains only scenery, though it is painstakingly assembled.[23]

Farrell's desire to show history as a discursive process in which human agency is problematical, a Marxist insight that history is 'a process without a subject', is invisible to Sullivan because the critical tools for reading his work, though available, were only just being assimilated by British critics. Those like Sullivan found his work too experimental, wanted him to deal with some essentialist 'human truth', but paradoxically his work is not experimental enough for those reading from the perspective of the postmodern novel. He is caught between the prevailing literary critical models of the modern and the postmodern, a digressor (like B.S. Johnson) whose experiments are located in a literary cul-de-sac somewhere between these two 'isms'.

A further reason why it was easy for early reviewers and critics to misjudge Farrell is that his writing changed rapidly over the course of a relatively brief career. Those critics of the 1970s who had read his first novel, *A Man from Elsewhere* (1963), would have remembered it as almost too predictable for its period – 'angry-provincial-philosophical-kitchen-sink', heavily indebted to the pessimistic late modernism of Samuel Beckett and Jean-Paul Sartre. It tells the intellectual disillusionment of a post-war-communist young man who vents his political dissatisfactions against a dying older man, a writer and war-hero, who seems to epitomise the failure or compromise of leftist ideals.

In *The Lung* (1965) which followed, disillusionment was personal rather than public, and the gloomy didactic seriousness of *A Man from Elsewhere* was rather unexpectedly replaced by the manic black comedy of personal illness as a metaphor for separation from society. In its examination of ways in which the past continually irrupts into the present, this novel begins to reveal Farrell's gift for a bizarre and often grim humour which seems to combine Beckett with *The Goon Show*. The failed hero, temporarily confined by polio to a community of the sick and the mad, transgresses all kinds of bourgeois boundaries, confronts the misunderstandings of his past, lost opportunities, fragmented meanings, and the question of his own sanity.

This serious comedy is elaborated and refined in Farrell's excellent third novel *A Girl in the Head* (1967), where a wickedly analytical satire of the 1960s takes shape in an understated deadpan irony which again, can easily be misread. This novel demonstrates a highly self-aware use of the textual conventions of heroism and romance. Farrell seems able to stand outside the preoccupations of his contemporaries, casting a mocking, calculating eye on the generation which introduced sexual liberation, the mini-skirt, flower-power – and French literary 'theory'.

After this there seems a hiatus. It is the moment when Farrell's Marxist interests, growing all the time, turn his attention backward from the contemporary world to the earlier epochs from which it sprang. In this view, historical novels are not a return to realism, but a move in the direction of the self-awareness of postmodern fiction, a Marxist project conceived by Farrell during his two-year stay in Paris in the early 1960s. Ronald Binns has discussed Farrell's admiration for the work of Georg Lukács and points out the relevance to Farrell's work of Lukács's view that the historical novel should 'rouse the present' and demonstrate the complexities of a moment 'which contemporaries would experience as their own pre-history'.[24] With this context, the trilogy can be read as an attempt to show, through hindsight, the processes of an inexorable dialectical materialism.

Farrell is concerned less with the of loss Empire than with moments that explain the loss. His fictions examine the process of decay, the small continuous subversions which propel change. He is interested in historiography rather than history. In this he prefigures one of the greatest of the later postmodern writers, Umberto Eco, in whose view historical novels should 'not only identify in the past the causes of what came later, but also trace the process through which those causes began slowly to produce their effects'.[25]

One of Farrell's major techniques for achieving this is one that we would like to call, variously, 'intertextuality', 'intratextuality', and 'interdiscursivity', but our use of these terms needs some explanation. What began for us with an interest in Farrell's use of his non-fiction references in the trilogy quickly led to a realisation that other writers' fiction is an even more puzzlingly insistent presence in his novels. Novels, plays, and poetry, both antecedent and contemporary, are quoted or suggested with almost staggering frequency, brought to the surface of Farrell's work by the narrator or through the characters. They can be recalled by direct mention, by subtle references to plot, characters, or action, or by implications of style or genre. Binns comments perceptively on writers Farrell particularly admired, and on many novels which can be seen to have affected his writing, but the critical concept of 'influence' that Binns uses for dealing with this has also been problematised by recent theories. 'Influence' and 'allusion', terms which would have traditionally been used to describe and evaluate one author's debts to others, have entered into lengthy debate with the newer term, 'intertextuality', and some of the implications of all three of these seem necessary to assess accurately the subtlety of Farrell's playfully serious manipulation of the artworks of the past and present.

'Influence' is not wholly satisfactory to explain Farrell's usages, partly because they go far beyond what is usually suggested by this word, but also because it has implications which might again associate him with an unthinking liberal humanism. The idea of 'influence' suggests that the writer consciously[26] accepts and implicates himself in the continuity of the Western literary tradition and therefore the re-statement of its values, both literary and social, in each generation. Even if 'influence' is interpreted in the extended terms of Harold Bloom's later proposal (in *The Anxiety of Influence* [1973] and *A Map of*

Misreading [1975]) that the relations between a writer and his antecedents is *unconscious* as much as conscious, a result of willed misreading and an Oedipal act of challenge to the literary father, still the writer is not freed from the implications that he accepts but merely modifies canonical values. Misreading is effective only in allowing a release of the individual writer from the burden of the past, it is not an act of rebellion against the underlying nature of the tradition itself. Thus the idea that Farrell is 'influenced' by Joseph Conrad, Richard Hughes, Malcolm Lowry, and so on, just like his use of documentary material, seems to relegate him to the position of conservative re-writer of the capitalist/imperialist status quo.

There are two difficulties, though, in using the term 'intertextuality' to apply to the kind of deliberate effects Farrell achieves. As Susan Stanford Friedman discusses in 'Weavings: Intertextuality and the (Re)Birth of the Author', Julia Kristeva, in inventing the term, did not intend it to indicate a *voluntary* use of other texts by an author. For Kristeva and for Roland Barthes, also closely associated with the concept, 'intertextuality' is a condition of the production of all texts, a statement of the inescapable, unwilled, inadvertent presence of other texts from the culture in any writing. It speaks of the way in which all new writing draws inevitably on the 'already said' of the culture. The difficulty is that Farrell's 'mosaic of quotations' (Kristeva) from other literary texts, visual arts, and music, is extremely deliberate, and does appear to imply various kinds of intent. Kristeva has objected to what she sees as the 'banal' misuse of the word 'intertextuality' to apply to such a situation as Farrell's which includes 'the study of sources'. A number of feminists have, though, argued against Kristeva's attempt to delimit the term, and have defended the use of intertextuality for both willed and unwilled echoing of other texts. Taking refuge behind Susan Stanford Friedman's compelling argument we are using the term throughout this book with a freedom that Kristeva would not approve, but that has become available through the debates of many recent scholars.[27] 'Intratextuality' refers to cross-references between Farrell's own works, and 'interdiscursivity' is Linda Hutcheon's term for the drawing of attention to relations between different discourses.

The second difficulty of 'intertextuality', a problem also included in Friedman's discussion, is related to critical distrust of the 'intentional fallacy' and to the perceived 'naïvety' of biographical criticism. Both 'allusion' and 'intertextuality' in our usages imply a now-suspect authorially intended meaning which the author reinforces by the quotation of other writings. A corollary of this is that a reader who recognises the quotations is, as Thomas Schaub indicates, 'confined within the steering mechanisms of the text … which are themselves ideologically driven'.[28] It is enough, perhaps, to concede that while we may pay attention to recorded authorial intention, we also recognise that 'writers cannot remain in total control of the systems of reference their words bring into play'.[29] Thus the intertexts 'planted' by Farrell may of course exceed both his own intention and the functions ascribed by any one reading. We also agree with Nancy K. Miller in her feeling that even though reinstating the author as producer of the text 'may betray a naive faith in origins ... ' it is sometimes a critically productive addition to 'Foucauldian "indifference" or Barthesian "anonymity."'[30] An approach which allows a cautious use of biographical matter has the advantage of allowing us to show that Farrell's manuscripts for the trilogy give evidence of a process of revision in which he can be seen working towards various refinements of the theme of liberal humanism in the process of being revealed as an untenable set of discursively transmitted ideologies.

Farrell's comments on his intentions and his views about the novel in the twentieth century are extant in interviews, conversations recollected by friends, and very importantly, in a large body of regular reviewing which he completed between 1970 and 1972 and which gives fascinating insights into the range of his reading and his opinions about writing. All his reviews are intensely personal – he often says what he responds to as a reader, or employs auto-biographical anecdotes for illustration. But the reviews are also searchingly analytical – one is always conscious of the considered thought of a writer sympathetically assessing through the work of other writers the technicalities of novel writing, the problems of style and structure, recalcitrant material, aesthetic decisions, failures of openings and endings, the need to deal with certain scenes, details, dialogues. From our reading of these sources and our exploration of the intertextuality in the trilogy, it began to emerge how much the Empire trilogy is connected with a developing Marxist exploration in his work of the relations between culture and society.

Farrell's creative investigation proceeds in the same years as profound changes in Western Marxism which he was certainly aware of through the work of English Marxists Raymond Williams and Christopher Caudwell. But Farrell's fluent French may also have allowed him to read developments from the French intellectual left (Lacan, Macherey, Althusser, Foucault), before they were translated into English.

In *Troubles*, the first-written of the trilogy (though not the earliest in chrono-logical setting), the central, most prominent intertextuality takes an apparently unsophisticated form: 'gobbets' of genuine newspaper articles from the *Irish Times* 1919–21, which are inserted apparently randomly into the novel. Although these are never introduced or glossed in any way, the implied reader for them is Major Brendan Archer, the main character, who thus becomes, inside the fiction, what Barthes claims each reader is outside the fiction: 'the space on which all the quotations that make up a writing are inscribed without any of them being lost'.[31] Archer and the external reader are thus in similar, yet not identical positions. Both are making attempts at reading the situation in Ireland, and of Ireland in relation to a larger world-history of the time, yet the raw material on which they operate is significantly different. For Archer it is 'brute events' of experience, plus various kinds of texts which encode the ideologies of the time, even when they are apparently unrelated to the situation: race-riots in Chicago, the plot of a movie appearing at a Dublin picture-house. The 'external' reader, by contrast, works from 'facts' and texts already selected by Farrell and mediated through the narrator; but the 'external' reader is also presumably influenced by the unwilled intertextuality Kristeva proposes, and by two senses of distance from this material, Farrell's sense of distance, and the reader's own, now almost a generation further on. Whatever the multiple effects of this, Farrell is still able to count on setting up through the Major a liberal humanist position always in doubt about the veracity of its own conclusions.

By the time of the next novel, *The Siege of Krishnapur*, further complexities have been added. Firstly, the operations of genre itself are always in question in this novel giving the intertextuality extra bite (as in the opening which recalls in various ways E.M. Forster's *A Passage to India* [1924], and in other passages which recall Rudyard Kipling's *Kim* [1901], but also Kipling's actual life).[32] But Farrell also introduces two other overall destabilizing effects as well as a multitude of minor local ones. In this novel the two liberal humanist 'reader representatives', the Collector and Fleury, are a generation apart, and the differences between old and young opinions in any given period, as well as views which are closer and more distant in time from the events narrated, are dramatised in the novel itself. Farrell uses allusion and intertextuality to associate the Collector with Matthew Arnold, to dramatise that older humanist conviction that it is the finest consciousnesses of each age which must decide the path for human progress and create the institutions which will make it possible. The entire form and tenor of the novel, though, enact a completely opposing view, the insight of Marx, contemporary of Matthew Arnold, that it may be the economics and the institutions of a society which decide its consciousnesses. Here we have, brought together in apparently unresolvable contradiction, the two 'grands récits' of the late nineteenth and twentieth centuries, liberal humanism and Marxism. Both are undermined by Farrell's insistence on culture as discourse, display, and performance.

The Singapore Grip investigates further twists of the intertextual. At one point in this novel Walter Blackett, capitalist exploiter, contemplates the Japanese bombing of Singapore in a passage which has been cited as a finely ironical presentation of distorted Hegelian idealism:

> Certainly, it was not easy to see a common principle in the great mass of events occurring at any moment far and near. ... He believed that each

individual event in a historical moment was subtly modified by an intangible mechanism which he could only think of as 'the spirit of the time'. If a Japanese bomber had opened its bomb doors over Singapore in the year 1920 no bomb would have struck the city. Its bombs would have been lodged in a transparent roof that covered Singapore like a bubble. ... The spirit of these times, unfortunately, allowed the bombs of an Asiatic nation to fall on a British city.[33]

This is certainly allusion, but it is also both intertextuality and intratextuality, referring as it does to the ideological momentum within the trilogy which has demonstrated liberal humanism from the benign muddle-headedness of the Major in *Troubles*, champion of gentlemanliness and morality, to Walter Blackett's ignorant idealism which conceals, even perhaps for him, but never for the reader, liberal humanism's connection to a viciously immoral capitalist imperialism. The Major, who returns as a minor character in *The Singapore Grip*, is now significantly dressed as a devil, ready to take part in the carnival which is to celebrate fifty years of Blackett and Webb's commercial reign (–cum–exploitation) in Singapore. Ostensibly a symbol of 'Inflation', the Major's costume indicates that even his benign tolerance may turn out to be evil. Ronald Binns concedes the high level of interest in economics and imperialism in the novel, but believes that Marxism is also treated with some irony, perhaps through Ehrendorf's First and Second Laws. We hope to show that if it is read intratextually with the other two novels *The Singapore Grip* reveals the postmodern defeat of pantomine devils, not by the forces of good, but by the apocalyptic magnitude of new evils unimagined by old devils. The power, desire, and knowledge for which Faust sells his soul are no longer private bargains focused on the angst of the tragic hero and his separation from God, but public manifestations of a new scale and kind of anarchy and violence.

In *The Hill Station*, the novel Farrell left uncompleted at his death, Marx 'comes out', as it were, into the open. He makes a personal appearance as 'a familiar bearded leonine figure'[34] working away in the British Museum while the characters in the novel are pursuing their daily routine in British India some years after the Mutiny, oblivious that they are coming ever closer to the death of the British Empire, signalled in this novel by tropes of disease and exhaustion. At one point in this novel someone releases a pig, the very figure of carnival and misrule, into a church service. The resulting fracas certainly symbolises the disorder of a church divided against itself, but also hints that an upheaval of old ways may be necessary and cathartic when new energies are released.

Julian Barnes, a writer who seems very close to Farrell in his bizarre humour, in his Francophilia, and in his postmodern creative investigation of the discourses of literature and history, has his main character in *Flaubert's Parrot* use a pig as simile for the slipperiness of the past:

> How do we seize the past? Can we ever do so? When I was a medical student some pranksters at an end-of-term dance released into the hall a piglet which had been smeared with grease. It squirmed between legs, evaded capture, squealed a lot. People fell over trying to grasp it, and were made to look ridiculous in the process. The past often seems to behave like that piglet.[35]

Our aim is to show that far from trying to stop this vitality Farrell revels in the liveliness of the past, and particularly in its transformative heretical possibilities for fiction.

1 / A Sketch from Life:
J.G. Farrell in Context

In his review of Hilary Pyle's biography of Jack Yeats, Farrell made the following comment:

> One of the difficulties in writing about artists is that very often the poor fellows live such outwardly uneventful lives that the harassed biographer is driven to recording the most trivial detail in his attempt to flesh out his portrait to proportions that come anywhere near matching the stature of his subject.[1]

For good and ill this is not true of Farrell. His childhood was lived during the Second World War, he moved between Ireland and England during his teenage years, and suffered a prolonged and life-threatening illness in his early twenties. He lived in Paris during the anti-Vietnam War protests, worked in Arctic Canada, and at various times travelled in America, Morocco, and Asia. He died by drowning in his forty-fifth year. Even the more mundane parts of his life were transformed by his idiosyncratic ways of seeing and his gift for language and humour:

> One rainy day in New York last year, in the course of a kerbside dispute over a taxi, a bizarrely dressed lady with strangely piercing eyes attempted to turn this reviewer into a frog. Although she was unsuccessful, it was a disconcerting experience nevertheless.[2]

In fact anyone looking closely at Farrell's career has the impression that, like many artists and writers, he was living two lives which continually fed each other. On the imaginative level which he would probably have considered more important, his life was occupied with an intense amount of reading, both fiction and non-fiction, and similarly with writing. His negotiations between his reading and his writing are to some extent the real story of his life once he seriously decided to become a writer, but this is the life which can hardly be grasped except as the trace it leaves in the novels. Apart from this, as his narrator says in *Troubles*, 'The rest was merely the "being alive" that every age has to do',[3] and the external details appear straightforward enough.

James Gordon Farrell was born in Liverpool on 23 January 1935, the son of an English father and an Irish mother, and one of three boys. His father's family, though originally from Ireland and despite their Irish Catholic name, had been long settled in Liverpool and were Protestant. Farrell himself described his father's family as 'very warm'. His mother's side of the family, who were from Ireland, apparently claimed a distant relationship with the dukes of Bedford, which led to family discussions about whether or not they could be considered members of the Ascendancy, and no doubt inspired the Dongeon family's comic claims to Huguenot ancestry in *A Girl in the Head*. Before J.G. Farrell was born his parents had lived in Chittagong in what was then the north-east part of Britian's Indian Empire, where his father had worked in the rubber industry, and this somewhat colonial family background no doubt influenced his 'Empire trilogy', indirectly if not directly.[4] It may well be that the sense of dislocation experienced by Farrell's central male characters owes much to his own sense of never quite belonging due to his family's middle-class, ex-colonial, Anglo-Irish background. Caroline Moorehead's profile of the writer points to this sense of dislocation when she refers to the fact that '[a]t school he was addressed as an Irish boy; in Ireland he felt English', and this may explain why '[a]t 19 he emigrated to Canada'.[5]

Farrell was born at a time when, as Benny Green puts it, 'the Empire reached its apogee in terms of sheer acreage'.[6] Although in literary terms the Empire had reached its apogee in terms of interest some years earlier, many of the writers who depicted the Empire in their work were still prominent during the time when Farrell was growing up – including, notably, Rudyard Kipling, John Buchan, Joyce Cary, Somerset Maugham, and E.M. Forster. To some critics Farrell's own work has seemed to be a continuance in a slightly more ironic and self-aware mode of that 'resolute de-politicising of imperialism' which has been the achievement of Kipling, Conrad, and Forster, who had endeavoured to make the personal view of Empire replace the political.[7]

On the outbreak of the Second World War, Farrell's family moved to 'Boscobel', a large Victorian house in Southport, an upmarket Victorian seaside resort now a popular retirement centre in Lancashire. This house, which was badly damaged by a German bomb in 1941, undoubtedly inspired the rambling Victorian edifices which appear in both *A Girl in the Head* (where the Dongeon family home is actually named 'Boscobel'[8]) and *Troubles*, and his memory of the bombing probably influenced Farrell's descriptions of the Residency in *The Siege of Krishnapur* and the damage which befalls the home of the Langfields in *The Singapore Grip*. In an interview with Malcolm Dean Farrell himself makes a connection between his own wartime experiences and his treatment of possessions in *The Siege of Krishnapur* and *The Singapore Grip*:

> I remember as a child during the Blitz how adults in pyjamas would
> assemble in our air-raid shelter clutching the most extraordinary objects.
> During the Indian mutiny, Cawnpore was made almost indefensible by
> pianos and stuffed owls and other bric-à-brac. It's human nature. I don't
> mean to sound superior. If Kensington were besieged tomorrow I
> wouldn't want to leave my own stuffed owls behind.[9]

The war was to have an effect on the whole body of his fiction, especially on
A Man from Elsewhere, and on the grotesque images in his black comedy. And
it was during this wartime period as a young child in Southport that Farrell
first started writing stories: 'My first began "bang, bang, bang the Indians are
coming ..." I still think it is not a bad beginning. It even had a love element
but my father advised me to leave this out until I was older'.[10]

The love element remained problematic even in Farrell's mature work, where
there is frequently both an interrogation of romance as fictional convention
and an ambivalence towards sexual relations. Many of his male characters,
although strongly motivated by sexual desire in terms of plot, actually produce
an impression of asexuality. Sayer in *A Man from Elsewhere*, Martin Sands in
The Lung, Boris in *A Girl in the Head*, the Major in *Troubles* and *The Singapore
Grip*, and both the Collector and Fleury in *The Siege of Krishnapur* all give the
impression of being asexual. None of these characters, nor any others for that
matter, are convincing sexual beings; little importance seems to be attached to
sexual tension, and when the characters do engage in the sexual act itself it is
normally used by Farrell for comic purposes. Perhaps the character in Farrell's
fiction who is most nearly a sexual being is Harry Dunstaple in *The Siege of
Krishnapur*. Harry's is a kind of late-Victorian sexuality, where the pursuit of
women is displaced by his pursuit of adventure, but even this is subordinated
to satire of the genre. In *A Girl in the Head* the title itself points to the intellectual approach to sex which is evident in all Farrell's fiction, where sex is kept
in the head, a cerebral presence rather than physical manifestation in the
novels. This emotional distance is another feature which makes Farrell difficult
to place even among his contemporaries. The 1960s was a time when physical
sexuality was being celebrated openly – as in David Lodge's *The British Museum
is Falling Down* (1965), Margaret Drabble's *The Millstone* (1965), and Muriel
Spark's *The Prime of Miss Jean Brodie* (1961), which, while not describing the
sexual act, is alive with sexual tension, and at the end of the decade comes John
Fowles's even more explicit investigation of sexuality *The French Lieutenant's
Woman* (1969).

From the age of twelve Farrell's childhood was divided between England,
where he boarded at Rossall School, a minor Church of England public school
in Fleetwood on the Lancashire coast, and Ireland, his parents having settled

in Dalkey, on the coast outside Dublin, after the Second World War. Farrell's experience of the journeying between the two locations is succinctly captured in a line from *The Lung*: 'Ah, yes, those nightmare journeys back to school in the mail boat over the wintry guinness-black Irish Sea!'[11] – a passage which vividly recalls Dylan Thomas, a significant literary figure in the late 1940s when Farrell would have been travelling backwards and forwards across the Irish Sea. As this suggests, Farrell was sensitive to the literary climate of his time; he read and thought about literature from an early age, and absorbed a wide sense of literary culture.[12] Farrell seems to have loved his time in Dalkey, and delighted in his environment. A passage in *The Lung*, in which Martin Sands recalls his own boyhood summers in Dalkey, is probably as autobiographical as any part of this novel and conveys strongly a sense of blissful summer holidays spent in Ireland:

> It seemed to him in retrospect that all those Dublin summers had been thickly coated with sunshine, all his memories were crystallised with it like sugary golden fruit. He had a vision of girls with white teeth and sunburned faces. A lonely boy, cloistered in a boarding school throughout his adolescence, a girl for him had been as graceful as any unicorn ever was, and as mysterious. He saw the green vertebrae of Dalkey Island sleeping peacefully in the shining water. Girls and the fresh sea wind that modelled their summer dresses to the shape of their bodies ... slender nervous hands always ready to anchor their skirts against a particularly lecherous gust. But the smell of the sea! It washed through the room with the purity of love itself while in the darkness silken hair streamed out on the wind, rich with salt and the sun and smiling faces. (46)

Farrell's sense of being distanced from women, which also comes through clearly here, may in part account for what Ronald Binns refers to as 'a romantically melancholy view of male-female relations',[13] and his failure to create any female characters to rival the depth of his lone male figures.

It is not only the Ireland of his boyhood that is recalled in *The Lung*: the novel is littered with locations from Farrell's own life. The streets of Oxford, where he attended university, are described in considerable detail as Martin Sands meanders through them early in the novel in a manner reminiscent of the way the Consul wanders through the streets of Cuernavaca at the beginning of Malcolm Lowry's *Under the Volcano* (1947), and there are references, too, to France, and to the Lancashire coast.

Farrell's early life was spent almost entirely near the sea, on the Lancashire coast in Liverpool, Southport, and later Fleetwood, or on the Irish coast at Dalkey. And it was to the Irish coast, to the isolated Sheep's Head peninsula in

Bantry Bay that he moved only four months before he was drowned there while fishing. In what turns out to be a prescient passage, Farrell describes in *The Lung* a drowning that could almost be his own: ' ... the drowned sheep that we came upon half-buried in the sand, glass-eyed, fleece matted with sand and salt water, legs spread as if it had died in the act of beautifully moving. It must have wandered into the sea from a farm beyond the spray along the Wicklow coast ... and drowned alone in the boiling surf' (139). The sea, then, was an important location in his own life, and one that plays a significant part in each of his first four novels. It is perhaps appropriate that the obituary in *The Times* should, in a lovely Freudian slip, wrongly refer to his first novel by the Hemingwayesque (or Ibsenish) title, *The Man from the Sea*.[14] The coast, particularly a beach, is a marginal environment – neither quite land nor sea – which suited Farrell's temperament and fitted with his own sense of dislocation. His French teacher at Rossall remembers the young Jim Farrell 'as a boy who got on with everybody but was always slightly apart, not one of the pack'.[15]

The sea, which is so clearly an important environment in Farrell's work, is also evocatively portrayed by some of his favourite writers: Joseph Conrad, Richard Hughes (whom he later met) in his novel *In Hazard* (1938), which Farrell first read at the age of eight or nine, Malcolm Lowry, Proust, and Pierre Loti whose novel *Pêcheur d'Islande* (1886), a story about Breton fishermen, was unfashionably prescribed as a French textbook at Rossall. After leaving Rossall School, Farrell taught for a year at a prep school in Dublin. Dissatisfied both with Dublin (as Oscar Wilde, James Joyce, and Samuel Beckett earlier had become in their turn) and his job there, he left for Canada to gain experience which he hoped would help him become a writer. 'Propelled by dreams of Hemingway'[16] and no doubt by Lowry and others too, he worked as a firefighter for seven months on the DEW (Defence Early Warning) line on Baffin Island in the Canadian Arctic. He then travelled around Canada and the United States.

In 1956 Farrell, then twenty-one years old, went to Brasenose College, Oxford, to read Law. Farrell at this stage potentially enters into an élite group of his age – British, white, male, heterosexual – reading a subject traditionally the reserve of the upper-middle classes or above, at one of the nation's two most prestigious educational establishments. To all external appearances Farrell – a keen sportsman, with public school behind him and now at Oxford – fit the mould of the traditional élite of nation builders. However, two factors interrupt his alignment with this ruling group, a group that was already beginning to have its privileges and assumptions profoundly questioned: his Anglo-Irishness and a period of serious illness. After only one term his university career was interrupted when he collapsed in the changing rooms after a game of rugby. He was diagnosed as having polio and had to spend the next six months in an iron lung. Debilitating though the disease was on a personal level, Farrell's was not an isolated case, and the disease may not have set him apart as much as it may have done at another moment in history. Nevertheless, the sudden dramatic change in his life and circumstances, from a position of physical and intellectual power to weakness and dependence, would have made him aware of the shocking vulnerability of the human subject. It appears that Farrell himself was prone to dramatising the change, as John Spurling explains in his memoir of the author:

> The myth grew up, partly promoted by Jim himself, that he had entered the lung as a stalwart 'hearty' and emerged as a white-haired, emaciated novelist. It was not quite so. He had been, certainly, a fine games player at Rossall, but the master responsible for the school magazine recalled that Jim could have filled it all by himself, 'but we had to let the others have a look in'.[17]

(At Oxford, too, he contributed interviews to a short-lived magazine entitled *Oxford Opinion*.) While, as Spurling reveals, the polarisation from stalwart hearty to emaciated novelist was not to be taken too seriously, Farrell's promotion of this myth nevertheless suggests the deep impact his experience in the lung had on him. Illness was to become a major metaphor in his work, not only in his second novel, *The Lung*, a black comedy which in part fictionalises his experiences in an iron lung (which Spurling describes in his memoir as trademark Farrellian comedy).

Farrell returned to Brasenose College in the autumn of 1957, this time to read Modern Languages, and three years later he graduated with a Third-Class Honours degree in French and Spanish. This change of direction, from Law to Languages, which was evidently influenced by his illness, may also have owed something to a growing interest in Socialism:

> His mother remembers Farrell developing into a passionate socialist and coming home in the holidays to rail against his bourgeois background. Farrell's friend the journalist Malcolm Dean identified the novelist as 'a romantic socialist idealist' ... and recalls how Farrell used to mock people who spoke disdainfully of 'seychellists'.[18]

As Binns goes on to say, 'Farrell's years in France seem to have reinforced these leanings to the left'.[19]

Immediately after coming down from Oxford Farrell spent three years working as an English teacher in various parts of France, including a spell at a school in a northern suburb of Paris and another at the *lycée* in Mende in the Lozère.[20]

It becomes clear from each successive novel that as time passed Farrell was progressively influenced by the developments in Marxist theory which were contemporary with his residence in France, where Marxism was being expanded into an extended range of left-wing positions – expounded by Sartre, Macherey, Althusser, and others – each giving very varied accounts both of social relations and the functioning of literature and history within those relations. These theories were also being evaluated by British Marxists including Christopher Caudwell and Raymond Williams, whose work would almost certainly have been read by Farrell.

During this time in France he wrote *A Man from Elsewhere*, his first published novel, which deals extensively with a moral problem in post-war left-wing politics. He was later to disown the book: 'I'd been telling people for years that I was a writer and I really had to write it. It actually got quite good reviews, which confirmed me in my belief that the people, the critics, who are supposed to know the difference between good and bad, *don't*'.[21] This is a rather surprising admonition of critics coming from a man who himself worked both as a publisher's reader and a reviewer. Yet Farrell apparently rejected the book 'to the point of fantasizing that one day he [would] buy up every remaining copy and pulp it'.[22] This may have been due in part to the nature of the socialism expounded in that work which appears rather naïve in comparison to the more subtly developed positions evident in later novels.

Farrell returned to England in 1963 and lived for the next few years in London, writing, and earning money when he needed it by teaching English to foreign students and reading manuscripts for Hutchinson's – including *A Weekend with Claude* (1967) by the then unknown Beryl Bainbridge, for which he earned a fee of four guineas.[23] At this time Farrell was living in relative poverty in what he always described as a greenhouse (actually a conservatory) in Palace Gardens Terrace, near Kensington Gardens, which Brigid Allen describes as 'freezing cold in winter, stifling in summer, barely furnished, and private only in the sense that he was inhabiting it on his own'.[24] This greenhouse was later to appear in his third novel, *A Girl in the Head*, as Boris's first Maidenhair Bay address, described in detail,[25] from where he is 'rescued' by the Dongeons.

In 1966, on the strength of his first two novels, Farrell was awarded a Harkness Fellowship and spent two years in North America. His initial plan to enrol at the Yale Film School with the intention of training to become a script-writer appears to have been quickly dropped, and he soon moved to New York, where he spent most of the next two years. The American literary context of this period would also exert a visible influence on Farrell's writing. Discussing American fiction of this period Bergonzi suggests that the 'absurdist or comic-apocalyptic fiction … grapples with the "incredible reality" [of mid twentieth century America] and tries to understand it, if not make it wholly credible'.[26] This was a vibrant re-thinking of realism in the American novel, which, like the French novel, was political in a way that the English novel was not in the 1960s. The sheer comic energy in Farrell's Empire trilogy makes those novels stand out like a beacon amidst the overwhelmingly dull post-1960s English novel, and links his work to that of American writers like Thomas Pynchon and Saul Bellow.

These influences may have contributed to Farrell's decision to reject the contemporary settings and styles of his first three novels, all of which he later disowned or dismissed as unimportant – though without these books in print it is difficult to see his later work in context.

Farrell returned to London from New York with just enough money to rent a cheap bed-sitting room in Notting Hill. There he turned his attention to a new subject which he had started to think about while in the United States, the decay of the British Empire, and began work on the first of a loose trilogy of novels that was to confirm his position as one of the twentieth century's most gifted writers.

It should be emphasised, though, that his interest in the decay of the British Empire is not an entirely new departure for Farrell. Indeed all his novels have, to a greater or lesser degree, a war or siege mentality. In *A Man from Elsewhere*, *The Lung*, and *A Girl in the Head* there are sexual sieges and counter sieges, while in *Troubles*, *The Siege of Krishnapur*, and *The Singapore Grip* the sexual sieges remain but are complicated by physical sites of siege – the Majestic Hotel, the Residency, and Singapore itself – and ideological metaphors of siege.

By focussing on Britain's loss of Empire Farrell chooses this as the major event in twentieth-century British history, an event with global implications that many other moments of British history did not have. Farrell referred to 'the decline of the British Empire' as 'the really interesting thing that happened during my lifetime'.[27] It is a subject that allows him to challenge the whole idea of Western capitalism, the ethics and philosophy that underlie Western liberal-humanism. In terms of the effect it had on Britain's standing in world terms, the loss of Empire is a more significant event than either of the World Wars, and the repercussions were much greater. The trilogy reveals Farrell's awareness that the British sense of collective identity had moved during the nineteenth century through the profound change from 'nation' to 'Empire'. By the end of the nineteenth century the experiences of colonisation and imperial power allowed the British to imagine themselves as a 'master-race'. Farrell demonstrates this but goes further to dramatise the shock to British culture of having to lose this certainty of sovereignty when the Empire began collapsing around its makers. This mood was exacerbated by pessimism after the Second World War. John Osborne's *Look Back in Anger* (1956) captures the mood of the period perfectly. Jimmy Porter is the classic rebel without a cause, a young man whose desire to be heroic is stifled by the negativity of his times. But significantly in Osborne's play there is also sympathy for Jimmy's father who had been in India, whose world order has been shattered by history.

Farrell's interest in Empire came at a time when these effects of Empire were beginning to be analysed by a small number of British writers of both fiction and non-fiction. Raymond Williams's influential work *Culture and Society 1780–1950* (1958) pursued an academic study of British culture while James Morris's *Pax Britannica* (1968) entered this territory through the form of popular history. Perhaps the first of the fiction writers to chart the decline of Britain's Empire was Anthony Burgess, whose Malayan trilogy, *The Long Day Wanes* (*Time for a Tiger* [1956]; *The Enemy in the Blanket* [1958]; *Beds in the East* [1959]), plots Malaya's progress to independence. This is an ambitious project, published at a time when most writers seemed content to share a collective British unwillingness to acknowledge the far-reaching cultural effects of the loss of Empire. The next writer to treat the loss of Empire in such an ambitious way was Paul Scott in his *Raj Quartet* (*The Jewel in the Crown* [1966]; *The Day of the Scorpion* [1968]; *The Towers of Silence* [1971]; *A Division of the Spoils* [1975]), a work Farrell admired tremendously, and which overlapped with his own Empire trilogy both in dates of publication and (in the case of *The Singapore Grip*) the historical period covered.[28] Scott's quartet, which depicts in detail the loss of India, the 'jewel in the crown' of Britain's Empire, is carefully charted over a period of five years from the 'Quit India' riots of 1942 to the aftermath of Partition and Britain's final withdrawal in 1947. The longer term effects on those who had been part of the Raj administration are examined in his postscript to *The Raj Quartet*, *Staying On* (1977).

In his review of *A Division of the Spoils* Farrell calls Scott's tetralogy 'a literary achievement of impressive dimensions' and concludes:

> had a work of this quality been written fifty years ago, by now I feel sure it would have its established place in English literature. Its two great and time-resisting virtues are, first, the extraordinary range of characters it so skilfully portrays and, secondly, its powerful evocation of the last days of British India, now quietly slipping away into history.[29]

While Burgess and Scott treat the last gasps of Empire in their fiction, Farrell's trilogy, though continuing and developing this interest in the loss of Empire, has a quite different relation to history than these works. It treats three disjunctive periods and places of Empire – from the Indian Mutiny, or Great Revolt, of 1857–58 to the fall of Singapore in 1942 – with a proto-postmodernist emphasis on the textual transmission of history as much as on its actual events. Farrell emphasises both the multiple interrelation of the novels and the sense of progressive reappraisal achieved by a kind of internal intratextuality between the three novels:

> I prefer to think of them as a triptych rather than as a trilogy with each panel presenting a picture of the Empire at a different historical watershed and by their association shedding, I hope, some light on each other. I can't promise that I won't add other Imperial panels and turn it into a polyptych.[30]

(And it could be argued that *The Hill Station* would have been the next panel of that mooted polyptych.) To writers of Farrell's generation, the idea of a set of novels working as a series would have been familiar from several well-known contemporary and slightly earlier examples. L.H. Myers's *The Near and the Far* tetralogy (1929–40; first published collectively in 1943), Joyce Cary's two trilogies (1940–53), and Lawrence Durrell's *Alexandria Quartet* (1957–60) were all published in the three decades before the first volume of Farrell's trilogy or triptych appeared in 1970. Two distinct approaches to the idea of a series of novels are evident here. The stories in some, like Burgess's trilogy and Scott's quartet of novels, are essentially chronological in nature. In others, like Cary's two trilogies, and particularly Durrell's quartet, the stories are presented in layers, giving multiple versions of the same events and conveying a late-modernist sense of a shifting subjective sense of reality. This latter pattern is closer to the one that Farrell adopts and extends. Farrell's idea of a triptych could be read as analogous to the three mirrors on the type of dressing table that would have been both common and fashionable when Farrell was a child. Each mirror (novel) may emphasise the reflection of a particular dimension of Empire – political, military, and economic – but together their series of cross-reflections present an indivisible three-dimensional picture of the whole.

Troubles won the Faber Memorial Prize, and was his first commercial success. It was followed three years later by *The Siege of Krishnapur* which won Britain's prestigious Booker Prize and brought Farrell a financial security he had not previously enjoyed. At the award dinner the normally shy Farrell surprised many people by attacking the Booker-McConnell company for exploiting its black work-force in the West Indies. By all accounts Farrell's attack was an impulsive gesture made quite simply because he believed the multi-national firm should be paying its employees higher wages. It was not a stand strong enough, however, to prevent him accepting the £5,000 prize-money, part of which he used to make an extended trip to Singapore to research the third novel in his 'Empire' trilogy (which turned out to be a more thoughtful and considered attack on the economic exploitation of native work-forces by companies like Booker-McConnell), or from spending 'a large part of it on cases of wine which almost completely filled the bathroom of his tiny flat'.[31] Farrell's impulsive gesture at the Booker Prize dinner illustrates well the inherent contradictions between socialism and bourgeois liberal-humanism that he becomes more aware of as his novels progress, between two sets of values which in our society cannot be cohered. *The Singapore Grip*, which details the fall of Singapore to the Japanese during the Second World War, approaches the decay of the Empire from an economic angle. It is some measure of Farrell's success that this novel, a main choice of the Literary Guild, had an initial print run of one hundred thousand, whereas his early novels had runs of three thousand.[32]

In 1979 Farrell bought an old farmhouse on the isolated Sheep's Head peninsula in County Cork and returned to live in Ireland. Only four months later, on 11 August, at the age of 44, he was drowned while fishing off some rocks near his home. Ironically, drownings, near drownings, and metaphors of drowning are to be found everywhere in Farrell's fiction. His unfinished novel, *The Hill Station*, was published posthumously in 1981.

Farrell's death was, as Benny Green so succinctly asserts, 'a loss which contemporary English fiction is hardly equipped to sustain'.[33]

2 / A Soft-Spoken Anarchy: *A Man from Elsewhere* and *The Lung*

In the opening chapter of J.G. Farrell's first novel, *A Man from Elsewhere*, the main character, Sayer, finds with 'vague disquiet' that his watch has stopped for the first time in 'more years than he could remember'[1] and yet, in a phrase repeated three times with slight variations, he is vividly conscious that 'the world continued to revolve with terrifying speed as it circled the sun' (15). Catching sight of the time on a clock in a jeweller's shop window, he is astonished to find that a journey across Paris which should have taken him less than an hour has actually taken him three hours. By the end of the chapter he is 'in search of a watchmaker' a phrase which, recalling Paley's famous argument for the existence of God, links Sayer's worries about time with existential questions about the transience and meaning of human life.[2]

Similarly, in Farrell's second novel, *The Lung*,[3] the next of his alienated unheroic heroes, Martin Sands, glances at his watch in the first chapter, only to find that like much else in his life, it has mysteriously disappeared. He later gives a variety of implausible explanations for its absence, but the truth is that his watch has become useless, he is about to enter into an experience of illness which will isolate existential questions by appearing to be outside time. Memories of the past will coexist with puzzling images of the present and speculation about the future. 'Time passed', says the narrative as Sands lies on his back in the hospital unable to move; an oft-repeated refrain of the other patients is 'Time goes so slowly here'; and Sands's name itself suggests phrases like 'sands of time', 'shifting sands', or the idea of sand slipping through one's fingers or an hourglass in which time is running out.

The recurrent emphasis on time in these two novels, linked as it is with a strong sense of pessimism about the human condition, shows Farrell anxious in his early fictions to take up ideas prevalent in English and European writing since the beginning of the century. The themes and technical experiments of literary modernism were informed by new theories about the nature of time, and from the middle of the century two world wars had added to the difficulty of believing in any religious or humanist view of time as the onward progress of humanity towards some ideal of perfection. It seemed instead, as one commentator has said, to be 'a kind of existence, which has lost both form and principle and in which life no longer goes forward …'.[4] *A Man from Elsewhere* and *The Lung* each explore in different ways a world in which human life has lost its meaning, has become simply a period of time to be filled somehow between birth and death. Gretchen, the young woman in *A Man from Elsewhere*, tells Sayer that she has been born into 'a generation of morons'. 'Yours', she adds, 'was bad enough, but mine is worse' (87).

Gretchen recognises that there are 'too many, far too many, problems ahead … The future had not been changed by the present. All that could be done was to make time stand still for a while. And it was too late even for that' (138). She has previously been gazing up at a clock over the bar in a cafe:

> The numbers had been replaced by the letters of an aperitif advertisement and it took her an irritatingly long time to discover that the clock had stopped at a quarter past three. Not that the time made any difference. (132)

Time here is symbolically concealed by an advertisement for the alcohol which palliates the grim condition of being human.

A Man from Elsewhere is a book about war; it explores the influence of the past on the present and future, and interrogates heroism in the aftermath of the Second World War. Set in the summer of 1961, it follows Sayer's mission on behalf of the Communist Party to investigate some apparently dubious events of the war in occupied France which might discredit the well-respected, elderly writer Regan, now terminally ill. Regan has previously defected from the Party, and the prospect that he may be awarded a prestigious 'Catholic Prize for World Peace' makes it likely that his defection will be publicised and justified. The novel dramatises (without resolving) the opposition between a decayed liberal humanist ideal represented by the dying Regan, and the apparently impersonal Communist ideology of the younger man, Sayer.

Ronald Binns identifies strong influences from Camus, Sartre, and Existentialism on this early work, in the similarity between Farrell's first title and Camus's *The Outsider* (1942), in the political concerns of *A Man from Elsewhere*, and in the 'ambiance of Farrell's fictionalized France [which] is that of a then-fashionable ennui and despair'.[5] They are also evident in aspects which Binns does not mention, in the episode of the Algerian in *A Man from Elsewhere*, in Regan's view that '[i]solation [should] become a state of grace and the outsider a hero of society' (98), and in Farrell's whole concern with the concept of heroism. These influences stem partly, no doubt, from Farrell's study of French at Oxford and his two years living and working in various parts of France, including Paris, during the writing of *A Man from Elsewhere*. But just as evident in this work are influences from other European and British novelists. Behind *A Man from Elsewhere* also lies George Orwell's and Arthur

Koestler's disillusionment with Russian communism, Graham Greene's exploitation of popular genres to examine some implications of Catholic morality, Robert Musil's *The Man without Qualities* (1930–32), and above all, Samuel Beckett's Murphy, Malloy, Malone, and Moran, for whom the experiences of mind and body fail to cohere, and whose farcical tragi-comic attempts to cope with life echo throughout Farrell's six completed novels.

Beckett, like Farrell, was an Irishman escaped to France. His completed trilogy (*Molloy, Malone Dies,* and *The Unnamable*) was first published in English in 1959, and it may not be simply coincidence that the bleakness and absurdity of life is played out in Farrell's early novels in characters whose names begin with the letter M: Mado, Marie-France, Martin, Marigold, Monica, Michael, Max, Mélanie, Marie-Thé, and Mick (Slattery).[6] Farrell's penchant for given names which begin with the letter M is parallelled by his liking for family names beginning with the letter S: Sayer, Sands, Slattery (to name but the central male characters in his first three novels). On a number of occasions his characters carry both letters: Martin Sands and Marigold Slattery in *The Lung*, or Mick Slattery in *A Girl in the Head*. There is also Martin's vision of Simon Magus in *The Lung*, whose initials not only reverse the more usual M.S, but coincidentally anticipate John Fowles's 1966 novel *The Magus*, one of the influences which moved the English novel in the direction of the metafiction and magic realism so crucial to Farrell's later fictions.

As Frank Kermode has pointed out, 'the images of tragedy and the hero surely do brood over existentialist thought in general', but 'the existentialist man repeats the gestures of the tragic hero in a context which is not tragic but absurd'.[7] Sayer's single combat with Regan for control of the past is in part a neo-Romantic 'agon' with its Oedipal struggle between dying older man (father, god) and young rival (son, mortal). It could almost, as well, be a metaphor for the start of Farrell's own writing career – the kind of Oedipal conflict proposed by Harold Bloom in *The Anxiety of Influence* as the model for the struggle with the literary 'patriarchy' through which each new young (male) writer absorbs and overcomes tradition by 'misreading' it, in order to establish his own voice. The heroism of the battle between Sayer and Regan ('the reigning one'?), is undermined because the battle is fought in a comfortably bourgeois setting, and further, Sayer knows that the Party's real interest is not in 'truth', but only in evidence that will blacken Regan's name. Sayer eventually comes to see his 'heroic' quest for truth as no more than the work of a garbage-man filling his cart with trash: 'He could be proud of himself. He had rummaged through the filth without flinching at the smell of decay' (177).

Luc, the film-maker in *A Man from Elsewhere* (whose name is perhaps a wry nod in the direction of Jean-Luc Godard), produces war films but despises himself for heroising the war in trashy commercial features which consist mostly of 'clichés and patriotic grunts' (60). During his incompetent attempt to defend a drunken Algerian, he enters a café knowing he looks ridiculous because he cannot help being conscious of seeing his own actions through the heroic mode of B-grade movies:

> As he paused on the threshold he had a fleeting image of a Western film on which he had once worked and the feeling of absurdity increased. He was the hero flinging open the door of the saloon. ... Nobody had paid the slightest attention to his entry. (164)

The bathos in the last line of this passage was to become a recurrent technique of Farrell's. Here it repeats the rather more subtle but equally complete deflation of Luc's earlier claim to heroic status. When he dons the blue working-trousers and sweater that he believes will ally him with the freedom he imagines the working-classes enjoy, he also mentally adopts a new profession: thinking of Voltaire, he tells the unconvinced lorry driver that he is a *cultivateur* (145). Significantly, this is also the profession of Audin's son Serge, inscribed on the monument to the three executed war heroes (45). Audin, whose name repeats that of a Norse god of war (65) has made a 'shrine' out of his son's room in memory of his death in the war. Gretchen accuses all the men of being obsessed with the war which has now been over for years, as she reminds them. Yet the philosophical consequences of the war are made clear in a fragment of conversation from a minor character, Simon:

> Take any moderately sensitive person of my age in a world without values and you'll find he's really up against it. It's hard to carry on when you simply don't believe in anything, when you know the next war will be the last and that there's sure to be a war. ... (57)

Although in context this is the trite conventional anguish of a rather inane young man, the nihilist mood of this speech pervades the novel. Regan thinks to himself looking back over his work that 'he had done nothing more than express his own confusion and the confusion of his time. The old society was irrevocably shattered and the new one he had been unable to recognize' (107).

In spite of Gretchen's tirade at dinner against making heroes of people who kill each other, she wants to see Sayer as a prince, a knight in armour, a role that seems possible when he saves her from the attentions of the leather-jacketed youths in the café (134); but later in the evening Sayer-the-hero is knocked unconscious by the youths and dragged about the beach tied to a motor bike. He in turn must be rescued by the medical students camping nearby whose German nationality is a further irony. The old idea of heroism, of a prince or knight rescuing the maiden, is outmoded, temporary, impossible to sustain in the modern world. War has, paradoxically, both destroyed and re-established ideals of heroism. The discourses of heroism, stubbornly persisting in the culture and now apparently reinforced by the banalities of popular film, confront reality in *A Man from Elsewhere* and reveal themselves as either horror or farce. In the first of two related scenes Luc fails as a knight in armour because the Algerian's is not a cause he understands. In the second scene which follows shortly after, Luc 'rescues' the 'damsel in distress' (166), a seventeen-year-old virgin who is locked out of her bedroom (deliberately the reader suspects). But what he actually unlocks is her metaphoric chastity belt; the knight in armour is lost to a night of amour.

When Regan invites first Luc then Sayer to accompany him on his potentially suicidal car journey into the village neither is prepared to endanger their lives without reason. Sayer, in a phrase which hints at knights-in-armour heroism, tells Regan he is 'not interested in these feudal activities' (67); both need a reason to risk their lives, there must be a point in it. Yet Gretchen, who loves Regan, is immediately prepared to accompany him. Heroism seems now to be not the active movement towards some useless goal, but the passive heroic courage of merely struggling to go on into the future at a time when going on seems futile. In *A Man from Elsewhere* the experience of being locked in time is felt by Regan as an impulse to give up in despair. He remembers a period after the death of his wife

> when time had seemed to stand still, when the future had seemed a towering mountainface and each new hour a breathless, painful step in its ascent. In constant danger of slipping back he had hauled himself into the future with numb and bleeding fingers. (110)

This is the heroism of Beckett's Watt, or Murphy, or the Unnamable for whom physical endurance takes the place of metaphysical experience – summed up in the oft-quoted final words of the trilogy 'I can't go on, I'll go on'.[8] In a world without meaning, the time between birth and death must be filled with the repetition of cycles, rituals: in *A Man from Elsewhere* the shift workers in the factory in the first chapter are seen moving from the automated regimen of the factory out through the gates towards the 'rituals' of the day; Audin's axe-chopping takes on a Godot-like repetition. Heroism in this world is the courage to face whatever is. This leads to the ironies of the title: in an existential sense there is no elsewhere; 'the world is all the case that it is' in Wittgenstein's terms, and the word 'elsewhere' in Farrell's usage refers to the terrible knowledge of being imprisoned in the present, inescapably in time and in the world.

And yet, as in Beckett's works, the series of lone male characters at the centre of Farrell's six novels are all, in another sense, 'men from elsewhere' (and both Regan and Sayer are specifically described as men from elsewhere), radically displaced post-war persons, geographically, culturally, and psychically separated from any sense of belonging, struggling to make sense of ever more complicated contingencies which threaten to engulf them. Here Farrell anticipates Salman Rushdie and others in his recognition of the exile or migrant as a central paradigm of twentieth-century writing and life. In his introduction to Günter Grass's *On Writing and Politics, 1967–1983*, Rushdie suggests that migration

> offers us one of the richest metaphors of our age. The very word *metaphor*, with its roots in the Greek words for *bearing across*, describes a sort of migration, the migration of ideas into images. Migrants – borne-across humans – are metaphorical beings in their very essence; and migration, seen as a metaphor, is everywhere around us. We all cross frontiers; in that sense, we are all migrant peoples.[9]

Displacement, Rushdie would argue, like Farrell, is a feature of the post-war world, not just the post-colonial one. Unlike the traditional liberal humanist hero of realist fiction, Farrell's heroes never have all the facts, or a sense of control over their experience; there are always large areas of their situation which remain mysterious to them. Sayer alone is convinced (at least at first – his conviction is undermined during the course of the novel) of some possibility of arriving at a stable truth, the later 'heroes' get less and less confident with each novel.

Sayer begins grudgingly to admire Regan, not for his political views, but for his courage in the face of his own impending death, exemplified in his reluctant admiration of Regan's refusal to take the morphine offered him by his doctor (152). Regan, in turn, acknowledges Sayer's commitment to social change, but neither of these men gain any comfort from their idealism. Regan sees nothing but 'chaos, self-delusion, and fatigue' (105). In *A Man from Elsewhere*, however, Farrell has not yet the skills to link his subversion of the heroic with his ideological criticism. The anti-heroism works more effectively because it is demonstrated in the situations of the novel, whereas the ideology is largely presented in dialogues, debates Sayer has with Regan and Luc which fall short of any satisfactory investigation of either the communist or liberal humanist positions. In the end Sayer's and Regan's positions seem similar, and equally flawed, but it is difficult to know whether this is the impression intended.

Luc tries to convince Sayer of the value of Regan's novels, particularly of their doctrine of the importance of liberal humanist promotion of individualism, of standing alone outside the comfort of any party or group, but the irony is that in the end it may be Regan who has sacrificed personal relationships to principles, while Sayer, who thinks personal relationships 'a waste of time' (17), tries to save Gretchen. Regan himself wonders if the differences between himself and Sayer are merely part of the change from youth to age, 'inevitable evolution from revolt to conservatism ... for not only had the man himself changed but also the truth had changed, as it will for ageing men' (105). (This is a perception which Farrell reworks later in *Troubles*, and again in *The Siege of Krishnapur* when Fleury and the Collector seem to change ideological positions during the novel. It is also present in *The Singapore Grip*.)

It was perhaps the bleak seriousness and pessimism of *A Man from Elsewhere* and Farrell's subsequent move towards comedy which caused him later to dislike the novel and to talk of buying up all copies for pulping; but even in this novel there are flashes of bizarre humour very similar to Beckett's. In the early pages Sayer watches from the window as an old woman stops to exchange words with an old man walking a dog. He thinks that

> [c]onsidering the speed of [the earth's] revolution, the old man and the woman were doing very well to keep their balance. The dog was standing squarely on four legs and so deserved less credit. (15–16)

And then there is the black comedy of the mistakenly premature announcement of Regan's death, the consequences of which look so clearly forward to the grotesqueries of the Empire trilogy. The house is inundated with flowers and Regan experiences with grim satisfaction the sense of what his own funeral and obituaries will be like.

Farrell's debt to Beckett is obscured in *A Man from Elsewhere* because Farrell adopts what appears to be a realist style, including a plot with more straightforward development than the disorienting, unfathomable proceedings in *Malloy*, *Malone Dies*, and *The Unnamable*. *The Lung*, though still realist to begin with, moves rapidly closer to a kind of theatre of the absurd as the novel continues. The displacement which Martin Sands undergoes in this novel is not merely geographical, but involves a state of being, from health (perhaps) to illness, though the whole tenor of the work implies fundamental questions about 'normal' health and sanity.

There is a sense, too, of a Beckettian (or perhaps Brechtian) influence in Farrell's use of italics in *The Lung* (50 and 65). The italics (which temporarily shift the narrative to the present tense, and which, like the fictional story Martin is writing about 'Max', form a meta-narrative of their own) are clearly intended to read like stage directions and suggest that like the events in a stage play, life is a carefully directed, pre-determined drama. These stage directions describe a hospital room where Martin Sands '*is in a light feverish sleep*'. On the wall above the bed (again anticipating Rushdie[10])

*is a framed picture he has not yet seen. It is a print of 'The Young Raleigh',
showing a small boy sitting on his heels, arms clasped round his knees, and
listening spellbound to an old seaman who, right arm outstretched, is pointing
towards the horizon.* (50)

The print of 'The Young Raleigh' shows Raleigh's life being 'pointed out' for
him by the fisherman's pointing hand, and thus implicitly by the discourse of
adventure and imperialism in the story the fisherman is telling. This emphasises
an idea of life in which determinism and contingency together defeat any willed
human choice. The whole thing is futile in Martin's view, as a particularly
Beckettian exchange with Nurse Phelps suggests:

> 'Nurse, has it ever occurred to you that we are all just waiting for a
> tragedy to happen ... like the death of the people we love or our own
> death ...'
> ...
>
> '... and that it doesn't make any real difference whether this tragedy
> happens tomorrow or in twenty years time since there's no avoiding it
> ...'
> ...
>
> '... and that everything we do, absolutely everything, whether it's
> playing marbles or being the Prime Minister, is just a way of passing the
> time till it happens ... even the things we enjoy like going to the cinema
> or making love ...' (75)

The events of *The Lung* begin on an Easter Monday, ironically the day after
the Resurrection, with a hackneyed prophecy made to Sands about his future
by a fortune-teller; the novel finishes just a year later. With an irony typical of
Farrell's later work, Sands only meets the fortune-teller because he believes he
is entering a refreshments tent at a fair where he ventures in dire need of an
alcoholic drink. In the last few lines of the novel, Sands realises that it is Easter
again already, but the question of whether his alienation, weltschmerz, angst,
has been cured along with his illness is not so easily decided by reference to
this hopeful Christian symbol. For one thing, his recognition that it is Easter
sigificantly comes by his seeing the chocolate easter eggs in shops, signs of the
commercialisation of the ritual. He admits to the doctor that he is 'a little'
changed, but the affirmation of life in the last few lines is equivocal and guarded
and very reminiscent of Beckett: 'Perhaps. No. Yes. Perhaps' (207).

Farrell's use in these two novels of a circular form – based in *A Man from
Elsewhere* on place, Paris to Paris, in *The Lung* on time, Easter to Easter – is
reminiscent of Lowry, a writer Farrell particularly admired, and one can see

further reflections of *Under the Volcano* in Martin's dark glasses, in his drunkeness, in the effects on him of his wife's infidelity, in the repeated animal imagery, and in the symbolic sign in the hospital gardens which points down to the earth (the grave or hell). The form can also be seen, though, as a post-Sartrean effort to resist full closure, an attempt to reproduce in fiction life's refusal to provide any place to rest in a conclusion except death.[11]

The novel begins at a church where Sands is supposed to be attending a wedding, and it ends with the possibility of his own wedding. But the optimism apparently offered by the neat bourgeois traditionalism of this form is undermined by a number of ironies and absurdities. The woman with whom he leaves the hospital and whom he may marry is the daughter of his former wife (by another husband). In the last lines of the novel he thinks farcically to himself in a parody of pseudo-autobiographical fiction: 'I married my exstepdaughter and we had ten children and lived happily ever after. It was just terrible' (207). The ludicrous elements of the situation are exacerbated by the reader's knowledge of the contingencies Sands has experienced during the past year, the frightening and near-fatal paralysis of an unexpected attack of polio, medical treatment in an iron lung which resembles an instrument of medieval torture, and any number of incidental indignities and embarrassments related to the physical body in which the mind seems to be imprisoned. There remains no certainty at all that anything outside the hospital will be an improvement, or that such difficulties can be avoided by exercise of the mind and will. The *mens sana in corpore sano*, the healthy mind in a healthy body which has been the ideal of the liberal humanist subject since the Enlightenment looked back to the classical world, seems now merely a matter of luck, or unluckiness (signalled by the black cat which follows Sands's fishy shoes at the beginning). These saturated images of grotesque physicality and disease take up the unheroic visions of the body already evident in *A Man from Elsewhere*: the unnamed girl Sayer leaves in the first chapter accuses him of being 'inhuman … a piece of cold meat hanging in a butcher's' (16). Luc too thinks of himself as 'a clockwork toy' (113) and 'living meat' (168).

Martin Sands in his iron lung exhibits a state of being like that of Beckett's Murphy who seems to enact a Cartesian split into mind and body, eventually half man, half rocking-chair. Hugh Kenner sees Beckett's 'Cartesian Centaurs' as half-man, half bicycle,[12] and Sands, too, becomes half man, half machine as the lung breathes for him. But Kenner's ego-cyclistical Centaur refers only to the earlier Beckett heroes for whom motion is still possible; Farrell's Sands is more like Beckett's later Hamm in his dustbin, or Krapp, a voice and a taperecorder, or Winnie in *Happy Days* (1961), buried first to the waist and then up to the neck. The human here is reduced to a perverse tendency to continue to exist, though to what ultimate end is not clear in either Beckett's or Farrell's work.

The overriding trope in this novel, though, is that of the pervasive sickness of the individual and collective human condition, again reminiscent of Camus, this time *The Plague* (1947), and other writers of the period (including perhaps Colin Wilson, whose existentialist novel *The Outsider* was published in 1956). William Golding in *The Hot Gates* (1965) links the idea of a diseased morality with the post-war recognition of the inhumanity of 'civilized' man:

> there were things done during [the Second World War] from which I still have to avert my mind less I should be physically sick. They were not done by the headhunters of New Guinea, or by some primitive tribe in the Amazon. They were done, skilfully, coldly, by educated men, ... men with a tradition of civilization behind them, to beings of their own kind. ... I believed that the condition of man was to be a morally diseased creation ...[13]

The idea of the dis-ease of the times had already been suggested in *A Man from Elsewhere* after Gretchen's outburst about war films:

> At length the conversation was resumed with another topic, but uneasily, as if everyone were aware that what they had been talking about, although never mentioned, had its roots in all human morality and behaviour, decaying roots which belied the healthy appearance of their conversation and in some way imparted to them all a diseased future. (62)

Both time and illness were to become preoccupations throughout Farrell's later novels, and sickness has been cited by a number of critics as a metaphor for diseased and dying colonial regimes in his Empire trilogy. But what these early novels so clearly show is that his interest in time and his tropes of disease are well established in his earliest work and originate in Farrell's perceptions of the period contemporary with his writing. His characters' (and Farrell's own) personal experiences of illness and the dislocations of time are translated into themes which seek to probe, if not the possibilities, then the impossibilities of human life in the mid twentieth century. This point is vital because it explains the motivation of his later explorations of history. In his hands the writing of history is not, as the modernists had felt it to be, a retreat from the problems of the present, but rather an attempt to explain the problems of the present by analysis of past mistakes, thus providing groundwork for vital changes. Farrell, writing with a socialist conviction established during his student days, acts on Georg Lukács's admonition that the historical novel is doing its work properly when it 'bring[s] the past to life as the prehistory of the present'.[14] From these first two novels he is involved in the dialectic between humanist and antihumanist conceptions of the subject which form so significant a part of the movement from modernism to postmodernism (whatever the disagreements about the definitive form of either).

Sayer's name, ironically pointing to his ineffectiveness, and highlighting the fact that whatever else he may have been Regan was a 'doer', was an early indication in *A Man from Elsewhere* of Farrell's interest in language, an interest that he carefully developed in *The Lung*. The most obvious play with language in that novel is in his use of puns, in both English and French. At the most obvious level puns remind us that words can have more than one meaning, that language tells many stories, that no story can be told as if it is the only one. His language games also point back to other writers, to the infinite intertextuality of literature. When Farrell writes '... the sloe eyed, the slow wide ... ' (113), he is instantly recalling Dylan Thomas's 'sloe-black, slow, black' in the opening of *Under Milk Wood* (1954), which in turn must recall all those writers who influenced Thomas himself, and so on. His punning in French serves a more specific purpose, acknowledging the influence of the *nouveau roman* in general, and specifically of Alain Robbe-Grillet (who wrote the screenplay for *Last Year in Marienbad* [1962], one of the most famous and influential art-films of the early 1960s). At one point in *The Lung* Louis, Sally's French lover who is visiting Martin, says slyly to the nurse with pimples, '*Y'en a qui ont perdu la fleur mais qui ont quand même conservé des boutons ...*' (106) ('There are those who have lost the flower, but preserved the bud ...'). There is an obvious sexual pun here, but also a triple play on the meaning of *boutons*, which can mean buttons and pimples as well as bud. Martin imagines Louis standing in front of a mirror and saying to himself: '*Tu es une fine braguette, mon vieux ... mais oui!*' A deft flybuttons! (106) ('You are a great seducer!'). Here the English highlights the pun on the word *braguette*, which can mean both seducer and flybuttons, and also links the two French sentences through their common play on words for buttons. This punning is also reminiscent of Robbe-Grillet, the titles of whose novels *La Jalousie* (1957) and *Les Gommes* (1953) were translated into English as *Jealousy* (1960) and *The Erasers* (1966). However, the former can also mean 'venetian blinds', and the latter too has suggestive ambiguities. Each translation offers a different clue to possible interpretations of the novel.

Farrell's use of the comedy of the grotesque shows marked development between *A Man from Elsewhere* and *The Lung*, and in the latter novel Farrell's attention is particularly concentrated on severed images of body parts, a preoccupation which gains in extent and savagery in the Empire trilogy. Harris shows Sands the photographs of his former fast-bowling which reveal the surrealism of life stopped in mid-action:

> To Sands they looked like stills from the film of some exotic dance. There
> were pictures of Harris with his arms lifted in wild ecstasy, of Harris
> bowed almost to the ground, one arm floating gracefully behind, after
> delivery ... of him in an agony of flailing limbs as he prepared to release
> the ball ... of him suspended in mid-air as he dived to hold some catch
> ... of him with his hands clutched to his mouth in the tyranny of despair
> at some missed chance ... (105)

When Harris tears up these photos they disintegrate into fragmented images
of a hand clutching a ball, a pair of boots in the air, dismembered body parts
which recall again the terrible dependence of the identity on keeping the mind
and body together.

The curious and grotesque antics of the human body show gross disjunction
between action and meaning in the scene of Sands's premeditated seduction of
Marigold. Because of the weakness of his arms and hands he knows he will
be unable to undress her and so plans to chop away her undergarments with a
pair of scissors he has previously concealed. Farrell describes the detail of the cold
steel sliding between her bra and the skin, so that the act is less like tenderness
than attack, less a meeting of emotions and more the complex gymnastics of sex
as 'a sort of eight-limbed Australian crawl' (59), as Gretchen sees it in *A Man
from Elsewhere*. Earlier, in *The Lung*, Martin, while Marigold kisses him, 'evolve[s]
a way of breathing out of the corner of his mouth, something after the fashion
in which a swimmer breathes while doing the Australian crawl' [154]).

The slapstick/burlesque of other scenes is a reminder that the context of
early Beckett is also that of Charlie Chaplin. During his convalescence Sands,
standing in the lavatory of the village pub, reads a question in the graffiti on the
walls. This question, like most of the questions in Sands's life, has no answer:

> The question seemed to be rhetorical. Disappointed he pulled the swing
> door and stood on the threshold of the lounge. For a terrible moment
> he thought the others must have left. The swing door, forgotten, swung
> and hitting him a solid blow in the back, dropped him. He lay on the
> dirty floor beside an empty cigarette packet and a half nibbled meat pie.
> For the sake of appearances he groaned. Actually he was feeling quite
> comfortable. The ceiling was yellowish and innocent of jokes, most
> restful to the eye. (191)

Similar moments of slapstick humour persist through Farrell's fiction to his
last completed novel *The Singapore Grip*.

Sands's recuperation in the hospital has been accompanied by the collateral
antics of the four men who share his ward and who seems to represent various

kinds of sane insanity. They are Wilson, with his obsession that cars ought to be banned because they cause so many accidental deaths each year; Harris, the former professional cricketer who has somehow lost his ability to believe in the importance of the game, and Exmoore, the clergyman who finally confesses 'the worst', his realisation that he wanted his congregation to love himself, not God, that his 'gorgeous rhetoric' has been nothing but the words of an actor seducing his audience. The fourth member of what amounts to a Greek chorus is 'old man Rivers', the silent, basketmaking geriatric in the corner. Each of the first three, in actions which comment ironically on the health and sanity of normal society, gives up their identity. Wilson commits suicide after it is discovered that on his trips to the village to 'buy postcards' he has actually been slitting the tyres of the fiendish motor vehicles. Harris tears up into little pieces the newspaper cuttings and photographs of his bowling heyday in a move which destroys forever the old identity which has been his continual solace. It is revealed that Exmoore has previously been called 'Moore' but has changed his name in what the doctor calls 'a joke of some kind' (110), but which is primarily a statement of a once-certain identity now lost.

Each of these men also convey hints of a once-heroic status. Wilson is called 'the invisible Wilson', while Harris, the incredible fast-bowler, is known as Hurricane Harris, a phrase which seems to come from one of the *'Boy's Own'*-style comics of the period. Exmoore, with his paisley silk dressing-gown, his cane, his cigarette holder, and his air of decadent aristocratic eccentricity, is associated with the references to Byron, Napoleon, and Don Quixote (as well as Noel Coward) which foreground in this text the failure of traditional, aristocratic literary heroism. Byron died during the inglorious ineptitudes of Missalonghi; Napoleon survived one exile and imprisonment, but not the next; Don Quixote tilted at windmills. Sands himself recovers his breath when placed in the iron lung, and feels 'like Johnny Weismuller in a speeded-up Tarzan film he had once seen when Lady Jane was being hotly pursued by crocodiles' (66). But the illusion of joy soon vanishes as he discovers that he can only only breathe as the machine dictates, and is actually 'as horizontal and as petrified as a stone crusader' (66), that is, a dead hero.

What seems to take the place of literary/historical ideas of heroism in *The Lung* is some almost incommunicable idea of freedom and life represented by a recurrent image which flashes into Sands's dreams and waking moments, the image of a fox and a pyramid of oranges in a waste of snow. The vividness of the orange and rust red against the white are never fully explained in the novel but seem to act as some kind of surreal affirmation of the persistence of vivid life, the exotic, the barely imaginable wild Other, against a background of whiteness, coldness, blankness, sterility, pseudo-domesticity, represented by winter in the English hospital. It seems likely that the fox is an image which stems from Farrell's acknowledged admiration of Richard Hughes's novel *The Fox in the Attic* (1961),[15] a reminder of the wildness that coexists within domesticity. In *The Lung* the fox's tail is wounded and the living red of blood follows it in the snow like a sign, a banner.

In spite of the comedy though, the bleak note of *A Man from Elsewhere* persists in the friendship between Sands and the young girl, Monica, who thinks he is a hero. As he leaves the hospital he asks the doctor about her mysterious illness and is told reluctantly that she has leukemia (and in this she is a forerunner of Angela in *Troubles*). At first he thinks of the waste of her life, 'her growing up for nothing. Her body developing into a woman's body for nothing. All her desires and dreams and personality conceived for nothing' (204–05), but later he tells Marigold bleakly: 'I was thinking about Monica … You know, I'm not sure she isn't better off dead' (206).

Bergonzi has commented on the way reality in America continually outstrips in outrageousness anything that fiction can offer. Farrell's particular line on this, now and in the next four novels, is his fascination with the surreal relations between the life of the mind or internal, private world and the equally extraordinary but unsynchronised life of the external public world. Life is always stranger than fiction and the challenge is to find a fictional means of rendering this. Reality lies just exactly in the continual adjustment and readjustments the individual makes without even noticing how odd some of these manoeuvres are.

These two first novels mark Farrell's years of exploration for the form he needed. Although he was still to write one more novel set in contemporary England before embarking on the historical genre that was to be his forte, the two first novels hold together as a group. And while neither *A Man from Elsewhere* nor *The Lung* is a great work – both are perhaps pushing in too many directions, diffusing interest rather than concentrating it – they are significant works within the context of Farrell's total oeuvre. They point to many of the themes and ideas that would later be developed in *A Girl in the Head* and in the Empire trilogy. Farrell's own sense of a change of direction after this is indicated by the change in his authorial signature, from 'James Farrell' to 'J.G. Farrell' for the novels from *A Girl in the Head* onwards (though this may also have been to separate himself from any confusion with the much better-known American writer, James T. Farrell, author of the 'Studs Lonigan' trilogy).[16]

3 / The Hero as Text: *A Girl in the Head*

Like Farrell's first two novels, his third, *A Girl in the Head* (called *The Succubus* in an earlier version[1]) focuses on a central male character alienated from the world in which he lives. The impoverished Anglo-Polish aristocrat Count Boris Slattery wanders from mid-summer to early autumn around Maidenhair Bay, a middle-class English seaside town he morosely describes as 'an insignificant little tropolis', 'the cemetry of all initiative and endeavour'. During this time he muses on his past and the apparently random contingencies which made him alight from a train in this place 'all those years ago' (15).

He was at the time (or so he claims in not-always-plausible asides), a 'lonely, rather distinguished figure' (16) in crocodile shoes, from another world, 'a world of summit discussions and top-level talks' (15). By accidentally saving Granny Marie-Thé, he met the Dongeon family, owners of 'Boscobel', a decaying Victorian mansion. The house is named after one in Southport owned by Farrell's family for several years, and in some ways anticipates the symbolic role of the Majestic Hotel in *Troubles*.[2]

The Dongeon family, as their name indicates, represent the suburban middle-class world which Boris believes has imprisoned him. Dongeon is an obsolete spelling of dungeon used as either a noun or a verb and Boris certainly believes himself to be a potential hero trapped in the dullness of the bourgeois-ordinary. Closely linked to the central theme of alienation in this novel (and already developed in Farrell's first two novels) is a sense of imprisonment which was also apparent earlier, but in this novel both alienation and imprisonment are treated with an ironic awareness of their almost clichéd status in contemporary fiction. If the iron lung which contains Martin Sands for lengthy periods in *The Lung* can be seen as a metaphor for modern society, then the same sense of imprisonment can be seen, more mockingly treated, in Boris's relationship with the Dongeon family. In apparently self-satirising capitulation to circumstances, Boris has married the Dongeons' ample daughter, Flower, and settled into the aimless life which is now the subject of lengthy passages of wry autobiographical soliloquy. These are interjected in italics between the omniscient narration.

Boris is a 'waiter'. He waits for time to pass. He spends the brief summer waiting for the coming of Inez, the teenage girl whose image in his head forms one of the referents for the title. Waiting is symbolic of the human condition, as Farrell had shown (via Beckett) in *The Lung*, even if the awaited one in *A Girl in the Head* is not Beckett's God(ot) but, suitably for the late 1960s, a fantasised female representing idealised sexual desire. Boris is also a (glorified) waiter at the local restaurant called 'The Groaning Board', a pun on Boris as the groaning bored. Throughout the novel there are references to Boris's habit of groaning at home (19), at the cinema (55), at the circus (192 and 196), on the beach (176), and frequently elsewhere. Although his groaning is usually an involuntary sign of existential anguish, it can also indicate repressed sexual desire (as when he watches Inez on the beach), and extreme contingent boredom (as at the circus). Only at the end of the novel after Inez has departed and other changes have occurred does Boris stop groaning, at which point the Dongeons are concerned about him and realise they would be reassured by a few heartfelt groans.

The pun as *différance* here opens up another chasm between the texts that society offers and the possibility of their real consummation in experience. The plentitude in one meaning of the phrase, 'The Groaning Board', hides the signification of an existence which starves Boris's soul (in spite of all Flower's activities in the kitchen). Hungry for something which he interprets as sexual action, but which may be love, he is always reduced to the unsatisfactory phrases, words, and then groans, which stand in place of whatever real consummation he desires. At one extraordinary moment he attempts to 'translate' sexual love into food by placing one of Flower's large breasts (still attached to its reluctant owner) into a frying-pan just to see what it looks like.

Boris's groaning also suggests similarities with the unheroic heroes of Saul Bellow's *Seize the Day* (1957), *Henderson the Rain King* (1959), and *Herzog* (1964), all tragi-comic existential groaners to a man, all troubled, like Boris, by women, alcohol, the past, and the transience and meaning of human life.

Bellow is not the only American whose work Farrell's resembles. His early travels around Canada and the USA and his two-year stay in America on a Harkness Scholarship (awarded in 1966) gave him familiarity with contemporary American fiction and its new phases of experiment. Bernard Bergonzi, writing in 1970 about *The Situation of the Novel*, acknowledges a body of critical discussion about the 'American-ness of American literature' as it was perceived in England at that time:

> We are familiar with the way in which the heroes of American novels are defiant solitaries, preserving their precious burden of innocence and freedom, ... everything, in fact, that John Bayley means when he refers to American literature as being peculiarly concerned with the Human Condition. We know, too, about the persistence of a strain of Gothic fantasy as a central element in American fiction, and ... we expect to meet a high proportion of freakishness and eccentricity. We have been shown

at length by Leslie Fiedler how the characters in American novels persist in moral childishness or at best adolescence, and find it very difficult to establish and maintain normal, mature sexual relations.[3]

These are the very qualities of which Boris is made. He is both imitation and parody of the American hero in an English setting.

Another intertextual influence strongly apparent here is that of Nabokov's *Lolita* (1955).[4] Like *Lolita*, *A Girl in the Head* is structured by obsession and pursuit. (As Binns point out, *Lolita* is the classic case of having a girl in the head). Boris, like Humbert Humbert, is an older man, also purportedly a middle-European emigré contemptuous of bourgeois Western domesticity and in loco parentis to the teenage girl whom he pursues. He too, is married to an older woman associated with stereotypical images of suburban-domestic dullness, while dreaming of a younger woman who represents all in life that is lost or never achieved over time.

As Binns has pointed out, Boris, wearing dark glasses, perambulating with alcoholic unsteadiness around Boscobel's overgrown garden and tennis court, the beach, the municipal gardens, and various pubs in the town, followed by the dog Bonzo, seems very like Malcolm Lowry's Consul in *Under the Volcano*.[5] Like the Consul too, Boris imbibes regularly from a silver flask, visits a cinema and sees a film whose action he relates to his own life, and has for one of his few friends a doctor, whose conversation continually invokes questions about human existence and meaning. Binns judges that Farrell does not achieve the tragic depths of Lowry's novel, but it is arguable that his intentions are very different, that Farrell simply uses Boris's resemblance to the Consul to emphasise the anti-heroic theme of his earlier novels, but now with an added parodic dimension.

Lowry's Consul conveys a Faustian sense of opportunities wasted, of a potentially fine and gifted man falling away from the possibility of heroic achievement because of the contingencies of his life. Farrell's anti-hero is quite different in effect. Although Boris implies in his soliloquies that his genius has been stifled by the Dongeon 'petits bourgeois' (110), the reader, mediating between the omniscient narration and Boris's own musings, knows that Boris is often self-deluding. The novel as a whole conveys the message that the belief in the possibility of heroic achievement is always illusion. Heroism exists only as a discourse constructed by a society in which it is no longer possible to believe.

It is also implied here that the alternation between optimism and pessimism, achievement and tragedy, is largely a matter of the difference between physical (and correspondingly psychical) sickness and health, part of the text written by the body. (But which is which? Is it healthy to be optimistic about humankind, or merely deluded? Is it sick to be pessimistic, or merely honest?)

The sense of the heroic-possible still present in Lowry is subverted in this novel by the kind of Beckettian absurdity so observable in *The Lung*, but now extended to apply to the individual's place in history. Walking through the town with Dr Cohen, Boris observes streets full of 'imposing Victorian houses, façades decorated with ornate masonry':

> What had happened to all the large, solid families who had once lived in these houses? They had been so sure that living in solid houses at the centre of a vast Empire they had a foot wedged in the door of eternity. Boris could find no satisfaction in the thought that they had deluded themselves. (87)

Architecture speaks as a text of the past here and introduces a question about the relations between past, present, and future which leads directly to the Empire trilogy.

The anti-hero of *A Man from Elsewhere* and *The Lung* now confronts history through visual texts also – photographs and 'vast historical' paintings – which, far from affording comfort or heroic models, reveal that the human is not just contingently but innately absurd. The narrative now changes to a first-person autobiographical form as Boris inserts himself into the text of history:

> The trouble about looking at these old photographs is that history leaks into the present through insignificant details. … It's the details that are so distressing. When I look at myself now in the light of these old pictures I get a most disagreeable sensation of being nothing but a detail myself. It's like looking at your face painted on one of those vast historical canvases. I look at myself. In close-up my face is commanding, terrible, awe-inspiring. Here I am … a great politician unrolling a map, or a general on a horse, or a renowned lover of the bluest blood surrounded by his mistresses. … But then, as I step back from the canvas, other parts of the picture creep into view with equal importance. Who the hell is that oafish character grinning vacantly as he scratches his armpit? He should be holding my prancing horse. And why is that dog allowed to chew a bone so near to me? It dilutes my importance. … Of course, I realize that it's nonsense to think of one's life as a meaningless detail rapidly receding into a mass of other meaningless details. But I confess that the thought has occurred to me from time to time. (26)[6]

The 'I' looking at 'myself' in history is a moment like Lacan's 'mirror-stage' of recognition that the 'I' who speaks is never the same as the 'I' which becomes the subject of the spoken.

There are strong echoes in this passage of the modernist anti-heroic stance of W.H. Auden's poem, 'Musée des Beaux Arts' (1940), in which both martyr-dom and miracle take place almost unnoticed 'While someone else is eating or opening a window or just walking dully along' and while '… the dogs go on with their doggy life and the torturer's horse / Scratches its innocent behind on a tree'.[7] Auden's ancillary point is that the artists, painters, writers, poets of every generation simultaneously re-present to the culture its own heroic myths and, in doing so, re-imagine the idea of the heroic for their own times. Demonstrating this is often the purpose of Farrell's calculated intertextual references, prominent in his work since *A Man from Elsewhere* but used with increasing effectiveness through the Empire trilogy. The sporadic deflation of the idea of the hero in the two earlier novels gives place to a new strategy in *A Girl in the Head*. Now Farrell constructs a cumulative assembly of fictional scenes and intertextual references which, like Boris's soliloquy quoted above, foregrounds many elements of the postmodern including the following:

> *a nostalgic conservative longing for the past, coupled with an erasure of the boundaries between past and present; an intense preoccupation with the real and its representations; a pornography of the visible; the commodification of sexuality and desire; a consumer culture which objectifies a set of masculine cultural ideals; intense emotional experiences shaped by anxiety, alienation, ressentiment and a detachment from others.*[8]

Farrell, like Thomas Pynchon in *The Crying of Lot 49* (1966),[9] a novel which he certainly read,[10] and may have had the chance to read before completing the manuscript of *A Girl in the Head*, also intertextualises Jacobean drama for its sense of a world of moral relativism. As Marguerite Alexander explains, 'Jacobean drama, like postmodernist fiction, is often morally ambiguous, [and] deals with relative values rather than absolutes'.[11] It is also meta-theatrical in its self-conscious use of stage directions and its obsession with tacked-on endings. At one point Boris, echoing Webster, thinks to himself 'My soul … like to a ship in a black storm' (95),[12] in which he sees himself afloat in a world of black, unintelligible daily existence. There is a Websterian sense in Farrell's fiction of a decadent civilisation (whether it be reflected in Maidenhair Bay, Dublin, Krishnapur, or Singapore) out of which redeeming human qualities occasionally surface.[13]

Boris waits, and while he waits he watches: a voyeur, a spectator, in the Baudrillardian sense that the 'members of the contemporary world are voyeurs adrift on a sea of symbols'.[14] The novel opens with him watching the beach from a tree through binoculars; he watches films, watches through windows, across the garden, through a hole he makes in the floor of his room, at the circus show where he sees Lady Jane and the lion. This seedy passive role is one of the first signs that he cannot maintain the conventionally active role of the literary hero. His early episode of reconnaissance from the sycamore tree is rendered absurd by the comments of his wife and in-laws from the ground, and by the fact that he has to be rescued by the fire-brigade. During his meditations in the tree the reader hears of Boris's recent and sudden slight heart attack, a *memento mori* which, together with the vision of the unknown Inez, is responsible for his present mood of preoccupation with the brevity and yearning of human life. But the incipient seriousness of this theme is always undercut by Farrell almost as it is conveyed: after his heart attack in the street, Boris is carried to the hospital recumbent on a stretcher with the potatoes he had been carrying ranged surrealistically around him as though he were 'a side of beef on its way to the oven' (8).

On his visit to the cinema with Alessandro, a young male guest of the Dongeons, Boris at first imagines himself, in a surge of lyrical clichés, as a romantic figure, 'strolling through a leafy forest dappled with sunlight, hand in hand with a beautiful, laughing girl whose white skirt swung like a lantern as she stepped down towards a waterfall' (54). Soon afterwards when the main feature comes on he appears to merge with the hero of the western they are watching until his drunken interjections cause their unheroic eviction from the cinema.

On another occasion he describes himself in heroic terms through the photograph of

> [a] human pyramid at a military academy near Jena with young Boris at the top flourishing a cutlass in one hand, in the other the regimental mascot (a white and smelly ram that I subsequently dropped while trying to get down, chipping one of its horns).
> ...
> The reason I mention the human pyramid, however, is that my position at the top of it seemed to me, as a younger man, to have a certain symbolic rightness about it (though the real reason for my elevation was that I happened to be the youngest and lightest cadet in the place). (103–04)

Boris's untidy descent from the pyramid[15] and the 'real reason' for his elevation continue a deflation of his heroism which falls further when he is addressed by someone in the street as 'Mick Slattery from Limerick!' (58). It appears that he may be neither aristocratic nor Polish at all. Though the reader can never be certain, Alessandro does call Flower 'Mrs Slattery' on one occasion (209). Similarly, the appellation 'The Gentleman Who Saved My Life' (110) given to Boris by Granny Marie-Thé (whose name is a pun on 'Marie' tea biscuits mentioned in *The Lung* [95]) is undermined because it has led him down into the

Dongeon household, a condition he apparently thinks of as a hell or purgatory state.

Boris begins to approach at this point the dilemma in which existentialists with a social conscience found themselves during the 1960s. Convinced that individual human life is meaningless and terrifyingly contingent, they still sought to discover social principles on which to intervene in history to alleviate the grosser kinds of injustice, and to theorise the processes of the individual in history. As Elizabeth Grosz so clearly puts it:

> By the Cold War period of the 1950s and 1960s phenomenology/existentialism and mechanistic marxism were the two extremes of French leftist politics and theory. Even though there were a number of individuals who attempted to reconcile the two ... they still seemed to be opposed. ... Where existentialism lacks a broad understanding of social and economic relations, or indeed any account of oppression and exploitation, marxism lacks a detailed understanding of the specifically ideological, cultural and interpersonal dynamics of capitalism, and, above all, an explanation of the lived experiences of bourgeois subjects.
>
> From the early 1960s Sartre attempted to integrate these apparently opposed positions. ... These political shifts and realignments ... provided at least some of the impetus for the emergence of an antihumanist and anti-reductionist marxism, represented in the 1960s by the work of Louis Althusser.[16]

Because of Farrell's fluent French, his two years of living in Paris, his interest in Lukács's Marxism and Sartre's existentialism, and his wide contemporary reading, there is little doubt that he was aware of these remakings of the French left-wing groups during the late 1960s. He shows in *A Girl in the Head* and on through all his later work that whatever ironic smile he might occasionally bring to this philosophising, he is deeply interested in two issues central to Louis Althusser's version of Marxism; first, the processes by which 'cultural products' (i.e. the artistic and literary works of a culture, or what Althusser calls ISAs, 'Intellectual State Apparatuses') act upon individuals and societies to produce, reinforce, change, question, and in other ways influence that society; and secondly, the imagined and actual relations of individual human subjects to history. In the Empire trilogy Farrell creates the action of each novel around these questions, but in *A Girl in the Head* Boris can only muse ineffectually on the muffling effects of his present life:

> And at this very moment, while [Boris] was standing in the nauseating unreality of Maidenhair Bay, people all over the world were dying

grotesque deaths in unromantic wars. Only in Maidenhair Bay could one
ignore reality in such a way. And it was surely a crime. (32)

As David Lodge makes clear in 'The Novelist at the Crossroads', this
question of social and historical responsibility became not just a matter of
theme in the 1960s and 1970s, but of technique.[17] Lukács had argued that the
impressionistic style of the modernists was socially irresponsible because it
focused exclusively on a solipsistic individual response to experience. He urged
a return to a realist style (in *Studies in European Realism* [1972]), arguing that
the task of the novel is to aid history to produce the unified human self. There
was a brief return to the kind of social realism Farrell had used in *A Man from
Elsewhere* in reaction to what now seemed for many reasons the experimental
dead-end of modernism, but this in turn was de-stabilised by what Robert
Scholes called 'fabulation', which can be seen with hindsight as associated with
the magic realism and metafiction of later postmodernism.[18]

A Girl in the Head is different from Farrell's two earlier novels in having the
comic as its dominant mode. There is an accompanying sense of the tragic, but
it arises, as it does in Beckett, out of the absurd disparity between the grandiose
philosophical and literary ideas humans have about humanity, and the insignificant thing humanity turns out to be when viewed through science and eternity.
It is not only himself that Boris wants to see as a hero. He thinks of the ice-cream
man on the sea-front as 'scanning the horizon for a white sail to appear, his
lover returning ... *Yseult des Blanches Mains* and all that sort of thing' (29). But
Dr Cohen calls this nonsense and says that the man is simply standing there
in a 'bovine reverie waiting for someone to buy his ice-creams'.[19] Boris also
sees the young man Alessandro as a Byronic hero (although significantly in *The
Lung* Byron is described as '[r]ather a pathetic chap in many ways' [27]).
Alessandro wears a scarlet cloak that Boris has given him (Boris bought it for
himself but never had the courage to wear it [12]) and often rides the white
horse which provides such a contrast for Boris's own unheroic Beckettian steed,
an old bicycle. In the following passage a gothic twist blends the Romantic/
Byronic hero with the screen vampire depicted by actors like Peter Cushing
and Christopher Lee in so many 'Dracula' films of the 1960s:

... he saw that Alessandro was trotting up swiftly on his magnificent
white horse, Starlight. Boris had seen a number of films in which stallions
reared up and trampled people to death, usually pregnant ladies. In
response to a sudden vision of Starlight's flashing hooves he at last
managed to struggle to his feet, breathing hard. Alessandro pulled the
horse up a few feet away and slid to the ground. He spoke a couple of
sharp words. The horse nodded, sneezed and waltzed back a couple of
paces, terrifying Boris.

Alessandro came over with his cloak swinging and billowing in the wind, identical in colour to Boris's streaming fingers. He said nothing but his dark eyes flickered from Boris's face to the hand that was scattering dark drops on the grey stones. Starlight, drooping his head in a bored fashion, had apparently abandoned the idea of trampling him to death.

'I tripped,' Boris said awkwardly. 'Silly. No, it's nothing. Just winded myself a bit ...'

'Let me see your hand.'

The boy reached forward and grasped Boris's wrist, turning the palm to the sky. Lifting it to his face he began to suck the blood from the palm. (100–01)

Another such appearance on horseback is followed by Alessandro's decidedly unheroic appearance in a borrowed female swimsuit rolled down and tucked under at the waist (130).

And ultimately, when Alessandro goes out looking for lost Inez he fails to find her, becomes lost himself, and has to be rescued by a cheerfully incompetent pack of Boy Scouts in one of those lengthy tragi-farcical episodes at which Farrell excels. Inez, who has fallen from her horse, is picked up by a passing grocery van which delivers her to Boscobel with 'two packets of cornflakes, a stone of castor sugar and four ounces of yeast' (182) – a deflation which recalls Boris on the stretcher with vegetables in the first pages of the novel.

Boris reads a phrase in Alessandro's biology textbook which recurs throughout the novel and which completes the demolition of the idea of the heroic: 'Living creatures ... ultimately consist entirely of chemicals. Basically, the story of life is a story of chemicals' (23). Boris is 'a piece of driftwood, inert, momentarily washed up there on the stony beach waiting (but not even waiting) for the tide to return and nurse him slowly and aimlessly out on to that undulating fusion of hydrogen and oxygen (or whatever it was)' (139).

Towards the end of the novel Boris becomes excited when he thinks that The Mysterious X, the magician, has looked into him during the performance and has seen something beyond chemicals, some internal essence. He stumbles backstage and confronts a disillusioning scene with Lady Jane and the lion in which he again finds that what seems to be exotic at a distance turns dull domestic at close range. Directed onwards, he finds The Mysterious X and demands to know what X saw in his mind:

'You must believe me,' muttered The Mysterious X. 'I saw nothing at all. Just pain maybe ... You'd hurt your hand. Pain and ... darkness. Just darkness ... Nothing.' (198)

The reader understands that this may be exactly what lies 'inside' human beings, nothing – just pain and darkness, but Boris refuses to accept this:

> 'You saw mortality and the death of love!'
> The Mysterious X grasped the white towel and dried his armpits mechanically. Tears were flooding from his eyes now and rimming the black mask.
> 'But I made a mistake, you see. I saw that the heart was a muscle. I saw ... You moved your head and the light changed ... and then I saw nothing but darkness.'
> 'And then?' Boris cried suddenly. 'Did you see an immortal soul? Did you see one of those?'
> 'I'm not sure,' The Mysterious X said miserably. 'I don't think I'd know one if I saw one.' (198)

Boris manifests most of the time a purely individualist, existentialist sense of weariness and disillusion, and indeed the novel as a whole is, like *A Man from Elsewhere* and *The Lung*, suffused by the sense of passing time. Binns suggests that Boris is like the Consul in being frightened by a sunflower, but in Farrell this is a symbol of transience and fragility, seen too in the seasonal or cyclical repetition voiced by many characters in the novel.[20] 'Snow in winter', Granny Dongeon says at one point, 'Apples in autumn, year in, year out' (18). And Boris takes up this same theme later:

> And the seasons! He was living alone inside an enormous clock. Beside him the cogs and wheels clicked over and over relentlessly, round and round in the same cruel circles. The same revolutions endlessly ending, endlessly beginning again, repeating, ending, beginning.
> ...
> Time passes and ends and begins again. Time passes.
> ...
> 'It's a long time since we ...'
> On the contrary. It was a short time. A short time endlessly repeated. And this was the very thing that nobody appeared to understand: that everything went in circles and not in straight lines.
> ...
> They were like fireworks exploding in the darkness. Each generation had a brief flash of glorious hope and after that ... yes, the separate sparks filtered rapidly through the layers of night to become extinguished long before they hit the ground. (55–56)

When Dr Cohen argues that life is completely meaningless and says that there is only one decent pass-time on the planet, chess, Boris is surprised. He demurs and suggests 'women and so forth', and his entanglement in the novel with women is closely allied to his search for meaning, identity, and history. Boris, in his state of apparently permanent delusion or confusion, believes he pursues women. The novel deals with his pursuit of at least seven women: Inez, Flower, Mélanie the au pair, June Furlough, Lady Jane the lion tamer, Ylva, and his mother (with the possible addition of 'some faceless girl cousin called Dilys or Penny' [204] who has become pregnant in the house in the recent past). This catalogue confirms the relevance of the epigraph from Webster's *The White Devil* (though Farrell does not name the play):

> Women are caught as you take tortoises,
> She must be turn'd on her back.[21]

Flamineo's aside to Brachiano clearly depicts men as the pursuers and women as the objects of pursuit who, like tortoises, are easily caught and easily controlled once caught. But it quickly becomes apparent that the epigraph is largely ironic – women manipulate Boris's pursuit of them.

His unsuccessfully realised desire to pursue women seems to be explained by the first of the two 'patterned' passages in the novel, contained within Boris's interior monologue which is in turn 'inside' the omniscient narrative of the main text. Boris tells the reader here (as though into a tape-recorder) how his mother deserted him as a child and how he once glimpsed her face in the doorway of a Munich beer-cellar and years later ran away from school to look for her in that same beer-cellar (42–45). The sense of loss and desertion Boris experiences in relation to his mother is repeated in his affair with the mysterious Ylva whom he failed to pursue when he had the opportunity, creating a regret which haunts him ever after.

The second patterned passage which describes his relationship with Flower (119–21) is partly explained by the first, but also elaborates the difference between Boris's unattainable women 'in the head' – his mother, Ylva, and Inez – and the disappointing ordinariness of the women he does capture – Flower and June Furlough. Boris loses his mother, and Ylva, and even Flower (in a sense with the miscarriage), then Inez, freedom, and youth. All this female loss is surrounded by mystery, as though the loss of the female represents the loss of all desire and power, things he never possessed, but tantalising images of what might have been possible, everything desired, always in the future. This is summed up by the overriding metaphor that the summer is almost over and 'the girl still had not arrived' (9). In a sense Boris's relationships with women, or more accurately, his stories to himself about his relationships with women, *are* his history, since we only know his history through his memories, real or imagined.

Inez (pronounced '*i'neige* ... like the French for "it is snowing",' as Boris informs the Dongeons [19]), is the most obvious object of Boris's pursuit. On the morning of her early swim, for instance, Boris is typically seen in the act of pursuing her. He follows her out of the house and across the garden 'treading like a cat', he crawls through a gap in the hedge, tracks her footprints across the sand, and discovers her naked in the sea. But Boris's successful 'pursuit' is immediately undermined when he is presented as a voyeur who must 'slink away before he [is] discovered' (114–17). And in fact it becomes apparent that Inez plays up to Boris to hide her alliance with Maurice, something that Boris only discovers on the last evening of Inez's stay at Boscobel, when after tracking her across the sand once more, he discovers her in the act of sex with Maurice (215–16), a mixture of strangely-positioned feet and legs which recalls Gretchen's thoughts about the 'eight-limbed Australian crawl' in *A Man from Elsewhere* and Martin Sands' discovery of his wife Sally on the couch with Louis in *The Lung*.

There are indications that Inez is well aware of the way she is manipulating both Boris and Alessandro. At one point she confides to Boris:

> 'I think [Alessandro's] probably got rather a crush on me.'
> 'What makes you think that?' inquired Boris uneasily.
> 'Oh, one can tell.' (176)

Her response to Boris's uneasy enquiry suggests, of course, that she can also tell that Boris has a crush on her, and the fact that his enquiry is 'uneasy' indicates that he is aware of this. Inez, rather than Boris, is in control of the relationship between them, as she also proves to be in her relationship with Alessandro.

It is Boris who is the pursued when the au pair Mélanie, having been moved out of her room to make way for Boris, keeps 'forgetting which bed she was supposed to be sleeping in' (124). Whereas Mélanie pursues Boris in a rather absentminded fashion, June Furlough (whose name means 'summer holiday', i.e. not the daily working world) actively pursues him. (There are hints that she is the girl with the 'sweaty olive countenance' [13] who lured him off the train years ago.) In the present action she 'picks up' Boris in the Capri café, leads him to the boatshed, and is in complete control of their sexual liaison which follows (90–98). Boris appears somewhat ludicrous throughout this episode and is wholly deflated when, after she unlocks her legs and releases him, she makes the ridiculously incongruous comparison between Boris and a tiger: '"You're all covered in stripes from leaning against the boat," June said, coming over and nuzzling against him. "You look like a tiger"' (96). Her own bare bottom is imprinted with two moons of boat varnish from a newly painted boat. The effect of this scene is to show that the fumbling practicalities of 'real' sexual acts are very different from Boris's effulgent romantic fantasies.

Boris's life eventually appears to be completely controlled by women. Even his marriage to Flower is not of his own making but was organised by the two Grannies, possibly, it is hinted, without telling him that she was already pregnant. She has a miscarriage only three weeks after their marriage and it is implied that they are married soon after Boris's arrival in the suggestively titled Maidenhair Bay. Boris is not the Don Juan (Dongeon?) he imagines himself to be, but Maurice Dongeon certainly is, with his trail of females anxious to pose for him and have private viewings of his art. Even Grandpa Dongeon has a slightly lecherous attitude to the Irish maids he claims are waiting to be trained, just 'crying out for it' (21). Boris is deceived and tantalised by women – his mother, Inez, Flower – in a writing of the female very much more considered than the cursory treatment of women in *A Man from Elsewhere* and *The Lung* (in spite of T. Winnifrith's naïve proposition that '[t]he title [of *A Girl in the Head*] is more appropriate in a way to the earlier novels where females – mysterious Gretchen and Marigold – are central'[22]).

Women are also closely connected with the curious egg symbolism in the novel. At one stage Boris comes into the kitchen where Flower is cooking, and in an unexpected act which astonishes her and the reader, throws six eggs, one after another, at the ceiling, where each smashes and drips to the floor. Later we come to connect this with Flower's miscarriage and the fact that the sexual act, the desired culmination of Boris's pursuit of the female, produces new life, but what could justify bringing new life into such a meaningless world? This also implies an added explanation for Inez's teasing statement to Alessandro (and the concealed watcher, Boris) that every month a pearl drops into her womb; she is not a real woman who produces eggs, but a fantasy woman who has ideal sex but no reproduction. The 'girl in the head' of the title is thus in a major sense unreal, an apparition, as hinted by the vaguely post-impressionist cover of the 1981 Fontana paperback, a drawing of a naked girl walking out of water.[23] There is something not quite real, not quite graspable about the female for Boris.

Farrell confirms this impression that the girls in Boris's head are not real but generic by setting them up alongside stereotypical images from the culture, especially from paintings and other works of art. At Boscobel he contemplates 'A Maiden's Honour' and finds 'an alarming resemblance between his own features and those of the wrinkled gentleman' (19) trying to buy the young girl from her mother or guardian. He also meditates on females in two other paintings, 'The Rewards of Luxury' and 'The Letter', and tries to persuade the reluctant Flower to dress up in Spanish costume and stand on the dining-room table in imitation of an illustration of Carmen that used to 'stimulate' him as a boy. Similarly, Inez is a 'Juliet' figure in Boris's imagination before he even sees her. He fantasises a conversation before her arrival: "'The orchard walls are high and hard to climb," Inez said to Boris, "and the place death, considering who thou art, if any of my kinsmen find thee here"' (19).[24] Later, Inez is shown coming out of the sea in a description deliberately evoking Botticelli's 'The Birth of Venus':

> Inez was now standing naked and motionless at the water's edge, with a serene half-smile on her lips as if at the recollection of some pleasant memory. Her slender right hand was raised to cover her breasts while the other trailed down absently over her sex. Her hair flowed down over her shoulders in golden waves. And there she stood, motionless, beside the sea. (116)

This is almost a paradigm case of the use of Roland Barthes's sense of inter-textuality as Jay Clayton and Eric Rothstein interpret it:

> A beautiful woman, Barthes notes, can be described only in terms of a citation of other women in painting, literature, and mythology: 'thus, beauty is referred to an infinity of codes: *lovely as Venus*? But Venus lovely as what?' (S/Z 34). The circularity of reference itself insures the effect of the real. 'Once the infinite circularity of codes is posited, the body itself cannot escape from it. ... Thus, even within realism, the codes never stop' (S/Z 55).[25]

Boris's women are imaginings from the culture, often seen synecdochically in bits and pieces; a head floating on the sea, an elegant leg getting out of the car, a white sweater, hands in a charming lap, never whole.

Boris wishes he could be like Maurice in his casual attitude to women (and the Boris/Maurice rhyme may suggest a deliberate opposition). He is jealous of Maurice's ability to believe in the solidity and importance of the world (86). Maurice, we have learned before, is 'made of' objects (21). Boris feels he could appear to be like Maurice: could buy all the same bits of costume and properties for the role, the pseudo-sailor jersey, the Volkswagen, and so on (86), but what he can never do is believe like Maurice, never 'act always in the sure knowledge that he had been born in the right place at the right time' (87). Recurrent images of the human subject as a collection of objects, as disparate limbs, or mechanical bits and pieces, often broken, as chemical compounds, or costumes for heroic roles, show Farrell dramatising the human as mere temporary conjunctions of disparate objects and fragments of language. This is at its most grotesque in the chapter in which Dr Cohen takes Boris to the hospital gymnasium and shows him a room full of crippled people exercising crippled limbs and deformed bodies and Cohen comments on the unreliability and frailty of the human body, a forerunner of Dr Ryan's comment in *Troubles* that the human body looks so solid but does not last. Like many modernists and postmodernists Farrell vacillates between this view of the human body as organic and not susceptible to control by the mind, and the contrary view of the human body as a machine as seen in the final chapter where Boris contemplates his own body as a ticket machine at the station. His work thus joins that

> series of more or less comic reflections on the 'disjunctive' human body in literature, perhaps culminating in Beckett. ... Such a disjunctive body determines the necessity for the modern and postmodern aesthetic obsession with the body – a body now firmly in time, but in a disjunctive time.[26]

Boris's disjointed musings on past, present, and future prepare the way for Farrell's fully postmodern considerations of history in the trilogy which immediately follows.

While there is an obviously Forsterian opening to *The Siege of Krishnapur*, E.M. Forster may seem an unlikely influence on *A Girl in the Head*. However, Forster's famous epigraph to *Howard's End* (1910), 'Only connect ...', does seem to inform one aspect of this novel. The bodily disjunctions discussed above are mirrored by disjunctions of language and communication. The smooth exchange of social discourses is continually disrupted by misunderstandings, silences, failures in communication.

Boris, of course, ultimately fails to connect with anyone (except perhaps with Dr Cohen, but by the time he realises this the doctor is already dead). Moreover, every character in the novel in one way or another seems unable to communicate with others. Maurice, in a series of wonderfully-realised comic moments, fails to connect with Granny Dongeon in his daily reading from the newspaper, while at the same time old Dongeon further exacerbates any attempt to communicate by constantly talking at cross-purposes. The following passage is a typical example:

> '"Forty-year-old Italian forbidden to see ward of court. Unhealthy influence. A manufacturer of artificial limbs, described by neighbours as a quiet and respectable..."'
>
> 'Funny people, those Italians,' old Dongeon said so close to his right ear that Boris jumped.
>
> 'Artificial limbs, Granny ... he makes them. He's an unhealthy influence.'
>
> 'I ran into a few of them in the war, you know,' old Dongeon went on. (22)

In the extracts that Maurice reads to Granny Dongeon, the 'real' world of the newspapers is absurd and unbelievable. This is certainly a movement on Farrell's part towards that fictional strategy of deliberate surrealism that Bergonzi comments on as an attempt to deal with a twentieth-century reality that is 'constantly transcending itself, moving to heights of absurdity or horror that leave the most extravagantly inventive novelist lagging behind'.[27] Granny's failure to understand the newspaper stories, and the inability of anyone else to communicate their meaning to her, also points to the failure of language to hold social conjunctions together.

Interestingly, Boris is most effective as a communicator when he speaks into the tape-recorder in the series of interior monologues which puncuate the novel. Either he chooses to communicate with himself (he is effectively talking to himself) because he finds it impossible to communicate with others, or he is trying to communicate with others through the medium of a machine because direct communication has failed. Ironically, the passages in which Boris addresses the tape-recorder are the most lucid in the novel, and compounding the irony, they describe in wordy detail several photographs, visual images that would normally be *shown* to others.

It is in this novel too, that Farrell first develops his metaphor of life as a game, which would later take a central position in his unfinished novel, *The Hill Station*. In *A Girl in The Head* Maurice (a successful collection of objects and consummate role-player) is, of course, the one who knows the rules and enforces them, even though his private behaviour shows far more 'transgression' than Boris's. The idea comes to the fore over a game of monopoly that Boris, the Dongeons, Alessandro, and the newly-arrived Inez have on her first evening:

> 'Don't go Boris. We're going to have a game of Monopoly before supper.'
> Boris looked at his watch and furrowed his brow.
> 'All right then. A quick game.' The thought of thrashing the Dongeon family before Inez was infinitely attractive.
> They began to play. After a few minutes a bitter argument broke out. Boris insisted that as he held all the railway-stations he could build hotels on them if he wanted.
> 'Have you never heard of a railway-hotel?' he demanded with heavy sarcasm.
> 'It's against the rules of the game,' Maurice replied calmly.
> The rule book was produced. It stated categorically that Boris was not allowed to build hotels on his railway-stations. For the rest of the game he maintained a sullen silence.

As it turned out, Granny Dongeon (helped by Maurice) quickly gained a stranglehold on the game. Boris retired to his room, speechless with rage, planning to compose an angry letter to the makers. (78–79)

The chapter ends here, with Boris thwarted. The next chapter picks up the thread the following morning when Boris, who has stepped out into the garden, is accosted by old Dongeon. The old man reminds Boris that he 'must play the game' (81) and that 'the game has rules and we must abide by them. Not just you or me. Not just Flower. We all must. The rules are the thing. We all must pull together. Abide by them' (82).

For Boris, finally, 'the girl in the head' comes to represent love unattained, that love he would like to propose as the answer to meaninglessness. 'At least love exists and beauty. That surely is something. That surely is not nothing' (207). But the implied question, phrased assertively at first, is repeated more tentatively and negatively, and 'outside the window the sycamore tree, pessimistic to the last, was invisibly drowning in quick-drying cement' (207–08). This last phrase is a reference to another of the curious newspaper articles read aloud to Granny Dongeon. Boris identifies himself with both the sycamore tree, and with the man in East Sheen who, the newspaper reports, had been buried alive in quick-drying cement the day before (207). Boris chops down the sycamore tree, either in an attempt to put it out of its misery or as a gesture indicating that his rebellious self has been cut off with the departure of Inez and Alessandro. The felling of the tree is connected with the destruction of the potted yellow chrysanthemum in the dining-room, Inez's parting gift to Flower, which had been 'smiling its mysterious golden smile into the surrounding gloom' (219). Boris seems to lapse into an equilibrium of defeat and silence until the short conversation with Flower which ends the novel. In this he tells her that life is 'really rather sad' and lacking in 'colour' and meanders into an apparently inconsequential story about an alcoholic he once knew, a story he has previously tried to tell Dr Cohen and which seems to refer to Boris himself. Flower fails to understand what he's saying, and his words, 'Oh, nothing', end the book.

According to George Brock, Farrell 'prefer[ed] to disown his first three novels and dismiss them as "casting around"'[28] – which Binns takes to mean 'the efforts of a young writer in search of a theme and not yet finding it'.[29] But this is to underestimate the quality and importance of the early works. It is not a theme Farrell is looking for in these novels – that is there from the beginning and surprisingly coherent throughout the whole body of his work – so much as a genre, which he was to find in his shift to the historical novel.[30]

4 / Newspapers, War, and Games: *Troubles*

Farrell chose to begin his three-novel historical study of the decay of Empire by writing in *Troubles* about a country to which, like many literary Irishmen, he was deeply though ambivalently attached. Significantly too, he chose a moment when the large-scale history of the decay of Empire is intertwined with his own family's history. His mother was brought up in Maryborough (now Portlaoise), and was the daughter of an Irish mother and an English father, well-placed to see anti-British feeling in the period. As Binns reports, she 'vividly remembers the impact which the 1916 Easter Rising made upon her, even though she was just a girl at the time and living far away from Dublin', and was also aware of IRA bombing of bridges in their locality.[1] Binns also notes that Farrell gives her father a brief appearance in *Troubles* at the final ball where he appears under his own name as 'the large and jovial ... Bob Russell, the timber merchant from Maryborough' (344).

When *Troubles* was translated into French some time after its English publication (the French version was never published), it was called *Un Amour Irlandais*, 'An Irish Affair', 'An Irish Love', or even 'An Irish Romance', and the difficulties of such a translation indicate something of the leap in subtlety and focus Farrell's writing achieved after *A Girl in the Head*. The ambiguous French title has the advantage of signalling the importance of the Irish setting; it also offers the ironical possibility of reading this blackly comic fiction as 'romance', but unfortunately it loses the multiple allusions of the phrase 'the troubles'. This applies in the novel to many kinds of unrest, dis-ease, and difficulty, from unrequited love to race riots, bicycle accidents, illness, financial problems, and unexpected pregnancy, but above all to the complex Irish struggle for independence from British rule, a struggle central to the novel. 'The troubles' originally meant the violence of the first Irish civil war between 1919 and 1921, the period in which Farrell's novel is set; but when Farrell was writing *Troubles* between 1968 and 1970 the phrase was also beginning to refer to a new period of conflict which began in Northern Ireland in 1968. Farrell later told an interviewer:

> I would go up to the British Museum newspaper library to read the *Irish Times* for 1920 and come back, buying an evening paper on the Tube. It was uncanny: exactly the same things were happening again, sometimes even in the same streets in Belfast.[2]

The 'haunting continuity of the past in the present' so fascinating to Farrell in *A Man from Elsewhere*, *The Lung*, and *A Girl in the Head*, thus proved to be organic in his new material. In *Troubles*, his first historical novel, Farrell extends this fascination into an exploration of the processes by which history is made, both as experience and as discourse.

The sense in his earlier fiction of individuals trapped in a flux of time which is both private and public gains focus in the trilogy from Farrell's profoundly Marxist sense of the ideological forces which create the discourses of history. As the decade of work on the trilogy passed, it is clear that Farrell was progressively influenced by the developments in Marxist literary theory after Lukács which were contemporary with his residence in France and his own early writing.

In writing *Troubles* he was no doubt also strongly influenced by several distinguished earlier literary treatments of the Irish struggle: W.B. Yeats's 'Easter 1916', Sean O'Casey's autobiographical writing as well as *The Plough and the Stars* (1926), Elizabeth Bowen's *The Last September* (1929), and Iris Murdoch's *The Red and the Green* (1965). Margaret Scanlan has carefully examined Farrell's allusions to Elizabeth Bowen in her article 'Rumours of War: Elizabeth Bowen's *Last September* and J.G. Farrell's *Troubles*', examining in detail these two studies of an Anglo-Irish 'Big House', of people deeply involved in a history they don't want to know about. They are, in fact 'constantly involved in strategies to put off knowing' about it.[3] Scanlan finds both writers equally persuaded that there was no tenable position for the Anglo-Irish at this time; their situation represents a central human problem of Empire, that of the private colonisers who after many generations feel 'at home', yet are separated by class, race, religion, language, and by the very fact of their implication in imperialist control, from those native peoples with whom they live. The reader of *Troubles* is given no direct lessons about history, but is made instead to experience the events and relationships of the present as a puzzling, unsimplifiable consequence of the total past.

The surviving notes and typescript drafts for each novel of the Empire trilogy show Farrell making significant changes in early stages, all apparently directed at dramatising more clearly through clashes between characters the conflicting ideologies in the historical moments he is treating. Working papers for *Troubles* show that Farrell made an early and substantial change to his original idea for what was to have been a single central character, 'the Colonel', a veteran of service in India now retired to Ireland.[4] 'The Colonel' becomes divided into the two important male characters who remain in the published version, Major Brendan Archer, the youngish Englishman just returned from the First World War, and middle-aged Edward Spencer, eccentric Anglo-Irishman, owner of the vast and decaying Majestic Hotel at 'Kilnalough' (from the Gaelic meaning 'church or burial place of the lake'[5]), a lonely promontory in County Wicklow.[6] This creation of two characters from one allows Farrell to present a more subtle, ambivalent account of the British view of Ireland. Edward becomes the spokesman for the old Anglican Ascendancy families, while the Major, a generation younger, has an Englishman's muddled tolerance arising largely from ignorance of the Irish situation. Of crucial importance to the kind of historical focus Farrell achieves in *Troubles* is his use of the Major to act as the reader's viewpoint for most of the novel.

The Major is usually addressed simply by his title, and while this may be, as Binns suggests, a reference to Somerville and Ross's famous Major Sinclair Yeates in *The Irish R.M.* stories (complete edition 1928) – both Majors become embroiled in making judgements on a culture they begin to realise they hardly understand at all – it is also a constant reminder that the First World War is a vitally significant context for the relations between Britain and Ireland in this period. British-Irish relations had deteriorated as a result of the persistence of the Irish leaders in maintaining contact with Germany during the War. This was exacerbated by the Easter uprising of 1916 in Dublin and the British insistence on treating those involved as war traitors.[7]

The Major and Edward Spencer are connected by the Major's meeting with Edward's daughter Angela in London in 1914 and his hasty engagement to her just before his departure for the trenches. The novel begins after the war and after the Major's recovery from shell-shock. He travels to Ireland to meet his fiancée and her family at their enormous hotel which, physically disintegrating at an accelerating rate during the novel, becomes a symbol for the crumbling of British authority in Ireland, but also for the outdated Victorian-Edwardian ideology of Empire in which the Anglo-Irish 'Big House' families are trapped.

The Majestic Hotel, massive, many-turreted, battlemented, balconied, with labyrinthine dusty corridors and decaying staircases spiralling upwards, is a Gothic house of ideas, reminiscent of Mervyn Peake's sprawling castle of Gormenghast.[8] As several commentators have noted, it conveys the sense of Ireland as a place of wildness, romance, eccentricity, and myth. The Major comes to this 'castle' like a fairy-tale hero-prince coming to claim his bride after adventures in war.[9] He meets her briefly at a mad tea-party on the afternoon of his arrival, but, ineffectual and unheroic like all Farrell's protagonists, is never again able to find her. He glimpses her in the distance and sets off in pursuit, even follows trays of food being taken to her room, but is always defeated by the winding intricacies of the hotel.

This surrealistic, dreamlike narrative of the Major's bizarre daily explorations is interrupted abruptly twenty-nine times during the course of the novel by sudden interpolations of prose passages very different in style and theme; these are extracts of Irish and world news from genuine newspaper articles published in the *Irish Times* between 1919 and 1921. The deliberate juxtaposition of these two kinds of text emphasises the contrast between the literary myth of Ireland as fascinating dream, and the hard-edged version of Irish and world politics revealed in the newspapers. However 'real' this latter version seems by contrast with the former, it is still not 'reality', but text, the same country through a different discourse. *Troubles* shows Farrell using the transitions between realist and fantasy modes he had experimented with in *A Girl in the Head*, but now with profound thematic relevance.

In one of the best early discussions of Farrell's work, Bernard Bergonzi acknowledges that Farrell's inclusion of the newspaper extracts establishes a global context for the 'troubles' and judges the device 'an effective if unsubtle way of emphasising the novel's historicity',[10] but Farrell's use of the newspapers achieves more than this. Through them he suggests his Marxist view that Ireland's 'troubles' are part of a world dialectical struggle (reports of Irish violence are placed alongside reports of race-rioting in Chicago, revolts in Amritsar, Afghanistan, and elsewhere); he uses the style of the journalism he quotes to evoke a sense of the period; he establishes the vital part played by the First World War in British thinking about Ireland at this time, and he explores his interest in the relationship between history as private flux of events and history as text or public discourse. The newspaper reports become vital parts of what Homi Bhabha describes as those 'scraps, patches and rags of daily life [which] must be *repeatedly* turned into the signs of a national culture'.[11]

In the early sections of the novel the Major's affairs of the heart are central; the rumours of Sinn Fein attacks and 'reprisals' on Irish people who work for the British are nothing more for him at this point than a curious, often irritating backdrop against which his own all-important concerns are enacted. His attempts to 'sort things out' with Angela (even to find her) are fruitless, and end suddenly when her family reports her illness and death. He finally learns she has died of leukaemia. That her mysterious illness should turn out to be a fatal disease of the blood is symbolically in keeping with her role as eldest daughter of the Anglo-Irish tradition. Many months later during the last grotesque ball, the Major looks down the great room and sees the same face, the face as an historical text, the same 'equine features ... repeated again and again all the way down the glittering ballroom ... from the oldest men and women to the youngest children':

> This was the face of Anglo-Ireland, the inbred Protestant aristocracy, the face, progressively refining itself into a separate, luxurious species, which had ruled Ireland for almost five hundred years: the wispy fair hair, the eyes too close together, the long nose and protruding teeth. (336)

This evolutionary attenuation is symbolically opposed to the fecundity and proliferation of the grossly, grotesquely luxuriant green plant growth, its roots deep in the nourishing Irish soil, which is gradually taking over the Majestic. Similarly, there is a symbolic contrast between Angela and her friend Sarah Devlin, with whom the Major becomes involved after Angela's death. Sarah is Irish and Catholic, and although apparently semi-paralysed early in the novel when the Major first meets her, gains strength and energy throughout the narrative, like both the greenery and the Irish cause itself.

Although it is typical of Farrell's fictional approach to heterosexual relationships that the female characters should be more symbolic than real, that their elusive appearances and disappearances should convey more about the Majestic and the aimiable uselessness of the Major than about themselves, in this novel their insubstantiality has considerable point – it conveys the fragmented nature of experience and the essentially textual quality of history. Angela's existence for the Major is for the most part a textual existence, and even his private life includes a clash between history-as-text and history-as-experience. Angela is most real for him in the long letters she has written to him during the war, full of detailed reality 'as hard as granite', and in the 'unbearable' detail of the many-paged last letter given to him by her family after her death. He find his textual impressions of her very different from the Angela he meets at the tea-party.

He also finds that the letters have told him everything and nothing about life in Ireland. He may know an encyclopedia of facts about her family, the names, pedigrees, and illnesses of all Edward's many dogs, 'the nature and amount of the dental work in [the Spencer family's] upper and lower jaws, where they buy their outer clothes (Angela had delicately omitted to mention underwear) and many more things besides' (14), but like the entries in an encyclopedia these amount to no coherent whole. They are lists rather than narratives. Her delicate omissions are also highly significant: the fact that she has a brother, Ripon, her own illness, Boy O'Neill's cancer, the state of the 'troubles' at Kilnalough.

The newspapers the Major reads seem at first to provide the corrective to Angela's myopic focus on domestic detail; they represent the wider and apparently more authoritative public text. He finds himself turning to them for explanations of mystifying events in his own experience. Some events are impossible for him to understand until they have been given shape and meaning by the public account which gives authority to a particular interpretation. The clearest example occurs when the Major, visiting Dublin as a break from the insanity of the Majestic, witnesses the assassination of a man in the street by another man wearing a sandwich-board. Although the whole event is inexplicable to him at the time, he begins to understand it afterwards through newspaper reports as the IRA execution of a retired English army officer. The Major finds that once the murder has been explained and recorded, it becomes part of that knowledge which is 'classified and accepted':

> It was odd, he thought. An old man is gunned down in the street and within a couple of days this senseless act is both normal and inevitable. … [The events] became random events of the year 1919, inevitable, without malice, part of history. The old man lying on the bridge with his watch in his hand was a part of history. (102)

The last sentence is almost a paradigm of Farrell's larger method. It moves the reader from the old man whose contact with the Major is purely personal, through the detail of the watch, whose time is both personal and public, into the 'master-narrative' of history.

The ironies of trusting in the power of text are symbolically emphasised by the assassin, who is revealed to have been wearing a sandwich board 'made not of wood but of iron', as a suit of armour. The board is inscribed with the words 'HOLY MARY MOTHER OF GOD PRAY FOR US SINNERS' (100) in the belief that 'Englishmen, Protestants, would turn their eyes away from the name of Our Lady, and these days so many people were being stopped and searched for arms …' (101–02). But neither physical nor textual armour saves the assassin; after the murder he in turn is shot by British soldiers and dies 'like an abandoned puppet' (100) having also played, unnamed, his part in the narrative of history.

The Major thinks back to this episode while staring out of the window of his hotel in Dame Street, Dublin. He considers the varied, intense life of the street, '… the gleaming motor cars, … the friendly faces, … the jaunting-cars with their nodding horses and … all the other things which would not be recorded …':

> A raid on a barracks, the murder of a policeman on a lonely country road, an airship crossing the Atlantic, a speech by a man on a platform, or any of the other random acts, mostly violent, that one reads about every day: this was the history of the time. The rest was merely the 'being alive' that every age has to do. (102)

Again it is emphasised here that it is only the acts that one *reads* about that become part of the history of the time. In Linda Hutcheon's words, 'the meaning and shape are not *in the events*, but *in the systems* which make those past "events" into present historical "facts."'[12] This perception aligns Farrell with those postmodern writers of history to whom she is specifically referring in this passage. Although the Major's concept of history is relatively naïve, he grasps two elements which are of central interest to Farrell, the idea of the 'history of the time' as a narrative construction in language, for which contemporary newspapers will become a primary source, and following from this, the tendency to the same kinds of selections and exclusion which make Angela's letters so inadequate as a description of 'reality'.

The Major's relationship with Sarah also proceeds by letter when, after Angela's death, he goes to London to be with his dying aunt. His last letter to Sarah (which he is never able to send because he does not have her address in France) is almost a desperate attempt to give himself the illusory permanence of text in defiance of the change, decay, and death all around him: '(… the kind of letter the Major was writing is seldom voluntarily finished before the Grim Reaper bids us lay down our pens)' (138).

He realises he has left Angela's last long letter unopened in the unused Imperial Bar of the Majestic, and when he returns and finds it still there months later, his reading of it takes place as a kind of melancholy-comic fugue against interpolations from a conversation between Dr Ryan and Edward. Dr Ryan is talking about how '[p]eople are insubstantial, … a person is only a very temporary and makeshift affair …' (154–55) and not listening to Edward who, taking little notice of the doctor, is talking about the vanished past of his own youth. Against this, the Major's reading of the 'intolerable detail' of Angela's record of her last weeks of illness brings the past directly into the present and also shows the tendency of the written text to say too much or not enough, to distort reality by its altered proportions, by its evasions, gaps, and silences. Even so, all these letters, long rambling outpourings almost like stream-of-consciousness, become signs of the private attempts and failures to communicate across the barriers of space, time, gender, experience, and even death.

Later in the novel the sinister possibilities of deliberate textual selection and distortion become apparent when, instead of helping him to understand the situation, the newspaper reports contradict his own experience. He has witnessed the burning down of cottages by the British Black and Tans and the Auxiliaries, but newspaper accounts attribute the violence to Sinn Fein. Evidence in the novel points to the fact that no textual construction can be relied upon to be free of bias, either intentional or inadvertent.

Although the Major at first assumes that his opinions will 'naturally' coincide with those of his host, Edward Spencer, both the Major and the reader grow uneasily aware that the gulf between them is widening as the novel progresses. Spencer, like the British Government, refuses to allow the Irish troubles the status of war because this would involve the admission that the Irish Republic already has a political identity. He persists in treating the troubles as the isolated personal acts of a few criminals, assessing each act of Irish rebellion against the 'rules of the game' as played in the recently ended 'real war' with Germany.

Early in the novel the Major is astounded by Edward's war memorial made 'in the shape of a gigantic book with open pages' (46) (an icon of history shaped in the visual image of text), where prayers are held before breakfast. Recruiting, he has been told, 'had been poor in Ireland. Connolly, the Sinn Feiners, Nationalists of every hue had declared that Irishmen should not fight in the British Army' (46), and Edward has admitted with anger that his own son Ripon refused to fight on the English side – yet somehow there on the lists is Edward's 'vast army of the dead' (46). Later, the living survivors also appear in the Victory Parade in Dublin, where Irish regiments are named as they appear in the march-past. Later still, the visiting undergraduate, Danby, reminds Edward that there were 'a hundred thousand Catholic Irishmen fighting in the British Army' (411).

Book and unicorn, the two devices of the Spencer family crest which support the 'gigantic' war memorial pages, each suggest life at one remove from reality, and hint at the often mythical conceptions of Empire the men were fighting to defend. Edward's patriotic idealism is undercut still further by the photographs of the young soldiers caught by the camera with their faces so dazzled by the sun that they look to be 'already in agony' (47). The Major's paralysis of memory and grief about the war is ironically subverted by the farcical rumblings of his own stomach and those of other guests waiting to start breakfast.

At first the Major sympathises with Edward and becomes 'tired of trying to comprehend a situation which defie[s] comprehension, a war without battles or trenches' (169), but as the novel goes on he becomes far less certain about Edward's easy distinctions between Irish rebels and English soldiers. The name Edward Spencer is not, of course, an accidental choice, but a sign of allegiances. As a Spencer, though the spelling is altered, he represents those paternalistic English assumptions about Ireland under the reign of the Ascendancy which can be traced back to the sixteenth-century Spenser's term of office in Ireland. As an 'Edward', he represents the troubles in Ireland seen through an Edwardian ethic which treats war as a kind of sport or game, to be played by certain rules 'natural' to all gentlemen, as in the 'Great Game' in Rudyard Kiping's *Kim*. One of the early newspaper extracts dealing with the Victory Loan brings sport and war into metaphorical conjunction: 'We have won the fight, but we have gone into debt in buying the "gloves". It was a glorious fight for humanity …' (75), and later, as the Major returns to England, the reader is confronted with this paragraph:

IN PRAISE OF BOXING

A man's last line of defence is his fists. There is no sport, not even cricket, which is more essentially English than boxing. … There is no sport in the world which demands cleaner living. There is no more natural sport. Low cunning will not help him, but a quick, clear brain, a hard body, and perfect training will carry a man a long way. (111–12)

Farrell here skilfully evokes the cultural-historical context, the nineteenth-century discourse of 'manliness' and 'Englishness', the ideal of the 'healthy mind in a healthy body' in which war and games are linked. This was still publically intact, as the newspapers show, but privately had come under question by many men and women with first-hand experience of the War – notably Wilfred Owen, Seigfried Sassoon and other poets of the First World War. These brief references draw attention to the ironies of a historical temper which embodies such idealistic and ambiguous attitudes to fighting, but Farrell probes this still further in several major episodes.

One of the first, which shows the most ludicrous side of this war-and-games spirit, comes through the Major's thoughts when he first meets Edward and recalls what Angela has told him in letters about her father's boxing career at university. Protestant Edward Spencer boxed against the Roman Catholic Kevin Clinch twenty years ago in his Trinity days:

> Time and again the elder Spencer had been battered to the canvas, time and again he had risen to demonstrate English pluck and tenacity against the superior might of his Celtic adversary. The Major imagined him stretched out at last, his fists still twitching automatically like the limbs of a decapitated chicken. What difference had it made that Edward had ended the contest horizontal and motionless in spite of all his efforts? Why, none at all. He had proved his point. Besides, the game's the thing, it doesn't matter who wins. Besides, Clinch was a stone heavier. (26)

Here, the personal is political in ludicrous detail. The image of the decapitated chicken and the bathetic cliché and common sense of the last two sentences pit the stubborn discourse of an idealistic imperialism farcically against practicality, a recurrent opposition in the novel. Farrell dramatises Edward's idealism as typifying the period by using a protracted series of fictional scenes and metaphors which demonstrate, often with manic comedy, the strong cultural links between war and sport.

'"Shinner"-hunting' is exposed as a kind of game in an early scene when residents of the Majestic, led by Edward, set out armed with the sporting accessories of Empire – tennis rackets, cricket bats, Zulu spears, guns – in a search for intruders. It is also apparent in the story Ripon tells the Major during this game/hunt: a man, apparently a 'Shinner' was escaping from the constables across country when he ran accidentally through a tennis court, and reaching the wire netting on the other side, began to climb. He was knocked to the ground by a volley of tennis balls, rackets, and other equipment thrown by the tennis party, who, getting into the spirit of the game, continued to throw things at him, long after the man lay insensible on the court. He later turns out to have been a member of the pro-British Royal Irish Constabulary (RIC), not a 'Shinner' at all. The same thing is evident too, as the crisis approaches in Kilnalough, when the old ladies from the hotel form 'war-parties' and insist on making forays into the town in what becomes almost a childish game of 'dares' until the Major puts an end to it.

During 1970 Farrell wrote a review of *The I.R.A.* by Tim Pat Coogan, and must therefore have read the book during the last stages of writing *Troubles*. In this review, entitled 'The Army Game', Farrell quotes from Coogan the words of a German spy, Herman Goertz, who parachuted into Ireland in 1940: 'Inside the IRA ... nobody knew what game was really played, not even their leaders. Their internal means of communication were as primitive as boys playing police and brigands'.[13]

In another passage in *Troubles* Farrell allows the Major's characteristically commonplace anguish to descend into a bathos which extends the games-war imagery and is at the same time a reminder that Britain itself was once part of someone else's empire:

> What dreadful days these were! The future of the British Isles could never have seemed so dismal since the Romans had invaded; there was trouble everywhere. The ultimate stunning blow arrived just two days before Christmas with the news that, in spite of courageous resistance by Hobbs and Hendren, England had been defeated in the first test match in Australia by the appalling total of three hundred and seventy-seven runs. (303)

But the satirical edge of Farrell's war and games imagery becomes more savage than humorous later in the novel when Edward shoots dead a young Sinn Feiner who has been attempting to blow up the statue of Queen Victoria in front of the hotel. The Major suddenly understands that Edward has been thinking like a big-game hunter, using the statue of Queen Victoria as a kind of tethered goat to attract his quarry. With a shock he realises that Edward probably does not see Sinn Feinners as people at all: 'He saw them as a species of game that one could only shoot according to a very brief and complicated season (that is to say, when one caught them in the act of setting off bombs)' (417). Faced with the Major's horror at his action, Edward simply keeps on repeating, in yet another recourse to the sporting ethic, that his tactic was 'perfectly fair!' The implication is that the Irish are not gentlemanly opponents but are reduced to the level of the quarry in field sports by their inability or unwillingness to play 'by the rules'. But the Major has gradually come to recognise the fundamental difference between the English idealistic glorification of war as a noble, manly game, and the practical Irish terrorism which has the sole aim of removing the British 'army of occupation'.

Farrell shows the naïvety of hoping that patriot and enemy can be lined up in simple opposition now as they appeared to have been in the private battle twenty years earlier between Edward and Kevin Clinch. The Major admits late in the novel that he is never sure which side he is on. He finds news of race-rioting in Chicago much easier to grasp because '[u]nlike the Irish troubles one knew instantly which side everyone was on' (113). 'Telling one from the other' becomes a very Irish problem in *Troubles* from the twins outwards. Ripon's story of the Shinner who escapes across the tennis court but turns out to be a member of the RIC is only the most obvious case of difficulty in knowing the enemy. On the way down to Kilnalough the Major tells fellow-travellers he is 'going to be married to a … an Irish girl' (15), but then wonders whether Angela would be pleased to be described as 'an Irish girl'. To the Major at first, and later to the Oxford undergraduates, Edward and his family are the mad Irish, but to Sarah and the Sinn Fein they are British and the enemy. Catholic Mr Noonan and Protestant Edward fail to recognise each other. Evans, the tutor, appears to take part with violent enthusiasm when Edward sallies forth to show the British flag at the local pub, but is later seen literally vomiting his disgust of the British onto their heads from the balcony above the ballroom. When Sinn Fein burn Edward's crops rather than let him give them to the starving Irish peasants the issue becomes even more confused. And is Murphy (whose name is another gesture towards Beckett) an Irish patriot, and thus a public hero, or is his final destruction of the Majestic an act of private revenge for the dramatic experiment on his salivary glands conducted by Edward?

This confusion at local level about the identity of the enemy and the complex interconnections between personal and political issues exists equally in national and international affairs as Farrell clearly demonstrates. Parnell, whose private life with Kitty O'Shea destroyed his public life and profoundly influenced the history of Irish-English affairs, was, Dr Ryan argues, 'the last man who could have preserved some sort of life for the British in Ireland but the damn fools didn't realize it, thought he was their enemy!' (156). De Valera's public flirtation with the Germans is parallelled by the private affairs between Sarah, a violent defender of the Republicans, and two of the enemy, Edward and Captain Bolton.

One newspaper item which appears at first to have little relevance actually draws attention to conventional stereotypes of patriotism, the problematical nature of which has already been raised. The Grafton Picture House is showing a film called

'The Coward', a dramatic episode of the American Civil War. It is a story of a man who was a coward, but who, when the test came, proved himself as ready to fight and die for his country as the most hardened soldier. (90)

Some issues raised in earlier scenes about connections between war, games, and the discourses of Empire are recapitulated and extended in another splendid scene towards the end of the novel. Set at a meal table, it centres around a group of Oxford undergraduates, led by the bumptious Danby, who have come to the Majestic to have a look at 'the Irish question'. The date of the novel's action has moved by this time to 1920, and young Danby and Co. represent the next generation of 'enlightened' liberal humanist British thinking about Ireland. They are too young to have seen service in the War, yet are better informed than either the Major or Edward about the background to the Irish struggle against England and are aware of the manifold sources of Irish dissatisfaction with unkept promises of the past. They argue on grounds of democratic principle for an Ireland they know only through textual history, against Edward, a spokesman for the old British view of Empire. It is another kind of duel for Edward, and as against Kevin Clinch, he loses. But, like the wider situation, this debate is a 'civil war', setting Edward against differently-minded British. Quoting Rousseau and claiming that Sinn Fein representatives could not take their seats at Westminster because 'they knew it wouldn't do any good', that nothing had ever been achieved for Ireland that way, they rouse Edward's wrath by suggesting that '[t]he original and *motive* violence comes from us British who have been violently repressing them since Cromwell and even before that ...' (408–09).

In spite of their better knowledge, though, the scene testifies that their purely theoretical knowledge of history cannot give them an adequate grasp of the realities of the situation. Their understanding is as limited in its own way as Edward's opposite knowledge of only the present. The situation at the hotel, by now a desperate one for the residents, appears to this jazz-age postwar generation of students as simply matter for humour. Unlike their older colleague Captain Roberts, who has returned to the university after War service, they read the situation as potential text because they cannot grasp its full reality. Their anticipation of the story into which this event will be transformed allows the genre of humorous undergraduate prank to silence the suffering involved:

> the undergraduates were absolutely delighted with Edward's outburst and were thinking: 'What a perfectly splendid old Tory! What a rare find!' The whole thing was priceless: the old ladies, the revolvers (what a shame they weren't loaded!), the decrepit palace around them – and brooding in the middle of it, John Bull! Never-say-die in person! The evening would make a rare saga when retold over beer-mugs in the buttery next term. It might be entitled: 'How Maitland Put His Cherubic Head In The British Lion's Mouth ... And Got It Bitten Off!' Only Captain Roberts, who had lost his taste for battles of any description

(even verbal), felt uncomfortable and heartily wished the meal were at an end. (410)

The words 'priceless' and 'rare saga' signal both the change in values and the potentially value-loaded oral transmission of portions of this history. Conflict between England and Ireland, profoundly serious for those involved, becomes here no more than an entertaining story. Episodes like this show Farrell's self-reflexive awareness of the suffering his own comic text may be accused of eliding, and ironise the complexities of the way in which events inevitably become narratives.

In spite of its ironic cast, though, young British lions baiting the old, it is the first real political discussion in the novel and Farrell places it close to the end where each word has acquired reverberations from the reader's knowledge of all that has gone before. Like Iris Murdoch's conversation in the final pages of *The Red and the Green*, from which he certainly learned, Farrell's debate in *Troubles* turns on the question of whether those involved in the 1916 Easter rebellion were cowards or heroes. Were they traitors and murderers attacking gallant Englishmen who were defending them from the Germans, or brave rebels attacking 'the army of occupation'? The reader knows by now that the opposing factions are too deeply attached to long-held mental positions to allow any easy judgement. This recalls Sarah's words of warning to the Major: 'In Ireland you must choose your tribe. Reason has nothing to do with it' (34).

Added tension in the reader's response to this scene comes from our knowledge that although the Major is supporting Edward on this occasion, it is only out of loyalty, no longer from conviction. The discussion actually brings to light how far his view has changed and how completely his confidence in the 'civilizing power' of the British in Ireland has vanished. The Major has more in common with the undergraduate War-veteran Captain Roberts; the similarity of their awkward positions is made apparent in the final part of the scene. On opposite sides of the debate, each is called to speak as a representative of returned servicemen. When Edward calls on the Major to confirm publically that men in the trenches felt 'stabbed in the back' by the Easter rebellion, the Major does reluctantly agree after a long sad silence. Danby instantly responds by calling on Captain Roberts to affirm that the servicemen had felt the Easter Week rebellion to be completely justified :

> Once again there was a pause and a seemingly interminable silence while everyone held their breath. ... But then at last Captain Roberts cleared his throat and murmured hoarsely: 'Perfectly justified ... We all thought so ...'
>
> ... But Captain Roberts was careful to avoid the Major's eye. (412)

When Edward leaves the room in fury and the meal breaks up in gales of laughter, 'Only Captain Roberts at one table and the Major at the other showed no sign of amusement' (413).

Danby and his fellow undergraduates may demonstrate their own absurdities, but they do bring to the debate a sense of the historical relations between Ireland and England which those like Edward refuse to contemplate. The owner and residents of the Majestic Hotel not only neglect to learn the lessons of history, they refuse even to admit the passing of time. Time is suspended here. The novel is full of confusions about time which produce the impression of historical stasis. The residents cling to the late-Victorian/early-Edwardian period which they nostalgically regard as the height of British civilization: Mrs Rappaport believes she is taking part in the Siege of Lucknow (a detail which anticipates the subject of Farrell's next novel), the Doctor expects the arrival of his wife who died forty years ago, and the twins appear at the ball in crinolines found in a trunk in the attic. Many of the guests have 'the appearance of wax figures, museum curiosities, unconnected with the present era, the seething modern world of 1921' (336). The clock over the reception desk at first tells the wrong time, and by the end of the novel has stopped altogether. Time is not rolling onward here, but retreating.

Yet Farrell is adept at making the sense of the stopping of public time, the atmosphere of a former age persisting, coexist with the feeling of change and decay in private lives. As Binns comments, 'Decay is everywhere in *Troubles*: in society, in the structure of the hotel, in the bodies of animals and human beings. The twins' names remind us that *Troubles* is a book with Faith and Charity but no Hope'.[14] Angela dies, and so does the Major's aunt; Sarah and Ripon depart; the dog Rover grows old; generations of cats turn from needle-toothed kittens into savage ginger toms and are finally slaughtered in scenes of gothic gore, only to be replaced by a plague of rats. (This last may be another of Farrell's wry comments on the cycles of history: when the bigoted loyalist Boy O'Neill boasts that the Auxiliaries will show Sinn Fein what for, the Major replies that the cure may be as bad as the disease.)

The card parties and the Ball, by which Edward hopes to recreate an atmosphere 'just like it was in the old days', seem at first to offer a hope of revival, but are actually the climax of doomed attempts to stop time and history. In a recent article on *Troubles*, Lars Hartveit reads the novel through Mikhail Bakhtin's conceptions of the carnivalesque. In this reading the spring Ball becomes one of the moments of 'pageant' or 'spectacle' in the novel which dramatise a community 'torn to pieces between the warring impulses of order and continuity (the past) and the vitality inherent in the process of change and renewal (the future)'.[15] Certainly the Ball, taking place among the irrepressible plant growth slowly breaking up the hotel, is the immediate precursor of even more dramatic change. Great white fists and muscled thigh-like roots of plants metaphorically show Farrell's conviction that change is as inevitable to history as it is to the human body. Significantly, many of these bulging roots come not just from Irish but from exotic plants, the acquired vegetation of Empire, formerly housed as potted plants in the hotel's Palm Court but now taking over. This symbol indicates Farrell's interest not only in what the Empire has done to its colonies, but in what it is doing to itself. These are some of the consequences of imperialist power reacting on the 'centre', part of what Ashcroft, Griffiths, and Tiffin in *The Empire Writes Back* (1989) call the paradox of the 'radically destabilizing effect' of imperial expansion on the coloniser's 'own preoccupations and power'.[16]

Even text is subject to change and decay. The giant letter 'M' falls off the hotel sign into an old lady's cup of tea, leaving the cryptic but suggestive message 'ajestic' (286); the letters of many epitaphs in the churchyard descend 'in dark flakes' to the ground (105), Edward's shaky shooting at cats causes 'a great plaster scroll bearing the words "*Semper fidelis*" to plummet earthwards' (327). The promise to be 'always faithful' cannot be kept here.

A hundred and twenty pages before the end of the novel, the rush of newspaper articles dwindles away. By this time 'the Major was perfectly numb to the daily horrors printed by the newspaper. He had become used to them as he had once become used to the dawn barrage' (317–18). Textuality and event are again aligned. The War is now 'history' and Ireland's troubles nearly end the Major's life when he is captured by the IRA and buried up to his neck on the beach in the face of the rapidly oncoming tide. True to form, this hero has to be rescued by a party of little old ladies.

Rumour and gossip now supplant even newspaper 'fact', and events proceed until the Majestic, descending in flames like Elizabeth Bowen's 'big house' in *The Last September*, reaches the condition in which it was described in the first pages of the novel, one of the casualties of time and history 'in those days'. Bowen herself praised *Troubles*, asserting that it is 'not "a period piece"; it is yesterday reflected in today's consciousness. The ironies, the disparities, the dismay, the sense of unavailingness are contemporary'.[17]

Bergonzi claims that for Farrell reality is indivisible, a comment which would not carry the approval now that Bergonzi meant it to have in 1979; but few contemporary readers would be able agree with this judgement. It is hard to consider Farrell's use of text within text without feeling that this is fictional metahistory, not merely the attempt to represent a particular time and place. *Troubles* marks the beginning of Farrell's investigation of the ways in which our reading of a particular historical moment becomes established and enters into a continuum of constant reinterpretation in the light of the always shifting present.

5 / Culture and Commodity:
The Siege of Krishnapur

I

Farrell said of *The Siege of Krishnapur* that 'It's just an adventure story dressed up in intellectual pyjamas'.[1] Why Farrell should specify 'pyjamas', instead of merely 'clothes', is a potentially interesting question, to which we will return; but even ignoring the pyjamas, this is a curious comment, and more ambiguously suggestive than may at first appear.

Farrell's statement seems to identify accurately the two elements of *The Siege of Krishnapur* which have made a number of critics uneasy since the novel won the Booker Prize in 1973: its (popular) adventure genre, and its intellectual, or ideological, position. But even to say this is to imply that Farrell accepts a now-suspect division between the form and the content of works of fiction. As the critic-narrator in Julian Barnes's *Flaubert's Parrot* says:

> Do you still think the novel divides, like Gaul, into three parts – the Idea, the Form and the Style? ... Form isn't an overcoat flung over the flesh of thought (that old comparison, old in Flaubert's day); it's the flesh of thought itself. You can no more imagine an Idea without a Form than a Form without an Idea. Everything in art depends on execution ...[2]

Recent critical theories (especially those based on various Marxisms) identify genre and ideology as deeply interconnected, and the implication against *The Siege of Krishnapur* seems to be that it must have the same ideological loading as the adventure genre. From the nineteenth century onwards, the adventure story has been the site of an influential discourse of heroism, especially, as John McLeod (citing David Trotter) shows, the story set at the 'outposts or frontiers of the Empire' where the idealized characters and situations form part of the 'myth of the colonizing subject [which] contributed to the construction of colonial identities'.[3] The adventure story is thus profoundly implicated in the ideology of imperialism. It can be argued, however, that Farrell was fully aware of the implications of the adventure story, and that his reference to 'intellectual pyjamas', rather than, say, 'overcoat', is a way of indicating his desire to dress this form in a set of startling ideas (not usually worn in public), which would re-work the genre and re-examine its ideologies. In many ways *The Siege of*

Krishnapur transforms the adventure story into a richly, darkly, ironic account of the British Raj in the mid-Victorian period; it also confronts a particular moment in the discourses of science, religion, and capitalism and their imperialist connections. An early example of postmodern parody, the novel has serious effects which place it beside other deliberate twentieth-century attempts to re-examine what Sara Suleri calls 'the rhetoric of English India'.[4]

The action of *The Siege of Krishnapur* is set during the so-called 'Indian Mutiny' of 1857 and thus it does seem to belong to a particularly ideology-laden sub-genre of the adventure story, the 'Mutiny novel'. In 1897 the author of an unsigned essay on 'The Indian Mutiny in Fiction' in *Blackwood's Edinburgh Magazine* claimed that '[o]f all the great events of this century, as they are reflected in fiction, the Indian Mutiny has taken the firmest hold on the popular imagination'.[5] Shailendra Dhari Singh, who has examined the remarkably consistent patterns of idealised-heroic-action and romance-as-reward in these novels, records that by the time of Indian Independence (1947) the Mutiny had been the subject of at least forty-seven novels.[6] Farrell's siege occurs in the fictitious town of Krishnapur ('city of Krishna'), where Mr Hopkins, the middle-aged 'Collector' of taxes for the District, heads a small garrison of British administrators and members of the military and their families. They become trapped in the elegant Residency on the Indian plain by the sepoy rebellion, defending themselves against attacks for three months before a relief force arrives.

This Indian siege provides another twist on a situation by now very familiar to readers of Farrell, and especially of *Troubles* – one person or a group of people, isolated both by ideology and geography, symbolically enacting humankind's existential condition by holding out in surreal defiance against opposition. In *The Siege of Krishnapur* though, pursuing his larger historiographical interests, Farrell turned to a time which chronologically precedes *Troubles*, a moment when he diagnosed that the threat to the British Empire began to be as much philosophical as physical. In an interview with Malcolm Dean Farrell said that his interest in the Mutiny came from the feeling that in the 1850s 'the Empire was at its most energetic thanks to the new technology of the Industrial Revolution and seemed to be offering (in many ways it was offering) a vast range of physical, social, and moral benefits'.[7]

In the same interview he emphasised that the Mutiny was crucial in 'destroying the myth of the grateful and obedient natives being led onwards and upwards by the paternal white ruler',[8] a comment echoed in the novel itself. Those still alive towards the end of the siege begin to realise that 'even if a relief now came, in many different ways it would be too late' because for them 'India itself was now a different place; the fiction of happy natives being led forward along the road to civilization could no longer be sustained'.[9] Postcolonial theorising had already begun in the 1970s when Farrell was writing *The Siege of Krishnapur*, and his awareness of tense contemporary debate may lie behind his apparently uneasy proposal that the Empire 'seemed to be offering (in many ways it was offering)' benefits to India.

Events in the novel are loosely based on the historical Siege of Lucknow (June to mid-September 1857), and Farrell incorporates a number of details recorded in contemporary eyewitness accounts of that particular siege, and of the Mutiny generally. He cites his most prominent documentary sources in an 'Afterword' to the novel, and these have been extensively discussed by Lars Hartveit.[10] Ironically, as noted in the Introduction, Farrell's attention to historical sources and his skilfull interweaving of documented events with fictional characters has tended to work against his critical reputation rather than for it. His acceptance of demands for 'accuracy' and 'verisimilitude' in historical fiction seem to imply adherence to a notion of history as a series of 'facts', subjective and elusive certainly, but ultimately amenable to the jigsaw-puzzle reconstruction of some master-narrative of 'truth'. As with *Troubles*, Farrell's documentary basis in *The Siege of Krishnapur* can be used to argue that he accepts a now-vulnerable view of history, not sufficiently aware that 'history' is 'always already' implicated in ideology both before and after any textual record.

For a reader immersed in the chronological development of Farrell's fiction, an argument which responds to this by linking his subversive use of genre with his use of history can begin by showing this novel elaborating the Marxist and historiographical interests already established throughout his early work. He seems intent in this novel on dramatising the comment of Marx which Ronald Binns so aptly uses as the epigraph to his chapter on *The Siege of Krishnapur*:

> I cannot part with the subject of India without some concluding remarks. The profound hypocrisy and inherent barbarism of bourgeois civilisation lies unveiled before our eyes, turning from its home, where it assumes respectable forms, to the colonies, where it goes naked.[11]

With a Marxist appreciation that 'the true bearers of ideology in art are the very forms, rather than the abstractable content, of the work itself',[12] Farrell satirises the adventure genre in *The Siege of Krishnapur* to show how narratives of history borrow and repeat the structures of fictional narratives.

John McLeod has discussed some aspects of Farrell's use of parody to undermine the literary conventions which underpin imperialist idealism, noting that Farrell's novel is 'deeply parodic of the conventional Mutiny novel's set-pieces',[13] but it has not been evident to all readers. Laurence Bristow-Smith, overlooking Farrell's irony, admires the novel in spite of the author's 'rather meek acceptance of the demands of the traditional adventure story'.[14] For critics who miss the parody (or find it insufficient, or too funny to be appropriate for a serious theme), Farrell's efforts to treat the past problematically in his own novel by, among other techniques, ironically juxtaposing 1850s and 1970s viewpoints, are just 'let-outs', a series of 'ruses' through which Farrell 'slides about quite opportunistically' to create 'an entertainment'. In this view, as voiced by P.N. Furbank, *The Siege of Krishnapur* is a cleverer-than-usual adventure story, but still a novel unable to bear comparison with the serious fictions of Thomas Mann and Stendhal (to whose work Farrell's had been likened by John Spurling) which express 'human truth'.[15] But in this novel Farrell has moved beyond the ontology of modernism and is far more interested in exploring the conventions which claim to represent reality than he is in arguing for some essentialist 'human truth'.

In two important scenes which frame the central action of the novel Farrell foregrounds the discrepancy between an event as 'raw' action, and the narrative into which it is subsequently transformed. Both cases draw attention to the artificial conventions of the adventure story and the way in which these colour certain individuals' thoughts about 'real' life and history. In the first, just before the siege begins in earnest, Harry and Fleury, in deliberately-used clichés of '*Boys Own*' ripping yarns, become 'firm friends' because they have 'an adventure together' while riding back to Krishnapur through mutinous countryside. A musket shot was 'almost definitely' fired at them:

> Harry clung to this *adventure*, such as it was, all the more tenaciously when he found that because of his sprained wrist he had missed an *adventure* at Captainganj.
>
> Those of his peers who had escaped with life and limb from the Captainganj parade ground did not seem to be thinking of it as an *adventure*, those who had managed to escape unhurt were now looking tired and shocked. And they seemed to be having trouble telling Harry what it had been like. ... It was hard to make any sense out of what had happened, and after a while they gave up trying. ... Strangely enough, they listened quite enviously to Harry talking about the musket shot which had 'almost definitely' been fired at himself and Fleury. They wished they had had an *adventure* too, instead of their involuntary glimpse of the abattoir. (emphasis added 94–95)

It is clear from this that only the embedding within a genre 'makes sense out of what happens', introducing distortion and evaluation as it does so. Without the recognisable form provided by a genre and its implicit values, the events become 'simply ... two or three terrible scenes printed on [the] mind' (94–95) having no story/genre to enable their interpretation.

In a scene with similar effect at the end of the novel the General in charge of the relieving force looks at the 'extraordinary collection of scarecrows' (307) who have survived the siege, and thinks of how this moment will be presented to the world:

> Even when allowances were made, the 'heroes of Krishnapur', as he did not doubt they would soon be called, were a pretty rum lot. And he would have to pose for hours, holding a sword and perched on a trestle or wooden horse while some artist-wallah depicted 'The Relief of Krishnapur'! He must remember to insist on being in the foreground, however; then it would not be so bad. With luck this wretched selection of 'heroes' would be given the soft pedal … an indistinct crowd of corpses and a few grateful faces, cannons and prancing horses would be best. (310–11)

'Interdiscursivity' here reminds the reader of the famous painting of 'The Relief of Lucknow' by Thomas Jones Barker and undermines any certainty about representations of history. The General's 'posing for hours' with a real sword, but on a trestle or wooden horse, to achieve a painting which only distorts the reality of the event, brings to attention the cultural blindness concealed within the quadrangle of 'life', 'art', 'truth', 'history'. The dated slang of Empire – 'rum lot', 'artist-wallah' – confirms that those who have 'trouble telling' about their experiences are influenced by values inherent in the language as well as in the genre. The General, finding the Collector a 'devilishly hard fellow' to talk to after the siege, reminds himself that the man probably has been through 'a sticky time'. The unpleasant Burlton earlier condemns himself with cliché, bragging that 'Jack Sepoy may be able to cut down defenceless people but he can't stand up to real pluck' (56).

But Farrell does not merely satirise this most obvious form of jingoistic language, he employs it suggestively against a range of other voices speaking for the mid-nineteenth century, a Bakhtinian heteroglossia which creates a dialogic form; Matthew Arnold as cultural critic calling out to the future to look back and appreciate the difficulties under which his own time was labouring, Coleridge on the literal truth of the Bible, Schleiermacher, Newman, Pusey, and the disputes of religion, the factions in the discourses of medicine, the 'science' of phrenology, the whimsical voice of Lewis Carroll among many other literary intertexts, and backwards further still to the debt that all these owe to their forerunners, among them Shakespeare and Milton, Plato and Socrates. Farrell's mid-nineteenth century is by no means monolithic or homogenous; indeed the besieged community is a microcosm of the divisions, the contending babble of discourses at work (and play) in early capitalist culture, a din of speakers, arguments and points of view which, it is clear, is only smoothed out by later generations into what Farrell calls ironically at one point, 'the spirit of the time'.

To avoid this 'smoothing out' himself, Farrell does not make any attempt to list or assess 'the causes of the Mutiny', though he does deal with them obliquely. References to the 'greased cartridges affair' which has been presumed by historians to be one of the major causes, are used in the novel only to illustrate the tragic lack of understanding of the Indians by the British and the unnecessary waste and futility of the whole situation. Other than this Farrell refuses to involve his story in the dubious retrospective logic of 'causes and effects' in historical discourse. The set of events known as the Mutiny, he shows, was an accretion of misunderstandings, mysteries never explained and perhaps unexplainable, trivia, and contingency. Any superimposed coherence will always be, in some sense, artificial. One part of Farrell's achievement is that he shows how the teleological drive of positivist fictional and historical narratives, always intent on moving towards the foregone conclusion of a glorious victory, must fail to capture the multifarious buzz of anarchic interconnections.

To reinforce his parodic, self-reflexive use of the adventure genre as a whole, Farrell presents his younger hero, Fleury, using techniques he had already experimented with in *The Man from Elsewhere* and *A Girl in the Head*. In these novels Farrell had already begun to investigate both the experience of the heroic and the textual conventions which encode it, using a range of carefully pointed allusions to heroic models in the Western tradition. Farrell calls in question the whole idea of the unselfconscious hero by making both Fleury and the narrative itself extremely conscious, even anxious, about his status as a would-be hero. Fleury is not, as in 'straight' Mutiny novels, the handsome, young, British male for whom heroism is simply an outcome of 'doing his job' while displaying the manly courage, self-discipline, and intelligence 'natural' to the superiority of his race. Fleury visualises himself as playing a theatrical and deliberate role, a position emphasised by the ironic language of the narration and the suggestive intertextual allusion. Almost Fleury's first introduction in the novel is by way of his clothes, the courage appropriate to heroes being evident only in the wearing of a lounging jacket 'daringly unwaisted'. Later, during a pause before an expected assault, he spends the time 'vaguely trying out various poses in his mind for daguerrotypes to appear in the *Illustrated London News*' (144). When Hari, the Maharajah's son, actually does make a dageurrotype of Fleury, he calls it the 'portrait of [a] very backward man indeed' (85), a phrase with multiple ironies.

The complicity of literature in creating heroic models is signified repeatedly. Fleury is, in the early pages, a self-made imitation of a Romantic poet, a Shelley or a Chatterton, a pseudo-Byron (having also a similar tendency to plumpness), with the addition of a little Keats (trying, in spite of size and good health, to look faintly tubercular), and a mention of Coleridge (199); a pale Romantic hero of a recognisable, if eclectic, type. Before Fleury's arrival in India, Dr Dunstaple is rather worried about signs from England that Fleury, when he appears, will be effeminate; there have been rumours of his disturbing tendency to play the violin in a ruined folly at the end of the rose-garden. But the doctor need not have feared; Fleury's only use of a violin emerges in an unskillful attempt to kill a besieging Sikh whom he strangles with the strings. 'Dobbin', his sister's nickname for him, links him with the clumsy but noble officer in William Thackeray's *Vanity Fair* (1848), and his strange 'sabre-whirling' method of combat (invented by himself), which makes his arms look like 'the sails of a windmill' (288) suggests both Cervantes's Don Quixote and Sergeant Troy in Thomas Hardy's *Far From the Madding Crowd* (1874).

Unfortunately, as the narrative shows, Fleury has been overtaken by a change of taste in the fashion of heroes, a manouevre by which Farrell demonstrates in this novel, as he had in *A Girl in the Head*, that the discourses of heroism, being socially constructed, are subject to change with inconvenient suddenness. Fleury's air of melancholy, formerly so much admired, is now termed 'hangdog'. Although at various points in the novel it is implied that the conventions of the hero require a reciprocal set of conventions for the heroine, Farrell does not show the same interest in examining female roles and stereotypes. These are considered only as they affect the male heroic. It is only because of Fleury's discomfiture that we learn that the young ladies have come to prefer Tennyson's 'great broad-shouldered, genial Englishmen' (36). We quite clearly come to understand, however, that what appears to be a personal choice of heroic models when Fleury begins to change from poet to 'hussar', is only the illusion of choice. The new-fashioned military hero is a necessity to an Empire in an early capitalist phase which must 'deterratorialize' in order to 're-terratorialize' in Deleuze and Guattari's words.[16] In a different formulation, capital must, by acquiring new dominions, be enabled to move its production from the centre to the margins where labour is cheaper and surplus value greater, and where it acquires a new supply of consumers for its commodities.

Althusser's 'Ideological State Apparatuses', among them literature and art, play their part in effecting this change.[17] As Farrell's use of intertextuality shows, at the very moment when the individual appears to be exercising freedom of choice about private behaviour, the literary conventions of the heroic and the romantic accomplish an ideological 'hailing-in'. As Paul de Man says, 'What we call ideology is precisely the confusion of linguistic with natural reality, of reference with phenomenalism'.[18]

Farrell's use of several references to Tennyson (including, on two occasions, the line from 'The Princess', 'the soft and milky rabble of womankind!' [27 and 154], which the Collector recalls when his eyes fall upon a group of women), reminds the twentieth-century reader that Tennyson was, by the time of the Mutiny, England's Poet Laureate and celebrant of failed heroics ('Half a league, half a league, / Half a league onward, / All in the valley of Death / Rode the six hundred'[19]). Tennyson wrote a poem on 'The Defence of Lucknow', in which the British flag, so ironically used in Farrell's siege, is celebrated with vigour if not elegance:

> Banner of England, not for a season, O banner of Britain, hast thou
> Floated in conquering battle or flapt to the battle-cry!
> Never with mightier glory than when we had rear'd thee on high
> Flying on top of the roofs in the ghastly siege of Lucknow –
> Shot thro' the staff or the halyard, but ever we raised thee anew,
> And ever upon the topmost roof our banner of England blew.[20]

If Fleury's response to this pervasive jingoism is deficient, there are other characters in the novel prepared to exhibit an excess of heroic fervour without worrying about its origin or meaning. Hearty Harry Dunstaple goes raging into battle in a most respectably idiotic charge against the enemy. He is immediately cut down and is at the point of death when Fleury saves him by tiptoeing up behind Harry's antagonist 'in unmilitary fashion' (150) and delivering a saving blow. Harry, echoing his Adjutant, says contemptuously of some of the Indian soldiers that 'they're no more use in a fight than the chorus at Covent Garden' (70), but from the detached distance which the narrative maintains, much of the military posturing and procedure is made to look operatically ridiculous.

When Fleury first arrives in Krishnapur he is taken on a visit to meet some of the other 'heroes' who prove to be a loutish group. Among them is the unpleasant Rayne, significantly the Opium Agent, at whose house the young Lieutenant Cutter demonstrates his idea of the heroic by riding his horse into the drawing room, jumping it over a sofa, attacking the cushions with a sabre, and terrifying the women and the Indian servants. Although he does act 'heroically' in the subsequent siege, Cutter's sudden death, when it comes, seems 'disconcertingly trivial'. In a further demonstration of the importance of language in the construction of the heroic, Farrell makes this seem at least partly because he dies without the opportunity for a last speech, or 'any valedictory comments whatsoever' (208). Fleury also has a 'struggle to convince himself that Cutter's heroic stature was not a tiny bit reduced' by the Christian name 'Foxlett' (208), which becomes public at the funeral. Towards the end of the siege when they assemble for an inspiriting speech from the Collector, the Magistrate refers to one of the most famous textual examples of the patriotic literary heroic (Shakespeare's *Henry V*) when he says sardonically, 'I suppose he's going to tell us that gentlemen now abed in England will be sorry that they're not here'(281).[21]

As most twentieth-century readers would know, Shakespeare is canonised, idealised historical fiction, written after the event and with a strong political bias. Farrell records the response that can be expected by those who try to challenge a heroic tradition when the narrator adds that 'nobody was amused by [the Magistrate's] loathsome display of cynicism' (281).

Both Fleury and the elderly General show resemblances to the White Knight in Lewis Carroll's *Through the Looking Glass* (1871), the second of his *Alice* books. These reveal the paradox that subversions of the heroic tradition are often at work in the culture at the same moment when other discourses are reinforcing it. The elderly General, at his first appearance, on horseback but swinging a cricket bat and more intent on sport than war, has to be helped to make an ungainly descent from the saddle. The comic expectations created by this scene prepare the reader for a similar one on the General's next arrival, again on horseback. At first the resemblance to the White Knight looks even closer as the General, 'instead of waiting to be lifted … plunged forward over the horse's head and slithered to the ground' (89). On investigation though, the comic deflation of the chivalric code takes a colder turn when the onlookers become aware as the General tries to stand that '[b]lood was running freely from [his] body and splashing audibly on to the baked earth' (89). The use of the grotesque in the passage which follows is a very typical example of Farrell's style which raises several opposing responses in the reader by combining images of blood, injury, and nursery food with ironic social observation and questions of value. Like most mock-heroic, it also gains from its formal language and the tone of calm explanation:

> The *sowars* were evidently trying to stop the flowing of blood by holding him first one way, then another, as someone eating toast and honey might try, by vigilance and dexterity, to prevent it dripping. The General's blood continued to patter on the earth, however, and all the way up the steps and into the hall where he was laid down at last, after some hesitation, on a rather expensive carpet. (89)

Fleury, like the White Knight, becomes more and more inventive as the siege progresses. Appearing on horseback with the 'Fleury Cavalry Eradicator' pointing forward over his horse's head 'like a pair of weird antlers', he seems to be riding a reindeer (184). He is too soft-hearted to use the fork though, when the appropriate moment unexpectedly presents itself. Fleury's inventiveness also has another point. Twice in the novel, he almost 'invents' things which the twentieth-century reader knows were not actually invented until some time later. In the first case his musing has led him to the brink of inventing a Darwinian explanation for the development of a fish's eye, but he feels such an argument would be absurd. Later, he wonders what would happen if you took a lot of daguerrotypes in slightly different poses and found a way of looking at them in very quick succession so that the image appeared to be moving. This time his attention is distracted and he does not pursue the thought. The distance in time between character and reader is used in these instances to make implications about the paths not taken in history – the 'almost-happened', the contingency of chance and possibility which inhabits the gaps and silences of the historical record.

Other commentators have also seen in the novel some deliberate references to Stendhal's *The Charterhouse of Parma* (1839), and to the novels of Charles Dickens, Elizabeth Gaskell, Anthony Trollope, Joseph Conrad, P.G. Wodehouse and Albert Camus.[21] The reminders of Forster and Kipling continually bring to the the reader's attention the textual struggles through which the British have sought to define and document their mental and physical struggles with the overwhelming reality of India.

The romantic conventions of the Mutiny novel are as relentlessly undermined as the heroic. Late in the siege Louise Dunstaple has a birthday, and Fleury, whose affections her way tend, spends ten pounds to buy a teaspoonful of tea. He then exchanges his gold cufflinks, a silver snuff-box, and a pair of shoes for two lumps of sugar, and makes her a tiny cake which he cooks on a hot rock. Not only are materialistic values ironised in this exchange, Farrell also emphasises, as he had in *Troubles*, the brute power of physical needs urging against the mind's control. Fleury and Lucy find their intimate dinner marred by almost unendurable heat, flies, smells, and the fact that she can hardly concentrate on listening to Fleury because in her starving condition she is so distracted by the presence of food. When they do eat they struggle painfully with the cake because it has baked hard while their teeth are loose from scurvy. Louise begins to weep silently because she has no-one with whom she can discuss the fact that she has not had her period for two months and fears she may be barren. Their romance is saved from a possible rival suitor who arrives with the relief party, but only because Louise and Fleury smell so repugnant. The stench they have become accustomed to keeps the newcomer, a former admirer of Louise, at a safe distance.

The short final chapter which describes an unexpected meeting between Fleury and the Collector in a London street twenty years after the siege seems a further reminder to the reader of the conventions of the Victorian novel and the ideological basis of these. It supplies information about the 'pairing off' of the couples and their subsequent fates. Louise and Fleury did marry and now have children, but this conventional 'happy ending' is marred by the fact that Fleury is planning, if not already involved in, an assignation with another woman. Harry has married Lucy, Miriam has married Dr McNab, but these 'courtships' have been entirely perfunctory and anti-romantic during the novel.

They take place as fragmentary asides during episodes of starvation, painful birth and death immediately juxtaposed, terrible wounds, cholera, heat stroke, and the stench of decay. Less 'love' than appetite and convention, this is the mating instinct of animals, the drive to seek comfort from the intolerable human situation (not just of the siege, but of the human condition itself).[23] It is the existential state of siege which brings about the forlorn attempt to draw close to another human being.

In a scene which again uses the mode of the grotesque, Louise finally strips off the flour-and-water poultice which she has been wearing on her boils and eats it. As readers we both laugh and recoil, but we know that we would not laugh if the same scene occurred in life. The grotesque thus has the almost metafictional effect of reminding the reader that we are not reading reality; this is fiction, which allows us a safe distance but demands in return that we examine our responses as we could not do in the immediacy of a 'real' situation. This appears to be one answer to those critics who maintain that *The Siege of Krishnapur* is too funny to present the full horror of the brutalities perpetrated by both sides in the Mutiny. There are many things Farrell does not say, but his blackly comic-grotesque descriptions, at least for some readers, produce a repulsion against physical violence which could hardly be increased by the most long-winded and seriously 'realistic' descriptions of carnage. By his use of the grotesque, Farrell adds to these scenes the terrible fact of their ultimate absurdity as political and social decisions. He also avoids that faint (and some-times not so faint) air of voyeuristic self-indulgence which can accompany the lip-smacking 'journalistic' description of violence and suffering. It has been one of the self-imposed tasks of most art-forms in the twentieth-century to break through the cocooning habits of genre and ideology to re-present the butchery of war with fresh eyes. Farrell's surreal grotesque is shockingly effective in this.

II

What Farrell puts under siege in his version of the Mutiny is not some isolated British outposts, nor even just the conventions of the adventure novel and its values, but the whole Whig view of history that underwrites the imperialist presence in India. Unlike other Mutiny writers Farrell does not celebrate the end of the siege as a great victory for the British. The colonisers may have won the battle (though at terrible cost to both sides), but there are no fanfares, no sense of a glorious success, merely the bathos of a few filthy, ragged, starving survivors so changed that, significantly, they are hardly able to communicate with their rescuers. Farrell shows that this temporary win is far less important than the fact that the British have begun the century-long process of losing the ideological war. The security of Empire is over.

The impression that this victory is actually a defeat is most forcibly demonstrated in *The Siege of Krishnapur* by the series of surreal images created for the reader by Farrell's treatment of the Great Exhibition, a use of documentary reference which becomes a brilliant extended metaphor in the novel. The Exhibition comes to stand, as John McLeod shows, for the fragility of imperial control and the hermeneutic difficulties of any approach to the past. Equally effectively though, it allows Farrell to provide a series of vivid and almost unforgettable scenes. In these, the artifacts of British culture, the sofas, chairs, ornaments, table-ware, paintings, and bric-à-brac which for the twentieth century so completely evoke the stifling domesticity of the Victorians, are taken out of the context which makes them familiar and placed against the irreconcilable 'otherness' of the Indian landscape. These images of an incongruous physical juxtaposition of cultures are at least as striking as any narrative of victory or loss.

In *The Siege of Krishnapur*, the Great Exhibition (actually held in London at the Crystal Palace in 1851), has been a major event in the life of the Collector, Mr Hopkins. His return to England to see it was followed by the subsequent spending of a large part of his personal fortune to export back to his Residency in India a multifarious collection of objects from the Exhibition. Ranging from his favourite 'gorse-bruiser' to busts and statues, these things signify to him, and he confidently assumes, to others, the pre-eminence of British civilization and the divine sanction for colonisation. Thus his accurate official title of 'Collector' has added ironic point in *The Siege of Krishnapur* – his 'collecting' represents the whole British philosophy which urges the accumulation not only of objects but of colonisable (usable) countries, a philosophy of dominion, possession, materialism, all in the name of 'the spread of civilization'.

One of the statues owned by the Collector is an allegorical group of figures called '*The Spirit of Science Conquers Ignorance and Prejudice*' (87), a phrase which sums up part of this ideological justification, and one which Farrell at first planned to use as the title for this novel.[24] A phrase which was sincerely meant and without irony in its time is full of irony in almost any circumstances now, but most particularly as the title for this self-aware fiction in which the Collector and his Exhibition voice the 'shaping concept of history' which justifies the enterprise of colonisation. Farrell's project thus seems to be in line with the advice given later (in 1984) by Fredric Jameson (from Marx via Althusser):

> as old-fashioned narrative or 'realistic' historiography becomes problematic, the historian should reformulate her vocation – not any longer to produce some vivid representation of history 'as it really happened', but rather to produce the *concept* of history.[25]

It is certainly true, as Bristow-Smith says, that the Collector represents the 'conscience' of British imperialism, since he embodies its most humane and idealistic side.[26] He occasionally mourns particular British failures to understand India, but he mourns these in the first part of the novel as temporary limitations, failures to proceed imaginatively enough with the great work of education.

He expatiates at dinner on the idea that the spiritual and the practical sides of imperial control are inseparable: 'every invention is a prayer to God. Every invention, however great, however small, is a humble emulation of the greatest invention of all, the Universe' (53). He envisages '[t]he spreading of the Gospel on the one hand, the spreading of the railways on the other' (50). His text for the first part is the Bible, his text for the practical side, the Catalogue of the Exhibition. He reads aloud from this after dinner to his guests:

> Let me see, Number 382: Instrument to teach the blind to write. Model of an aerial machine and of a navigable balloon. A fire annihalator by R. Weare of Plumstead Common. A domestic telegraph requiring only one bell for any number of rooms. An expanding pianoforte for yachts etc. Artificial teeth carved in hippopotamus ivory by Sinclair and Hockley of Soho. A universal drill for removing decay from teeth. A jaw-lever for keeping animals' mouths open. Improved double truss for hernia, invented by a labouring man ... (53)

In this passage Farrell uses the reader's displacement in time from the period of the action, which makes the list above so extraordinary to twentieth-century eyes, as a correlative for the shock of cultural displacement experienced in India by the Collector and his contemporaries. Yet some objects, like the 'aerial machine and ... navigable balloon', remind us simultaneously of how close we are and how far we have come from this unrecuperable strangeness of the past, the 'prehistory of our present'. The collection thus gains double point in the novel as both a conglomeration of physical objects extremely comic to the modern reader, but also as a textual record which stands, for the Collector at least, with the Bible as part of the textual authority for Empire.

As a catalogue, the Exhibition is a reminder of the textuality of the past, but as a series of physical objects, some of which may survive into the present, it draws attention to the ambiguities and interpretive distortions which attend apparently stable relics or traces. Changes in setting and context expose all objects unmercifully to the realisation that, taken out of their own time, place, and culture, their meaning is emptied out. The Residency is already a kind of museum, since the Great Exhibition is six years past at the time of the Mutiny, and there are hints in this of Kipling's father's 'Wonder Museum' at

Lahore, in which he tried to exhibit the whole of India, and Lurgan Sahib's extraordinary shop at Simla in *Kim*. It also prefigures Lifafa Das's peepshow in Salman Rushdie's *Midnight's Children*: there is something about India which urges upon the senses the idea of teeming multiplicity, a challenge to any kind of representation. This becomes an emblem of the challenge which 'reality' makes to art, and to the form of the novel in particular. Towards the end of the siege it is his thoughts about the millions of Indians living in poverty which form the ultimate challenge to the Collector's belief in the possibility of human progress towards equality. Debates on the usefulness and propriety of the objects which had been on display at the Great Exhibition recur throughout the novel, and as with the fashion of Fleury's heroism, Farrell's narration emphasises that a slippage in meaning is already occurring. The climax of cultural certainty which the Exhibition represented is already over, if indeed it ever existed outside its representation.

As with so many objects in Farrell's fictional worlds, the function of items in the collection is multiple and extends towards symbolic allusion in many directions. The objects line the walls of the Residency 'like armour', and later in the novel when the siege has reached the point where anything must be used for defence and weaponry, most of the objects from the collection are dragged out to reinforce the mud-built ramparts. They therefore become physically what they have always been philosophically and culturally, part of the aggression and defence of British ideology against the overwhelming alternative reality of India. The heads of Shakespeare and Keats are used as cannon balls against the sepoy forces, their meaning as cultural signifiers now reduced to their power as circular projectiles, a signifying system at which Shakespeare of the bald head undisputably outdoes Keats of the flowing locks. As Frances B. Singh points out, '[i]n the last defense of the compound, the very implements of civilization, progress and science become missiles of pain, horror and death'.[27]

In 'Exhibiting Empire in J.G. Farrell's *The Siege of Krishnapur*', which is probably the most powerful discussion to date of Farrell's use of the Exhibition, John McLeod reads *The Siege of Krishnapur* through Gayatri Spivak, Homi Bhabha, and Michel Foucault to reveal the collection as the display/performance of imperialist culture and order. McLeod argues that Farrell uses the collection to demonstrate the inherent fragility of the colonially imposed order. The gathering of objects in any collection or exhibition imposes a taxonomy which draws together under a new heading a group of disparate objects, but the new group is always threatening to disperse into its original individualities. Each single object is a startling reminder of the potential for separation and anarchy. While this summary does meagre justice to McLeod's subtle and persuasive argument, there is a case to be made that Farrell actually goes beyond this in directions again influenced by his Marxist interests.

The multiplicity of objects mentioned in *The Siege of Krishnapur* only partly consists of items from the Exhibition; the list from the catalogue above is only one of a series of lists and catalogues which abound in the novel. All are used by Farrell to characterise both the admirable fertile energy of the Victorian period and its less admirable rampant materialism. From the very first part of the novel the colonising culture is shown as an economy of production and consumption in which all the dominions of the Empire are ransacked for their contributions to British manufacture. At the picnic in Calcutta before Fleury's journey to Krishnapur,

> the Dunstaples' bearers unpacked before their eyes a real York ham, ... oysters, pickles, mutton pies, Cheddar cheese, ox tongue, cold chickens, chocolate, candied and crystallized fruits, and biscuits of all kinds made from the finest fresh Cape flour: Abernethy's crackers, Tops and Bottoms, spice nuts and every other delicious biscuit you could imagine. (30)

Fleury, when he unpacks at Krishnapur, proves to have many of those objects which support and solidify a bourgeois identity, either personal or public:

> books and clothes, Havanas, Brown Windsor soap, jams and conserves in miraculously unbroken jars, a cask of brandy, seidlitz powders, candles, a tin footbath, bound volumes of Bell's Life, more candles, boots in trees, and an ingenious piece of furniture designed to serve, in dire domestic situations which Fleury hoped never to experience, as both wash-stand and writing table. (45)

These are placed in a room already cluttered with official texts of the past which were once important to somebody:

> a collection of salt reports tied in bundles with the frail, faded red tape of India's official business. There were also blue-books, codes, and countless letters, some filed, some heaped at random. (45)

He goes from this room to a dinner with the Collector at which the dishes follow each other in glorious abundance: 'the fried fish in batter that glowed like barley sugar, the curried fowl seasoned with lime juice, coriander, cumin and garlic, the tender roast kid and mint sauce' are followed later by 'a cool and creamy mango fool' (48).

These lists combine a density of 'realist' metonymic detail with an implied comment on the submersion of this early capitalist society into a welter of objects. Farrell touches here on the complex and much-discussed relationships between base and superstructure which were under debate in mid-twentieth-century varieties of Western Marxism, the objects produced for consumption, the surplus value of labour which supplies and supports capitalism,[28] the submission of the human owners to the objects which begin to exert control over them. At one point when it becomes necessary to file down chains to prepare chain-shot for vegetation clearing (a scene which Binns regards as an ironic reminder of Joseph Conrad's French gunboat in *Heart of Darkness* [1899], firing randomly into the jungle[29]), the Collector remembers his fine British file. He would like to try out the file, but feels that he can't been seen to do something so menial or he would lose the respect of the natives.

Later, the garrison's cultural belief that doing one's own washing is 'low' makes all the siege community dependent on the dhobi, who is charging enormous prices. The Collector studies the dhobi's methods and then, in a maneouvre which anticipates by more than a century the Gandhian signature of cleaning latrines in his call for untouchable emancipation (and thus presents Mr Hopkins's actions as an undermining of the colonial/class system), begins publically to do his own washing (235). He feels proud of the independence signalled by his grey handkerchief, and at the same time remembers with 'amazement and disgust at his petty chauvinism' how delighted he had been when the British file won in competition against a foreign French file at the Exhibition (247).

Through Fleury, however, Farrell takes the difficult and potentially danger-ous step of trying to show that this zenophobia applies not only to the British culture but the Indian. Fleury disputes the relevance of the Great Exhibition, claiming that 'the Great Exhibition was not, as everyone said it was, a landmark of civilization; it was for the most part a collection of irrelevant rubbish' (82). It is irrelevant to Fleury because he does not accept the principles of taxonomy of the collection. In a visit to the Maharajah's Palace with the Maharajah's son Hari, Fleury suddenly recognises that all cultures validate themselves by the collection and display of artifacts. He treats the objects collected by Hari's fore-bears with the same disdain he has for the Collector's possessions, an attitude mis-interpreted by Hari as contempt for Indian culture. Neither India nor England are monolithic in this novel, divisions fissure their apparent homogeneity at many points; what is familiar and habitual in one's own culture becomes unrecognisably alien in another.

Farrell's technique of defamiliarisation and his ironic tone contribute at many points to this. When the Collector instructs that all possessions are to be used to shore up the failing defences, he is unmoved by pleas that people be allowed to keep small items, even 'things which you could not possibly do with-out, a set of fish-knives, for example, ... or a sketch of the Himalayas as seen from Darjeeling' (245). The humour and shock of this recurrent defamiliarisation build up to the moment when, with the garrison at starvation point, the Collector eats a large and lively black beetle 'with as much pleasure as if it had been a chocolate truffle' (285).

One of the deliberate consequences of this is a developing emphasis in the trilogy that any juxtaposition of cultures will bring about sooner or later a forcible recognition that all culture is constructed, time-and-place-specific, rather than natural or essential. There follows, for Farrell, the central and ironic fact of imperialism: that the colonising process will inevitably institute radical change in the colonising power itself. It is this process, the effect of colonisation on the colonisers, rather than on the colonised, that constitutes the fundamental focus of the Empire trilogy as a whole. As Spivak says, 'imperialism, understood as England's social mission, was a crucial part of the cultural representation of England to the English'.[30] The failure of Empire thus meant a crisis in 'the cultural representation of England to the English', which was still being acutely felt in Farrell's 1950s and 1960s Britain, and it was this which exercised Farrell. In the climate of newly-established postcolonial literary studies in the 1970s, however, this approach looked misguided if it was recognised at all.

The Collector's optimism and faith survive for some time into the siege. If the Collector is 'heroic' by virtue of his situation as a reluctant but committed leader, even that heroism is continually undercut by the detaching, objectifying distance through which readers are led to judge the error of many of his predictions and decisions. Again Farrell exploits the hindsight through which the present inevitably looks at the past: 'two wheels, he had been obliged to reflect, or even, come to that, a dozen wheels, would never match for speed and convenience the four legs of the horse' (201). The Collector's sickness, his attitudes to women, and his stubborn adherence to attitudes and ideas we know to be wrong continue the deflation of his heroism. His views are always undermined by the bathetic anti-heroism of the action and the wry voice of the omniscient narration. At one point the Collector thinks:

> ... How arid the eighteenth century was in comparison to our own. They did their best, no doubt, but they were *at best* only a preparation for our own century. ... Everything which they approached so ineffectually, we have brought to culmination. The poor fellows had no conception of how far Art, Science, Respectability, and Political Economy could be taken. Where they hesitated and blundered we have gone forward ... Ah!' He stumbled. (200)

His stumble is significant, an indication that to a Whig view, each 'age' in its turn looks to have 'hesitated and blundered' while its inheritors have 'gone forward' and 'brought to culmination' those earlier stumblings. Even the word 'arid' is important, making as it does, a correlation between the past (the British eighteenth century) in time, and the Indian continent (in space and culture). Both these, whatever their immediacy to the imagination, are in reality distanced in almost unbridgeable ways from the Victorian present in which the Collector is musing.

Telescopes cannot help the Collector's cultural myopia or his Whig view of history, but the siege itself provides the displacement which unsettles his deeply entrenched habits of sight and thought. His resulting illness (one of the recurring metaphors of disease and decay, both personal and imperial, here as in *Troubles*), is significantly a problem of the eyes. It leads him to retire to bed at noon, a sign of cultural and ideological disorientation. When he recovers he becomes not a collector but a disperser, giving instructions for the removal of everything possible out to the ramparts. He realises that his confidence in the superiority of his own time over all past times has quite vanished:

> He thought again of those hundred and fifty million people living in cruel poverty in India alone ... Would Science and Political Economy ever be powerful enough to give them a life of ease and respectability? He no longer believed that they would. ... This notion of the superiority of the nineteenth century which he had just been enjoying had depended on beliefs he no longer held, but which had just now been itching, like amputated limbs which he could feel although they no longer existed. (200)

By this time the Collector has begun to realise that the Exhibition was, as the Padre calls it, 'The World's Vanity Fair' (299). He remembers with horror that he had registered fleetingly but not thought about the large collection of shackles, fetters, bolts, and chains; all the equipment of slavery which had also been been exhibited.

It is no accident that Fleury has been sent to India to write a book on the progress of British civilization in India. In an early draft of the novel he is coming to investigate what might be the subject-matter for a tapestry to be presented by the Honourable East India Company to Her Majesty, Queen Victoria.[31] In later drafts Farrell pares away everything that distracts from his major themes and introduces more varieties of emphasis on the textual and discursive basis of British rule. The Collector is learning from a book how to run a siege, but ironically it is Cormontaingne's imaginary *Journal of the Attack of a Fortress* (171), which is not only fictional, but which predicts inevitable defeat for the besieged after a certain length of time. Dr McNab is known to have kept a diary of the progress of his wife's fever up to the time of her death. But India has the capacity to make the British realise just how much they have come to rely on texts, sometimes for good, at others for ill: when the Collector tries to write an order after the rains, the paper is too wet to accept the ink properly (227).

The salt reports and all the other documents from the Cutcherry make the besieged group feel 'safely padded' at one point, and later form a paper storm which gives them cover as they retreat to the Banqueting Hall.

> What an advantage that knowledge can be stored in books! The knowledge lies there like hermetically sealed provisions waiting for the day when you may need a meal. Surely what the Collector was doing as he pored over his military manuals, was proving the superiority of the European way of doing things, of European culture itself. This was a culture so flexible that whatever he needed was there in a book at his elbow. An ordinary sort of man, he could, with the help of an oil-lamp, turn himself into a great military engineer, a bishop, an explorer or a General over-night, if the fancy took him. (169–70)

In this novel it is not just the Exhibition nor the wider collection which characterises this society, but rather the proliferation of objects, and the discourses and textuality which bind them into a cultural whole. In many ways the Collector speaks in the first part of the novel for the liberal humanist view of Matthew Arnold, an association emphasised by the passage of meditation so strongly reminiscent of Arnold's most famous poem, 'Dover Beach' (215–16).[32] Fleury, too, speaks for Arnold, quoting directly from Arnold's *A French Eton* (1864), 'the words of a very dear friend … from Oxford, a poet (like myself), who is now working as an inspector of schools …' (118). Arnold's trenchant commentaries on the divisions in mid-Victorian life are contemporary with the period in which Marx was at work in the British Museum recording his very different views. For Arnold, it is the educated consciousness which must create the grand ideals necessary to direct the progress of society. For Marx, in an almost directly contrary view, the economic structure of society constitutes

> the real foundation, on which rise legal and political superstructures and to which correspond definite forms of social consciousness. The mode of production in material life determines the general character of the social, political and spiritual processes of life. It is not the consciousness of men that determines their existence, but, on the contrary, their social existence determines their consciousness.[33]

These oft-quoted words of Marx are discussed, as is Matthew Arnold's work, in Raymond Williams's *Culture and Society 1780–1950* (1958), a book which Farrell would almost certainly have known since Williams was, with Christopher Caudwell, the most prominent British Marxist cultural and literary historian of the 1960s. *Culture and Society*, and Williams's next book, *The Long Revolution*

(1961), would be obvious resources for any novelist of the time intending to write on Empire, especially a novelist with an already Marxist orientation.

It is not until Farrell's *The Hill Station*, a sequel of sorts to *The Siege of Krishnapur*, that we have, in a parenthetical aside, an image of Marx working in the British Museum while the events of the novel are taking place. It is almost as though, in re-reading *The Siege of Krishnapur* to write its sequel, Farrell had noticed how strongly the ghost of Marx haunts the ghost of Arnold in those pages.

By the end of *The Siege of Krishnapur* the Collector and Fleury have changed to opposite positions. In their last conversation Fleury voices the Arnoldian ideas (very close to those in Arnold's *Culture and Anarchy* [1869]):

> '... culture gives us an idea of a higher life to which we aspire. And *ideas*, too, are a part of culture ... No one can say that ideas are a sham. Our progress depends on them ... Think of their power. Ideas make us what we are. Our society is based on ideas ...'
> 'Oh, ideas ...' said the Collector dismissively. (313)

And the last words of the novel are almost a statement of Arnoldian views giving way in the Collector to a Marxist sense of how history is shaped:

> Perhaps by the very end of his life, in 1880, he had come to believe that a people, a nation, does not create itself according to its own best ideas, but is shaped by other forces, of which it has little knowledge. (313)

The sense of defeat implicit in this passage refers to more than the Indian Mutiny. Earlier sentences of the paragraph quoted above deliberately bring us back to the twentieth-century, both by a change to the present tense and by an indirect address to the reader. In this we get a direct implication of our common complicity in an indecision and inertia which prevents social change; but we are also excused with a tolerant and world-weary shrug:

> The years go by and the Collector undoubtedly felt, as many of us feel, that one uses up so many options, so much energy, simply in trying to find out what life is all about. And as for being able to do anything about it, well ... (313)

Another character who clearly illustrates a will to do social good which has been swallowed up by weariness and cynicism is the Magistrate: '... since he had shouted himself hoarse as a young man in 1832 he had been devoted to the radical cause, a supporter of Chartism, of factory reform, and of every other progressive notion which crossed his path' (258). Though he is the same age as the Collector his reforming enthusiasm has long curdled into a conviction of all human stupidity and self-interest. Towards the end of the siege when food is running short and there is a need to distribute the accumulated provisions and other goods which once belonged to those who have been killed, he realises that now he has an 'opportunity to *act*, not merely to argue'.

> Would he dare to grasp this chance and order the abolition of property within the community? ... He realized now that his belief in people was no longer alive ... he no longer loved the poor as a revolutionary must love them. People were stupid. The poor were just as stupid as the rich; he had only contempt for both of them. His interest in humanity now was stone dead, and probably had been for some time. He no longer believed that it was possible to struggle against the cruel forces of capitalist wealth. Nor did he particularly care. He had given up in despair. (258)

This passage and the disastrous attempt to auction the goods, which follows, seem to suggest that the fight against entrenched ideology requires an energy and enthusiasm which may only be sustainable in youth, especially with a youthful naïvety. To an older, more cynical view, a Hobbesian self-interest will be the emotion which outlasts most other human passions. This pessimistic final position of the Magistrate and the Collector, endorsed by the narrative voice, indicates clearly that *The Siege of Krishnapur* is as much a novel about Britain in the 1960s as about Britain in the 1850s and 1860s. It appears almost to be dramatising two of Raymond Williams's major insights in the chapter of *The Long Revolution* entitled 'Britain in the 1960s'.[34] Williams argues that the Labour movement, the unions, and other formerly socialist groups have become indistinguishable from capitalism in their practical operations, whatever the very different philosophical abstractions they still profess.

Williams claims too that what his Britain of the 1960s lacks is a sense of real community, and that this lack stems from deeply entrenched capitalist ideas of the individuality inherent in consumerism. This obscures, in Williams's view, the roots of actual mutual interdependence necessary for industrial production and services (an idea taken up much later and with variations by Gilles Deleuze and Félix Guattari in the two volumes of their *Capitalism and Schizophrenia*, *Anti-Oedipus* [1972] and *A Thousand Plateaus* [1980]). It is exactly a sense of community of the kind Williams wants which develops during the siege as the values of property and ownership fall away and interdependence becomes crucial to survival. Perhaps this remains the most hopeful aspect of *The Siege of Krishnapur*. The novel must otherwise be seen as Farrell's resigned portrayal of a misguided liberal humanist idealism and an ineffectual socialist reform both caught in the web of a romanticised capitalism, in 1970 as firmly as in 1857.

6 / The Theatre of Empire:
The Singapore Grip

Early in *The Singapore Grip* we learn that 'For a number of years now it had been Walter's agreeable habit to take his visitors by the arm and escort them along the row of paintings that hung in his drawing-room' (16). The series of paintings to which Walter Blackett proudly draws his captive visitor's attention are cargo being loaded in the East, unloaded in Liverpool, paintings of Rangoon which plot its growth from 'a sleepy little village' into 'a great modern city, now only surpassed as an Eastern port by Calcutta and Bombay' (17), paintings which depict the growth of Calcutta, Penang, Malacca, and paintings which show the development of Singapore, and the rise of Blackett and Webb Ltd. These visual images are neither for aesthetic purposes, nor are they ideologically neutral. Walter's commentary to his visitor, which accompanies the tour, actually charts the economic progress of the Empire in South East Asia. The paintings, and the rampantly imperialist narrative which accompanies them, provide a culturally-loaded summary of the history of Blackett and Webb and of Singapore itself. They are a simple and effective means of outlining the exploitative economic history which made Singapore what it was in the early 1940s. It is a technique that Paul Scott had successfully used in *A Division of the Spoils*, the final volume of his *Raj Quartet*, a book Farrell greatly admired, and which he had reviewed.[1] His own previous novel, *The Siege of Krishnapur*, had ended with a summation of the whole narrative action in the form of a painting of the siege in which military victories are revealed as the ideological constructions they are. In this novel, however, Farrell has moved away from the personal history of *Troubles* and the military history of *The Siege of Krishnapur* to a committedly economic treatment of Empire.

During another similar history lesson in *The Singapore Grip* – where Walter 'discours[es] fluently on the early days of the company' (43) with a young man from the *Straits Times* – some flesh is put on the skeletal picture presented by the paintings. Here, amongst other things, we learn that in the early days even opium had passed through Mr Webb's hands, '[a]nd human beings, too, of course' (44). The 'of course' is particularly telling; through only two words Farrell shows how the existence of such trade was an accepted component of the business of Empire, how for the Empire-builders the end invariably justified the means. The details of the suffering and hardship Walter's company,

Blackett and Webb, inflicted on the peasants in the nineteenth century are recounted without shame, even with pride by Walter (much to the discomfort of the Major), as is the destruction of traditional ways of life:

> The traditional village communities were broken up and the Burmese had to learn to travel about looking for seasonal or coolie work, from the producer's point of view a much more efficient and much cheaper system. 'The rice-growing delta had been turned into what someone called "a factory without chimneys",' summed up Walter with satisfaction ... (45–46)

The phrase 'a factory without chimneys' lends a Dickensian horror to the description. Such information, together with the Mr Webb's opposition to the 1926 General Strike in Britain, paints a deliberately Marxist picture of a company which exploits its labour, and which has expanded on the backs of its employees. There is a Dickensian dramatic irony, too, in the way in which Walter, like Mr Bounderby in *Hard Times* (1854), proudly voices opinions which appear outrageous to the reader. The bubble is further deflated soon after when old Mr Webb, now near death, is described thus: 'the old capitalist was really nothing but skin and bone' (49), a description that applies as much to western capitalism in its South East Asian Empire context as to Mr Webb, and anticipates the strong socialist fervour that followed the Second World War and ushered into the British parliament a Labour government which was to preside over the dismantling of Britain's Empire.

In a further manipulation of visual images Farrell later uses photographs to portray the changing colonial attitudes of the period. Dupigny, sitting alone in the Penang Swimming Club while Penang burns in the distance, looks at two framed photographs dating from about 1910. One of them

> showed a group of ladies and gentlemen, assembled this time for a picnic, perhaps. The padre was there looking young and vigorous, a watch-chain visible against his black waistcoat and with a white sun-helmet on his head. The ladies were still sitting in the rickshaws that had brought them; but only one coolie had remained to appear in the picture and there he was, still gripping the shafts as if he had only just trundled his fair cargo up. The European standing beside the rickshaw had reached out a hand as the photograph was being taken and forced the coolie's head down so that only his straw hat and not his face should be visible in the picture. (294)

Through Dupigny Farrell muses 'on the confident assumption of superiority embodied in that hand forcing the coolie to hide his face' (294). It is a confidence which, in 1941, in the face of impending Japanese victory in Malaya and the looming attack on 'Fortress Singapore', is no longer tenable. As Dupigny concludes, 'Whatever happened with the Japanese the old colonial life in the East, the European's hand on the coolie's straw hat, was finished' (294–95). The paintings and photographs (the metaphorical and proverbial writing on the wall) which record the history of the colony and its business houses ultimately point to the imminent closure of both.

And Farrell is not only pointing his finger of fate at the British Empire. Through the presence in Singapore of the Frenchman François Dupigny he is able to remind the reader of events in French Indo-China, while the American Jim Ehrendorf invites the reader to look ahead to the present of the novel's writing and to the French-American débâcle in Vietnam. The 'smooth and … flawless edifice' (21) is about to be demolished, the Singapore Grip is about to become a slippery signifier.

Manuscript material held in the library of Trinity College Dublin reveals that Farrell considered at least thirty-one titles for his previous novel, *The Siege of Krishnapur*, which was to become the second volume of his Empire trilogy – ranging from 'Difficulties', which has obvious links with *Troubles*, to the extra-ordinary title 'The Portable Steel Spectacles'.[2] There is no similar evidence to suggest that Farrell considered such a range of titles for the third volume of his trilogy. Indeed the phrase which gives the book its title – 'the Singapore Grip' – resonates through the text, each vibration providing Farrell with the opportunity to indulge his penchant for puns and other lexicographical games.

Significantly, the title phrase is introduced as Matthew arrives in Singapore in November 1941, quite literally as he climbs out of the plane in which he has completed the last stage of his journey: '"Don't forget to watch out for the Singapore Grip!" shouted one of the crew after him in a clamour of cheerful goodbyes and laughter as he jumped stiffly to the ground' (101). Shortly after-wards, as he makes his way across the city in the company of Monty, Joan, and his old friend Ehrendorf, Matthew, in an attempt to stimulate conversation, asks, 'Does anyone happen to know what the Singapore Grip is?' (108). It is a question that no-one shows any signs of having heard. What is to become a regular pattern of rhetorical questioning in the novel is established here. These questions are suggestively left hanging at the moment of their asking at various points in the novel, but their implications are taken up and explored later. The questions are all framed to focus attention from many directions on the ethics of the colonial enterprise in general and those of the rubber trade in particular.

A curiosity about the meaning of 'the Singapore Grip' is kept in the reader's mind through Farrell's deliberate plays on the word 'grip' (both noun and verb). These apparently almost self-indulgent word games serve the very important purpose of keeping the reader's attention clearly focussed on the central question of the novel: the meaning of the Singapore Grip and through that the sinister economic grasp of the Empire itself. This is particularly true of euphemistic mercantile clichés such as 'grip on the market' (45), 'commercial grip' (48), and, in the context of the novel, the oxymoron 'friendly grip' (250), which all highlight the exploitative stranglehold companies like Blackett and Webb Ltd exert on the colony of Singapore.[3]

Matthew, and occasionally the Major too, is frequently troubled by the way Blackett and Webb Ltd treat their native workforce, and the way the profit-motivated colonial enterprise itself operates in favour of its European 'partners'. Farrell's rhetorical strategy brings to the surface for the reader hints of the many dubious assumptions which underlie colonial and economic practices, and which people like Walter prefer not to think about. If they were to look too closely they might be forced to at least consider the morality of the Empire on which their businesses ride. In this novel the genuine, even if mistaken missionary idealism of the liberal humanist protagonists in *Troubles* and *The Siege of Krishnapur* has given way completely to policies based on a ruthless secular capitalism. Similarly these businessmen, smug in their complacent belief in Britain's hold on the territory, are unable even to imagine the vulnerability of Singapore. To contemplate seriously the fall of the city would be to recognise the vulnerability of their own empires.

A number of tantalizing answers to Matthew's question about the meaning of the Singapore Grip are offered at various stages in the novel. The first is given by François Dupigny who believes 'it is what they call here a certain tropical fever, very grave' (146). As Ronald Binns notes, drawing attention to possible intertextual connections between Farrell's novel and *War and Peace*, the Frenchman 'mistakenly assumes that the expression derives from *la grippe* (the French word for influenza)' – which, significantly, Anna Pavlovna is suffering from at the outset of Tolstoy's novel.[4] Matthew at first dismisses Dupigny's explanation, but later begins to accept it when he suffers a severe bout of fever himself: 'perhaps he had caught the Singapore Grip! Certainly an illness of some kind had taken hold of him' (198). The illness, of course, is colonialism, and its literal and metaphorical grip on this part of the world is the condition this novel investigates. The linking of colonialism and disease is a common enough literary strategy, as Jeffrey Meyers has shown.[5] It is one which Farrell has used and developed throughout his trilogy, and now, in *The Singapore Grip*, the colonial disease begins to infect the more sensitive members of the ruling élite whose consciences are not immune to the suffering of the colonised. Matthew, having inherited his father's business interests and taken up residence in the Mayfair has joined the colonial fold and his unease in this role is manifested in his illness.

But by the time of Matthew's illness Farrell has already skilfully planted vague suggestions of an altogether more interesting version of the Singapore

Grip in the minds of his readers, which proves to be at the centre of a dynamic and revealing series of significations:

> Words were whispered confidentially into Matthew's ear as he waded after Monty ... 'Nice girl' ... 'Guarantee virgin' ... 'You wantchee try Singapore Glip? More better allsame Shanghai Glip!' ('Do I want to try *what*?' wondered Matthew unable to make head nor tail of this rigmarole.) (191)

A further explanation of the phrase 'the Singapore Grip' is offered by Jim Ehrendorf, who after a moment's consideration 'thought it was a suitcase made of rattan, like a Shanghai Basket, as they were called, only smaller' (200). The intricacy of Farrell's word play can be seen here. The reference to a Shangai Basket links this explanation with the shadowy whisper Matthew had earlier heard, and puns on Ehrendorf's comment (which prompts Matthew to ask his question once more) that it is about time he 'packed [his] grip' (200).[6] This explanation is immediately dismissed by Joan, who authoritatively 'declared it to be a patent double-bladed hairpin which some women used to curl their hair after they had washed it' (200).

Much later Ehrendorf, prompted by another play on the word grip, explains 'that the expression, "the Singapore Grip", refers to the ability acquired by certain ladies of Singapore to control their autonomous vaginal muscles, apparently with delightful results' (498). But by this time we have been presented with enough colonial history to be quite sure, as Matthew is, that Ehrendorf is wrong. This is the point at which Farrell draws together the questions of Empire that have been troubling Matthew ever since his arrival in the East, and which are at the heart of this novel; Matthew's triumphant reply to Ehrendorf's explanation inverts the expression to make it one of colonial control (as opposed to the grip of a colonial prostitute on the European male), which also once more links the idea of colonisation with sexual power and money:

> 'No, Jim, that's not what the Singapore Grip is,' cried Matthew, his eyes flashing more than ever. 'I *know* what it is! It's the grip of our Western culture and economy on the Far East ... It's the stranglehold of capital on the traditional cultures of Malaya, China, Burma, Java, Indo-China and even India herself! It's the doing of things *our* way ... I mean, it's the pursuit of self-interest rather than of the *common* interest! ...'
>
> Ehrendorf sighed, thinking that in any case the Singapore Grip was about to be pried loose, if that was what it was. (498–99)

Matthew's position in relation to the notion of Empire is finally clear in his own mind, and the particular terms in which he speaks are also revealing for the reader. The emphasis on capital and culture, on self-interest and common interest, is an indication in this novel of further developments of Farrell's Marxist thinking. Binns suggests that '[t]he narrative explores the vocabulary and practices of capitalism, investigating the role played in business life by equity, bond-holdings, commodity brokers, stocks and standard profit'.[7] This is certainly true, but Matthew's linking of capital and culture suggests that Farrell is interested in later Marxist thinking about the relations between ideology and the 'cultural practices' of particular societies. And as Matthew's comment is the last mention of what has in certain respects been the controlling metaphor of the novel, it carries the full weight of authorial approval.

Moreover, Ehrendorf's suggestion that the Singapore Grip is a delightful vaginal embrace used by certain prostitutes of the colony – which in turn explains the offers whispered in Matthew's ear as he and Monty alight from their taxi in a red light district – intersects well with Monty's earlier reference to the 'colonial experience' soon after Matthew's arrival in Singapore and shortly before he asks about the meaning of the Singapore Grip. Matthew,

> who had been beginning to fear that he and Monty might have no common interest, became attentive and ventured to remark that he was interested, not only in political strikes and the relations of native workers to European employers, but also in ... well, the 'colonial experience' as a whole. (107)

As if by way of reply Monty has the driver take them through one of the many red-light districts of Singapore, and informs Matthew that '[t]his is respectable compared with Lavender Street yonder where the troops go. You could have a "colonial experience" there all right!' (110). This comment, which succinctly demonstrates the extent of common interest shared by Monty and Matthew, clearly equates the experience of colonialism with one of sexual possession (and oppression), and moreover, by using the metaphor of prostitution Farrell suggests that the people of Malaya and Singapore (and other colonised people too) have been forced to prostitute themselves for the economic benefit of the colonisers. By seeing the experience of Empire in terms of forced prostitution rather than rape (as Forster and Scott have done, for example, in *A Passage to India* and *The Raj Quartet*), Farrell emphasises the economic rather than military angle of Empire that is the focus of this novel.

Together these references (and indeed the whole complex web of sexual references that are woven into the fabric of the novel) establish the orientalised otherness through which the British regard Singapore, which in turn, via a simple binary opposition, is used to justify the colonial presence, while at the same time questioning and undermining any such colonial confidence. It is also important that Ehrendorf's suggestion is there because it holds an implication that both Ehrendorf and Matthew may be right in different ways. Matthew's is certainly the direct point being made here, but Ehrendorf's words are a reminder that the 'delightful' grip asserted by the colonised female on the colonising male has as its inverse the traditional male fear of the 'vagina dentata', the toothed vagina of the female which clutches its victim. This may be Farrell's warning that what at the moment looks like the one-way 'delightful' power grip in favour of the West may develop, or involve innately, a reciprocal grip by the colonised which the West might not enjoy so much.[8]

The exploration of the economic angle of Empire via the trope of prostitution is extended in a particularly interesting way in Walter's attempts to find a suitable husband – by which he understands 'a marriage soundly based on commercial logic' (52) – for his daughter Joan. Marriage is both another powerful symbol of male/colonial control, and one which returns the reader to the dynastic marriages of the great nineteenth-century realist novels.

Walter's belief that Joan's marriage is of importance to the business as well as to her personally is the driving action of the early part of the novel. Joan, we are told, shortly after her return from finishing school remonstrates against this exploitation of her person and protests that she will 'marry whom she please[s]' (15),[9] though we are later left in little doubt that she will go along with her father's wishes. After taking Joan to his nest in one of Blackett and Webb's godowns (a symbolically patriarchal space) he proposes that for the sake of the business she should marry Matthew Webb. Joan makes the following reply:

> 'But Father!' exclaimed Joan, laughing and jumping up from her chair to give her father a hug. 'How old-fashioned you are to deliver such a speech! I took it for granted long ago that you'd want me to marry Matthew for the sake of the firm. And the answer is "yes", of course. I don't care what he's like! You took such a long time to pop the question. I was beginning to think you'd never ask!' (99)

The form of this odd passage is that of a marriage proposal, which will join together both Joan and Matthew and also the two halves of Walter's estranged business empire. As Jane Austen, Charles Dickens, Anthony Trollope, and other practitioners of the nineteenth-century novel have demonstrated so well, the value-loaded language of the marketplace is, under capitalism, also the language of personal relations and of the marriage market.

But, the impression given here is that Walter has proposed to Joan and that she has accepted him, and the accompanying atmosphere is clearly sexual rather that familial. The scene takes place in Walter's 'little [love?] nest' (98) within one of Blackett and Webb's godowns which he and Joan reach by climbing a swaying ladder. As he follows her up Walter notices 'his daughter's strong thighs beneath her frock' (98), a gaze which later in the novel acquires overt sexual signification. After hearing the 'proposal' Joan jumps up and hugs her father, a hug which is scarcely innocent if one considers the passage in the context of two earlier scenes in the novel.

The first concerns Walter's visit to Joan in her bedroom where she is 'reclining on her bed in her underwear' (27), striking an obviously sexual rather than filial pose – one which casts her (like Gretchen in *A Man from Elsewhere*) in the role of lover rather than daughter. The scene ends with Walter playfully and vigorously tickling Joan while she lies on her bed. A second short intimate scene takes place in Walter's dressing-room when Joan returns Walter's visit. Here, with 'the moist, pink tip of her tongue … firmly gripped between her strong white teeth' (56), she ties her father's bow tie, a task that might normally be carried out by a wife, symbolically representing the ties of marriage.

This underlying current of incest is extended to contain Matthew, too, who is seen as almost a member of the family, and the object of Walter's and Joan's pursuit. The colonial experience is thus linked to sex as prostitution, and through a different trope to sex as incest. Critical commentaries suggest that incest motifs in nineteenth and twentieth century European and American literature are associated with the decay of previously dominant small power groups who struggle to maintain an undiluted line of ascendency by turning inward. William Faulkner's fictional Yoknapatawpha County is, of course, the prime example. In *The Singapore Grip* this incest and the drawing in of Matthew is another sign of the way in which they unconsciously see themselves already under threat, and are desperately attempting to maintain their hegemony.

The two tropes of prostitution and incest are used together in a later scene in which the sense of perversion is even more marked. Joan undresses in front of Matthew, the Major, and her father, and then, stripped to her underwear, at her father's behest climbs into bed beside Matthew:

> 'Oh, the little rascal', chuckled Walter. 'Oh, the little hussy! … And while Joan hung her dress on a coat-hanger to dry before climbing into bed Walter beamed at Matthew more expansively than ever. 'Well, there you are, my boy,' he seemed to be saying. 'There are the goods. You won't find better. You can see for yourself. It's a good offer. Take it or leave it'. (262)

The startling pseudo-fatherly language Walter uses to prostitute his daughter here, even acting as her pimp, also takes the reader back to the '*Boy's Own*' genre while at the same time the circumstances undermine the 'Happy-

Families' atmosphere of that form. Joan is here undressing before and *for* her father.

The expression of Matthew's own unease about Empire is used by Farrell to continue the debate on progress begun by the Collector in *The Siege of Krishnapur*. Progress in the colonial context is again defined (and again the economic angle is apparent) as that which enriches the coloniser, as Matthew volubly expresses in one of his many theoretical discussions with Ehrendorf:

> 'If by "progress" you mean the increasing welfare of the native then I'm afraid you're going to have a job proving the beneficial effects of these public works you make such a song and dance about ...' Matthew was saying ...
>
> 'I suppose you're talking about railways ... In our African colonies something like three-quarters of all loans raised by the colonial governments are for railways. True, they're useful for administration ... but what they're mainly useful for is opening up great tracts of land to be developed as plantations by Europeans. In other words, it's done not for the natives' benefit but for ours! ... ' (437)

Like Conrad, Cary, and others, Farrell is highlighting here the way that the benefits offered by Empire have in fact usually served to facilitate the economic rape of the colonies. This is perhaps most amply illustrated when Matthew is taken by Vera Chiang (whose initials stand for both Victoria Cross and Viet Cong – a mixture of Empire and anti-Empire) to visit a Chinese 'dying-house' which more than anything resembles the hopeless moribund living-death atmosphere of the opium den and crypt in Dickens's unfinished novel *The Mystery of Edwin Drood* (1870). Matthew's introduction by Vera as a 'son of Blackett and Webb' (342) brings forth a litany of complaints, which become increasingly difficult for Matthew to counter, about the way native smallholders in the rubber industry have been mistreated to the advantage of the big European Estates. When prevailed upon by one of the elderly inhabitants to read aloud the editorial opinion expressed in a faded cutting he produces from *The Planter*, dated June 1930, Matthew finds there, succinctly expressed, all that all that had been troubling him about the Empire:

> ' ... "In the hands of the producers of budwood lies the decision whether rubber planting will, in the far and remote future, become a native industry, or remain an asset of immense value to those European races to whose administrative skill and financial acumen ... (Oh dear, I don't like the sound of this) ... the development of Malaya and of the Dutch East Indies has been due ..." '

'More, sir, more!' croaked his audience.

"'... It is the honest unbiased opinion of many leading men outside the rubber industry that the less the smallholder has to do with rubber the better it will be in the long run for himself and for all others engaged in rubber production ...'" The match died. Matthew was left with the piece of paper in his fingers. He sighed. (346–47)

That self-interest rather than common interest is the motive which drives the moguls of the rubber industry is made abundantly clear when Walter expresses a willingness, even desire, to continue his business in partnership with the Japanese if need be: 'Yes, an advantage could be won for Blackett and Webb in concert with, say, Mitsubishi ...' (504). If the reader is tempted to see this as absurd, Farrell points to a parallel when Walter, defending his modest proposal, recalls an example from the First World War:

> 'War is only a passing phase in business life ... No, it was Lever of Lever Brothers who said that, not me! Yes, it seems that in the Great War he wanted, naturally enough, to go on selling his ... what did he call it? Sunlight Soap to the Germans ... He made quite a fuss when they wouldn't let him. He argued that the more soap they let him make the more glycerine there would be for munitions ... which is true enough when you come to think about it. If you want my opinion there's nothing like a spot of patriotism for blinding people to reality.' (539)

The reality to which Walter, like Lever, wants to use patriotism to blind people, is the reality of self-interest, of profit before all else. Once more patriotism is seen as the last refuge of a scoundrel, and profit the consuming creed of capitalism. However, while Farrell attacks capitalism through the somewhat Dickensian figure of Walter Blackett (his company and his ideas) he is nevertheless at least partly sympathetic towards him as a *character*. Indeed Farrell's barbs are aimed at the systems which produce the patriotism and nationalism behind characters like Walter, rather than at the characters themselves.

There is a seemingly insignificant scene in the middle of the novel where the Major recalls his visit to Japan and a day spent with a group of young Japanese officers, which leads to a discourse on 'the Japanese National Spirit' (274). The evening concludes with the Major being invited to sing his old school song:

> 'Alma mater te bibamus,
> Tui calices poscamus,
> Hanc sententiam dicamus:
> Floreat Sand ... ha! ... ha! ... lia!' (277)

Later, during the Japanese advance through Malaya the frightened young soldier Kikuchi (who lives forever in the shadow of his uncle, Bugler Kikuchi, whose death is held up as a model of the National Spirit and offered as an example for future generations to follow) hears his officer Matsushita singing to a circle of poisonous snakes. The song he sings is the Sandhall school song (a typically trivial example of the form) he learnt from the Major. The point of these two passages is to suggest that the imperialism which supports Empire is universal, and promoted (in Britain at least) by the public school system. Together the two passages warn of the dangers of idealism and nationalism (which were celebrated in Kipling's early jingoistic stories). By demonstrating how easily transferable such songs and the spirit behind them are, the second scene effectively highlights the danger of nationalism. It shows, too, that to condemn the nationalism that inspired Japan, we must also be prepared to condemn the nationalism that drove the British to its feats of Empire. (And indeed earlier Walter had exposed the dark side of British imperialism by putting forward the Japanese position [138–39].)

The dominant climate of self-interest is demonstrated in a wider colonial rather than economic context when Penang falls to the Japanese: 'The Major was doubly distressed to think that the Europeans had been evacuated from Penang while the rest of the population had been left to make the best of it' (321). That the British could abandon their Indian, their Malay, and their Chinese subjects – many of whom were on Japanese death-lists and did not survive the occupation of the Peninsula – whose unswerving loyalty they had deemed their right, again graphically illustrates the deceit upon which the Empire was built. (And, of course, parallels can be drawn with the American evacuation of Saigon, a city Farrell visited only weeks before it fell to the North Vietnamese.[10])

The economic context of the novel so far discussed is firmly tied to place and time through a meticulously constructed historical framework, the skeleton of which is provided by the fall of Singapore, a significant event which, like the Troubles in Ireland (which led to the division of the country) and the Mutiny in India (after which control of the country passed into the hands of the Crown) signalled a turning point in the fortunes of the Empire. But the fall of Singapore caused more widespread damage to what was in the 1940s already a misplaced confidence in Empire, as Farrell, with the benefit of hindsight and the strength of authorial presence makes clear:

> This Sunday, then, was the last day of the defence of Singapore, the last day of freedom for the British who remained on the Island … almost, you might say with hindsight, the last day of the British Empire in these parts. (556)

Throughout the novel the progress of the Malaya Campaign and the advance of the Japanese towards Singapore is carefully and faithfully recorded, both from the British perspective, and also, to a limited extent, from the Japanese. In a move which is in concert with Lukács's sense of the historical novel, Farrell includes a large cast of real historical figures, who are nevertheless never central characters in the novel: Wavell, Brooke-Popham, General Percival (whose book *The War in Malaya*, like the books of a number of other 'characters' in this novel, is listed in Farrell's bibliography), General Gordon Bennett, and others too numerous to list. In an interesting shift away from Lukács towards Freud, however, Farrell frequently enters the minds of these historical figures, to explore the thoughts and dreams that troubled them and caused them to make the decisions which have been documented.

Apart from the military references, which succinctly plot the progress of the war, Farrell introduces a number of specific references through which he carefully recreates the ethos of the times. Thus, for example, Ehrendorf tells the Blacketts how he and Matthew, together in Geneva in 1932, managed 'to make a quick trip to London that winter to see Gielgud's production of Rodney Ackland's magnificent play, *Strange Orchestra* at the St Martin's Theatre' (76), which may be another allusion to *A Passage to India*, where Mrs Moore and Adela Quested refer to a production of *Cousin Kate* they saw shortly before leaving England. Like all the details Farrell introduces, this is perfectly in keeping with the time period. *Strange Orchestra* was first performed in 1931. More interestingly, Farrell works into his novel what amounts to a list of the major films of the day (in much the same way as Paul Scott does in *Staying On*, his postscript to *The Raj Quartet*):

as January pursues its course the civilians and the Military are at least united in one pastime in the increasingly devastated and dangerous city ... they go to the cinema. They go to see *Private Affairs* with Nancy Kelly and Robert Cummings at the Cathay, or *Bad Men of Missouri* at the Alhambra, or Charlie Chaplin in *The Great Dictator* at the Roxy. Battered troops from up-country or new arrivals from Britain, Australia and India watch John Wayne in *Dark Command* at the Empire beside anxious and forlorn refugees from Penang and Kuala Lumpur. Together in the hot darkness they watch Joe E. Brown in *So You Won't Talk?*, *Mata Hari* with Greta Garbo and Ramon Novarro, and Henry Fonda in *The Return of Frank James* which, despite the boom and thud of bombs and anti-aircraft guns filtering into the cinema, has had all traces of gun-play removed by the Singapore censor in order not to give ideas to the city's Chinese gangsters. Perhaps as they sit there they are a little reassured by 'the first drama of Uncle Sam's new jump fighters': *Parachute Battalion* with Robert

Preston and Edmund O'Brien ... but no doubt they find parachutes too close to reality and prefer Loretta Young in *The Lady from Cheyenne*: 'It was a man's world until a low-cut gown took over the town.' They watch in silence with the light from the screen flickering on their strained faces. The week it is shown (by that time people will be wearing steel helmets in the stalls during air-raids) will see, on Tuesday, a massive raid by eighty-one Japanese Navy bombers on the Tanglin and Orchard Road district and, on Wednesday, an even more devastating raid on Beach Road. (329–30)

The inclusion of this long list of films, which intersects with details of the progress of the war, creates brilliantly the sense of unreality which pervaded Singapore at this time – what amounts to a surreal picture of an entire population fiddling while their city burnt. More importantly, they are seen receiving fresh transfusions of the ideologies which have brought about this conflict. Interrupting what at first glance looks misleadingly like no more than a list of films, are details of the arrival of refugees from Penang and Kuala Lumpur, the arrival of battle-weary troops and fresh troops from Britain and Australia, of the ridiculous concerns of the Singapore censor as the city is faced with destruction at the hands of the Japanese, of people wearing helmets as they continue to watch films during air raids, and of specific Japanese attacks.

Farrell's list is, of course, a selection which emphasises war films, spy films, westerns, and all the narrative conventions of heroism which these bring into play. Although Farrell's list is at first reminiscent of the list of film titles which punctuates Paul Scott's *Staying On*, the effect is considerably more sophisticated. Scott's film titles are used to evoke particular ages: the period of Lucy Smalley's youth is recalled via references to silent films such as *The Big Parade* and *Seventh Heaven*, while the 1970s is established through references to the films Lucy sees with Ibrahim on their Monday evening visits to the New Electric cinema, notably *Butch Cassidy and the Sundance Kid*. In *The Singapore Grip* by contrast, the scene which this list evokes describes a quintessentially postmodern moment when the representation of the real has become more real and more necessary than the real itself. The filmgoers of Singapore watch a variety of cinematic images of battles and conflicts from the 'Wild West' to the First World War and beyond, while simultaneously turning firmly away from the unmediated chaos of the present where battle is actually raging around them. They are preoccupied with the manufactured (and importantly) visual narrative in which they recognise an almost identical but improved version of themselves. The real of this, like the battle at Captainganj in *The Siege of Krishnapur*, has no narrative form or visual coherence and is therefore less apprehendable and less real than the satisfyingly genre-encoded films which reaffirm a recognisable ideology.

Singapore of 1940–41 is also a moment when the symbol of traditionally licensed revolt against state order, the carnival of misrule which Bakhtin sees as central to the novel form, has been both appropriated by the dominant regime (capitalism – Blackett & Webb's celebration), and also completely outdone in scale and dramatic energy by a new player from outside the symbiotic duality of rule and anti-rule. The apocalyptic imagery of fire and water which pervades the end of *The Singapore Grip* is a signal that the postmodern moment has arrived when the stability of the 'modern' mutually supporting antithesis has been broken asunder. Although as one critic has noted:

> It is not possible to give a precise date to the beginning of the post-modern period, as Virginia Woolf did for modernism ... we may, with Hassan (1985:122) 'woefully imagine that postmodernism began in or about September, 1939'.[11]

Farrell is demonstrating again his ability to recreate not just the surface of the period, but the concept of its own situation that it reveals.

As in *Troubles* Farrell makes considerable use of newspaper headlines and stories in the later parts of *The Singapore Grip*. He uses these extracts, taken mainly from the *Straits Times*, when he wants to move his novel rapidly towards its conclusion while still wishing to include details of the progress of the war. But this documentary evidence must be read in the context of an earlier warning that is there for an alert reader to pick up. Describing the Japanese-Chinese conflict of the early 1930s Matthew observes that '[o]nly the *Manchester Guardian* had condemned the Japanese and their British supporters' (189). This is a reminder that newspapers and other contemporary documentary sources are as subjective as any other, that they only tell one of many stories, more often than not the official one. This point is emphasised soon after when the first Japanese bombing raid on Singapore is described:

> when official estimates are made of this first air raid on Singapore ... there will be no mention of this old man for the simple reason that he, in common with so many others, has left no trace of ever having existed either in this part of the world or in any other. (218)

This passage also serves to remind the reader of the tenuous imperial hold Britain had on the colony at this point. The old man's lack of identity (his anonymous subaltern position, to use Spivak's term) is the direct result of the de-humanising workings of the British colonial system – a system which, in the face of the Japanese advance through Malaya, the British (morally as well as militaristically) are no longer able to defend, but which, ironically, they expected their oppressed (and now abandoned) subjects to defend for them.

In *The Singapore Grip* Farrell's interest in irony and relationships leads him back, via a series of carefully integrated allusions (and as Binns observes, Farrell's allusions are always discreet[12]), to Jane Austen. When Matthew meets Mrs Blackett for the first time, for example, she is reclining on her sofa (118) and is described in a manner immediately reminiscent of the famous description of Mrs Bertram in *Mansfield Park* (1814), discussed by Forster in *Aspects of the Novel* (1927) to illustrate his sense of flat characters. And indeed, like Austen's, Farrell's characters are frequently flat, tending towards caricature. There is also a Sir Thomas in this novel, the hapless Governor of Singapore, whose name recalls Sir Thomas Bertram's. It is worth remembering in the light of these Austenish allusions that like Blackett and Webb's success, Sir Thomas Bertram's fortune is built on plantation labour and thus a trade in human beings. Equally importantly, *Mansfield Park* is Austen's great novel about England in transition. Mansfield Park itself represents the 'true old England' under attack from new social forces, including the power of money as a value taking the place of all other values. In *Mansfield Park* England is saved, but in *The Singapore Grip* we have no Fanny and Edmund to save England.

But while Austen provides the tone for some of the domestic scenes in this novel, it is to Dickens that one must turn to consider the scope of the novel, and it is in Dickensian terms that the business practices of Blackett and Webb Ltd and their competitors are described. In an interesting reference to Dickens, Dupigny observes to Matthew, 'when you [British] think of France it is always in the manner of that *grand emmerdeur*, Charles Dickens' (124).[13] This allusion to Dickens's historical novel of the French Revolution, *A Tale of Two Cities* (1859), points both to Farrell's approach to the historical novel and to moments of shared concern – in particular Dickens's criticisms of the cruel exploitation of power are parallelled in *The Singapore Grip* by Farrell's exposure of the colonial enterprise. What Lukács calls the Marquis Saint Evremonde's 'between-the-classes position'[14] is repeated in Matthew who is neither part of the colonial enterprise, nor entirely apart from it. And, of course, this use of in-between characters is central to Sir Walter Scott's method of historical fiction. In *Waverley* (1814), for example, Edward Waverley finds himself (for personal rather than political reasons) uncomfortably between the Hanoverian and Jacobite causes.

A novel which makes a rather more direct appearance in *The Singapore Grip* is the one Ehrendorf was writing

> about a gifted young American from Kansas City who goes to Oxford on a scholarship and there, having fallen in love with an English girl who surrounds herself with cynical, sophisticated people, goes to the dogs, forgetting the sincere, warm-hearted American girl whose virginity he had made away with while crossing the Atlantic on a Cunard liner ... et cetera ... (283)

Ehrendorf, having rediscovered the novel in his refrigerator, wonders how he could write such rubbish, but can't quite bring himself to throw it away. Kansas City, of course, is where Dorothy comes from and returns to in L. Frank Baum's *The Wizard of Oz* (1900), and this may be a fleeting reference to that seminal novel of exile (and Farrell's own sense of exile has already been noted in the opening chapter). There is a second reference to Ehrendorf's novel much later when he sees 'himself as the ill-starred hero of his novel in its first version (innocent American abused by cynical Europeans)' (482–83). This first version is a clear allusion to Henry James, which together with the allusions to Tolstoy, Austen, Dickens, and others plot the literary tradition out of which Farrell is writing.

These allusions to other narratives reach their zenith in the openly metafictional and postmodern final chapter of the novel. In the opening chapter of the novel Farrell had directly addressed his reader, who may have been 'reading in bed or in a deck-chair on the lawn' (12). In the final chapter, completing a circular pattern already noted in the early novels, Farrell once more addresses his reader, and in doing so draws his story to a close: 'if you have been reading in a deck-chair on the lawn, it is time to go inside and make the tea. And if you have been reading in bed, why, it is time to put out the light now and go to sleep' (568). But while one story draws to an end (signalled by the authorial address to the reader), closure is resisted. As the novel reaches into the present – some forty years on from the historical events depicted in the earlier chapters – Kate Blackett sits at her breakfast table opposite her husband who is reading *The Times* for 10 December 1976. (The sense of the present is also established through the paintings by Patricia Moynagh and Mary Newcomb which adorn the walls.) He reads the following extract aloud:

> 'Listen to this, Kate,' he says. 'Here's something that might interest a rubber tycoon's daughter: "Plantation work pays less than one dollar a day." From Our Correspondent, Geneva, 9 December. "Millions of workers on rubber, sugar, tea, cotton or coffee plantations are earning less than $1 (62p) a day, according to the International Labour Office." Let me see, what else does it say? Trade union rights ... et cetera ... malnutrition ... disease ... Yes ... "Many migrant workers on rubber or sugar plantations live in conditions of acute overcrowding. Sometimes there are up to 100 workers in one large room." Daily wage rates ... And so on. There.' (567)

This short extract, which repeats in condensed form the history of economic exploitation that has just been told, is a metafictional device used in the Epilogue of Iris Murdoch's *The Red and the Green*, where in 1938 Frances's husband (like Kate's) sits at his breakfast table reading a newspaper which carries the headline '*Franco Threatens Barcelona*',[15] a headline which, in the context of the novel, recalls (and repeats) what Frances's husband calls 'that nineteen sixteen nonsense that your family was mixed up in'[16] – just as Kate's family was mixed up in the Singapore/Empire nonsense. The strong allusions to the ending of Murdoch's novel are particularly significant as they refer the reader back to Ireland and thus indirectly to *Troubles*, which also uses the ending of *The Red and the Green*, as has been discussed in Chapter 4 above. And, of course, a further link between these two panels of Farrell's tryptych is made via the deck-chairs occupied by the reader at the end of *The Singapore Grip* and the Major at the end of *Troubles*.

In his narrator's final comment, proffered from the privileged position of hindsight, Farrell is able to survey the post-Empire period and comment on the lack of change that has ocurred since independence:

> That man behind the newspaper, if it were Ehrendorf, let us say, and if he happened to remember his arguments of years ago with Matthew about colonialism and tropical agriculture, might he not, as his eye was caught by that headline 'Plantation work pays less than one dollar a day', have said to himself that nothing very much had changed, after all, despite that tremendous upheaval in the Far East? That if even after independence in these Third World countries, it is *still* like that, then something has gone wrong, that some other, perhaps native, élite has merely replaced the British? If it *were* Ehrendorf might he not have recalled that remark of Adamson's (passed on to him by Matthew) about King William and the boatman who asked who had won the battle ('What's it to you? You'll still be a boatman.')? (567–68)

In one sense this passage seems to sum up the pessimism that pervades each of the three novels in the Empire trilogy. Despite the fact that in each of the three novels the communities which had been built on untenable moral and political values are destroyed, there is a sense that the values on which those communities were built survive.[17] The anecdote about King William and the boatman is quoted by Adamson at the height of the Japanese bombing campaign in reply to a political question from Matthew:

> Once he admitted, reluctantly in reply to Matthew's question that, after the war, if he got back to Britain, he would vote for a Labour Government 'to change all this' and he gestured vaguely with a stick at the smouldering warehouses around them. After a moment's silent reflection he added: 'I read somewhere that the boatman who rowed King William back across the river after the Battle of the Boyne is supposed to have asked

the King which side won ... To which the King replied: "What's it to you? You'll still be a boatman."' (477)

Forty years later the man behind the paper (and the reader, too) knows that the change Adamson hoped to bring about by voting for a Labour Government did not occur. But as Farrell demonstrates through the philosophical Adamson, who 'calm but determined' (477) goes about his business of directing Singapore's auxiliary fire-fighting units[18] despite the impossibility of the task before him, 'at any stage of history, individuals can do no more than play their given or chosen social role'.[19] The optimism of the novel lies in such moments as Matthew's recognition that

> 'Surely there are people like this all over the world, in every country, in every society in every class or caste or community! People who simply go about doing the things that have to be done, not just for themselves but for everybody.' Such people, whether they were Socialists, or Capitalists, or Communists, or paid no attention to politics at all, because they were entirely committed to whatever job it was they were doing were bound to be the very backbone of their society ... (477)

(To which Farrell, in wry acknowledgment of his own privileged, distanced, authorial position, has Matthew add 'without them people like himself who spent their days in speculation and dispute could scarcely expect to survive' [477]. Moreover, as J.M. Rignall reminds us, the metafictional ending of *The Singapore Grip* 'obliges us to acknowledge that reading, too, is a form of privileged spectating'.[20]) Farrell's optimism is evident, too, in the final line of the novel (an undisguised allusion to Margaret Mitchell's *Gone With the Wind* (1936) – like *The Singapore Grip* a novel which depicts a system of economic and racial exploitation, the war which finally brings an apocalyptic end to that system, and looks ahead to a different, albeit uncertain future): 'Tomorrow is another day, as they say, as they say' (568).

7 / 'Finale in a Minor Key': *The Hill Station*

In the title of an article on *Staying On* Yasmine Gooneratne describes Paul Scott's novel as a 'finale in a minor key'.[1] In this apt phrase Gooneratne highlights the tendency of critics to view the novel as a minor postscript to Scott's major work, *The Raj Quartet*. Gooneratne's phrase provides a particularly appropriate description of Scott's novel and of Farrell's *The Hill Station* because a work performed in a minor key is not by definition a minor work, rather the minor key has connotations of sadness, even tragedy. In *Staying On* Scott takes up the story of two minor characters from *The Raj Quartet*, Tusker and Lucy Smalley, to create a powerful novel which looks at the lives of those who, staying on in India after Independence, were to become the last remnants of the British Raj. More than any other aspect of the work, what distinguishes *Staying On* from Scott's earlier quartet of novels is that it does not deal with any dramatic historical moment; there is a considerable sense of history as a continuum in the novel, a sense of past and future as well as the moment of the novel, as there is in Farrell's 'minor key finale' *The Hill Station*.[2]

The address to the reader at the outset of the novel – 'Nowadays the railway goes all the way up to Simla, but before the turn of the century it stopped at Kalka' (13) – along with later, similarly direct comparisons between past and present, emphasises the future, and thus the fact that Farrell is concerned less with a particular moment of history, than with looking more intensely at the internal relations between classes in British society in India. He is concerned in *The Hill Station* with the interrelation between the discourses of religion and medicine (which includes, by implication, science), at this moment in the 1870s. The 'middle-of-the-road' orthodox Anglican institution of the Church, deeply implicated in social hierarchies throughout the Victorian period, is shown in this novel testing its strength (as the Bishop tests his physical strength) against new forces of opposition from within and without.

Like Scott, Farrell takes up the lives of characters from an earlier work – the McNabs from *The Siege of Krishnapur* – but this does not necessarily make *The Hill Station* 'a kind of modest sequel to *The Siege of Krishnapur*' as Binns suggests.[3] Indeed Binns is so convinced that *The Hill Station* should be seen as a sequel to *The Siege of Krishnapur* that his discussion (barely two pages long) of Farrell's final novel is appended to his chapter on *The Siege of Krishnapur* and precedes his discussion of *The Singapore Grip* in what is otherwise a chronological approach to the novels. While *The Hill Station* would apparently have developed and concluded the personal histories of the McNabs – and conceivably of other characters from *The Siege of Krishnapur* too, through retrospective passages, or through news brought to the McNabs (as news of the Laytons is brought to Lucy Smalley by David Turner in *Staying On*) – the novel's importance lies not with the individual histories it might have furthered (Farrell provides and simultaneously undermines such conventional expectations of ending in the final chapter of *The Siege of Krishnapur*) but in the new dimensions it would have brought to his treatment of Empire.

Rather than view *The Hill Station* as an epilogue of sorts to the Empire trilogy, or even as the fourth imperial panel of a larger Empire polyptych, it may be instructive to consider it intratextually in relation to *all* the six novels Farrell had published previously. In a variety of ways Farrell appears to return particularly to the methods and interests of his earliest novels – which he had rather ambivalently dismissed and in the case of his first novel, *A Man from Elsewhere*, disowned – but with the added skills developed during the decade spent working on the trilogy.

The Hill Station is set in the British station of Simla, the summer capital of the Raj, in 1871[4] – late enough for the horror of the Mutiny to have faded from most British memories, and to be an object of vague stories to the younger generation: Emily, for instance, is aware that her uncle and aunt 'had met under strained circumstances … in some battle or other with lots of flies about and without clothes on' (92). At the same time, it is early enough for the threat of war with Afghanistan, which was constant throughout the 1880s, and the Indian Nationalist agitation that began in earnest in the 1890s still to be some time away. Nevertheless, as Farrell describes Emily being carried through town 'on the strong brown shoulders of her *jampanis*' (92) he simultaneously indicates that the end of this world of privilege has already been written:

> a few thousand miles away in London a familiar bearded leonine figure sucking a pencil turned a little in his seat in the British Museum to see the hands of the clock at the northern quarter of the Reading Room, and thought, 'Soon it will be closing time'. (92)

In this carefully judged passage Farrell acknowledges the shadowy presence of Marx behind his own fictional output as well as pointing to the monumental presence of Marx in historical terms – the first volume of Marx's *Das Kapital* had been published in 1867. The hands of the clock in the Reading Room signal not only the coming end of another day at the British Museum (for Farrell, perhaps, as for Marx), but also the beginning of the end to the privileged world inhabited by Emily, and the dismantling of Empire itself.

The final sentence of the quoted passage is an intertextual reference to at least two venerated British institutions, the library and the pub, both of which carry enormous cultural signification and are associated with pleasures of various kinds. The announcement of closing time comes as a warning in both places that that pleasure is about to end. 'The text' as Barthes says, 'is a tissue of quotations drawn from the innumerable centres of culture'.[5] The allusion here passes through to the line 'HURRY UP PLEASE IT'S TIME',[6] which is repeated several times towards the end of 'A Game of Chess', the second section of T.S. Eliot's poem 'The Waste Land' (first published in 1922). Eliot's poem itself is flush with intertextual allusions (though Eliot's modernist use of intertextuality differs from Farrell's postmodernist usage). Significantly, perhaps, 'The Waste Land' can be read as social criticism, a comment on the futility of post-World War One society, and indeed it has been interpreted as a protest against the old order – which in *The Hill Station* could be the world of privilege enjoyed by Emily and her class. The passage represents what Frank Kermode has called *kairos*, 'a point in time filled with significance, charged with a meaning derived from its relation to the end'.[7] Farrell's moment may not be a Biblical apocalypse, the end of the world, but for the British, when the moment came, the loss of Empire and the partial dismantling of the class system marked an end to the privileged world enjoyed by many.

The focus in this novel is on place as much as time, as Paul Theroux recognises when, commenting on the title chosen by John Spurling, he writes 'I have the feeling the name Simla would have appeared in the title, because its setting is as definite and necessarily particular as those in "The Siege of Krishnapur" and "The Singapore Grip."'[8] Simla is a place outside ordinary life, a location in which the working administration of Empire gives way to a hill station life of rest and recuperation from the rigours of the plains. The atmosphere of unreality and confinement evident in both *The Lung* and *A Girl in the Head* (but to some extent present in all Farrell's fiction) is repeated here; it is a time where the hours go slowly because they are not filled by the necessities of work, but marked out only by the repetitive patterns of meals and social occasions. A number of contrasts are specifically drawn to demonstrate the differences between Simla and the rest of India, particularly an element of social and moral laxity which is contrasted with the stricter hierarchies of the plains world. Simla itself, though contained, is also split, as Binns observes: 'Simla ... is a divided realm, both spiritually, in the clash between high and low church, and socially, in the descent from Elysium House to the Lower Bazaar'.[9] There is also another crucial contrast which Binns notes, 'between the remote, high Himalayas and the insignificant squabbles of Simla's men and women'.[10] This adds a Forsterian dimension which Farrell may have intended to develop in the completed novel.

In ways which resemble his intertextual responses to Malcolm Lowry's *Under the Volcano* in *The Lung* and *A Girl in the Head*, in *The Hill Station* Farrell responds directly to Thomas Mann's *The Magic Mountain* (1924), a point on which critics who have written about *The Hill Station* appear to concur. Binns believes the *The Hill Station* would have been Farrell's 'homage to ... Thomas Mann's *The Magic Mountain*',[11] while John Spurling suggests that 'the medical details of cholera in *Krishnapur* and of tuberculosis in *The Hill Station* are direct tributes to *The Magic Mountain*'.[12] And Paul Theroux makes the important observation that Farrell's major lesson from *The Magic Mountain* was 'in dealing with philosophical issues and mixing them with social ones'.[13] Mann's novel, which explores the moral and intellectual sickness of society (a subject of all Farrell's fiction) shortly before the First World War, is set in a sanitorium – and Simla, like Davos (the location of Mann's novel), was also a sanitorium. Farrell's extended metaphor of sickness places *The Hill Station* (with *The Lung* too) in a long line of major literary works, in which illness is a major theme.[14]

In his review of the novel Paul Theroux suggests that 'Farrell's boldest stroke is in setting the novel in the decade before Kipling showed his boyish face in Simla'.[15] Nevertheless, as Spurling's description of the novel as 'a comparatively plain tale from the hills'[16] signals, Farrell does inevitably write in Kipling's shadow, as must any post-Kipling British writer who chooses this Himalayan location. The novel he responds to in particular, despite its late 1880s setting,[17] is *Kim*. Farrell's postmodern interest in language games (evident to a greater or lesser extent in all his fiction, and particularly important in *The Singapore Grip*) is here developed specifically in relation to *Kim*. The popular view of the late nineteenth century as the period of 'The Great Game' is parodied in *The Hill Station* where various characters are frequently opposed in playing games, including croquet and arm-wrestling, or seen indulging in such Austenish sport as social mountaineering (91). There is also an Austenish irony, understatement, and implied social commentary in this novel, noticably in the sub-plot which involves Mrs Forester and Emily, but also in the general containment of the Simla community which resembles Austen's deliberately restricted worlds (Bath, from where Emily has come, Mansfield Park, Highbury, and so on, as well as the confined societies of Farrell's own earlier novels), and reveals the British community of *The Hill Station* to be less homogeneous than it appeared in his other novels. In a paragraph which seems designed to evoke Austen, Farrell reveals Emily reflecting on her position in Simla society:

> Emily, brought up a Miss Anderson of Saltwater House, could not help but feel that when she was with the McNabs she suffered a slight but perceptible loss of rank. She felt that people saw her as Miss McNab instead of Miss Anderson. (91)

And in a slightly later comment which playfully links Marx and Austen for the reader he adds 'A situation like this which might have meant despair for a girl of the *petite bourgeoisie* could be shrugged off with disdain by a Miss Anderson of Bath' (100).

The nineteen chapters we have of this unfinished novel represent about half the projected novel.[18] These chapters, though clearly unrevised, are enough to grip the reader, and John Spurling's informative essay included in the book, which draws on Farrell's notes for the novel, sets out the further directions the work would probably have taken. The major concerns of the novel are sickness, religion, and ritual. And beyond these three major concerns there is a sub-plot involving Mrs Forester (a 'fallen' woman) and the McNabs's niece Emily, through which issues of class are brought to the fore.

Binns suggests, in his brief discussion of the novel, that '[t]he real thrust of *The Hill Station* would seemingly have been less concerned with either religious ritual or social satire than with a development of Farrell's interest in the theme of sickness'.[19] Sickness has occupied a central position in much of Farrell's fiction. In the early novels Regan's illness and impending death provide the reason for Sayer's visit in *A Man from Elsewhere*, Martin Sands's polio dominates the narrative of *The Lung*, and Boris frequently appears to be ill in *A Girl in the Head*. Sickness continues to be central to the later trilogy as a whole, and as Binns rightly concludes, 'sickness is omnipresent'[20] in *The Hill Station*.

Even before we learn Emily's name we are told that 'one of her arms hung rather loosely at her side and ended in a hand whose shrinking tendons had drawn its fingers into a permanently clutching little fist' (17). It is soon evident that the Reverend Kingston is suffering from tuberculosis, his curate Mr Forsyth is sick with malarial fever, one of the young curates at Elysium House is 'worried by a swollen gland in his neck' (89), and judging by McNab's cryptic remarks, it appears that Mr Lowrie has a heart condition. More importantly, he is un-aware of this, oblivious that his future may be as short as those of the invalids he complacently watches making the fruitless journey in search of health in the higher altitudes. These invalids who make their way to Simla contrast with the 'boisterous young officers ... each one of them armed with a highly questionable sick-certificate' (14). The Bishop, too, at a later stage of the novel would have appeared to be dying,[21] and there are hints that rabies would have played a significant role in the novel. This is established in a particularly comic scene where a shopkeeper attempts to sell McNab a pair of leather ankle-protectors to guard against the possibility of being bitten by a rabid dog, and also in Farrell's notes. Farrell's Simla is thus a community built largely on sickness. When Farrell, in the opening chapter, describes Mr Lowrie's habit of inspecting the invalids to judge which of them will survive their journey, a guessing game, a thread of suspense, begins for the reader who begins to calculate who will survive *this* siege, of sickness.

Farrell's attention to detail, evident in his treatment of his exploration of cholera in *The Siege of Krishnapur*, is again displayed in his approach to tuberculosis in *The Hill Station*. He dedicates a chapter to opening up the medical debates surrounding tuberculosis, which he begins by looking back to his subject from the distance of the present: 'At that time it was widely believed in the medical profession ...' (127). Farrell then proceeds to outline the various beliefs about 'phthisis or pulmonary consumption, as tuberculosis used to be called' (127) that were current at the time – which can be seen as yet another manifestation of the fascination with epistemology which underlies the trilogy. But Farrell's interest here is not in the disease itself so much as in an exploration of the 'psychological and spiritual dimensions'[22] of sickness. As Jeffrey Meyers notes of the eight works of literature he treats in *Disease in the Novel*, they all

> portray what Freud calls the 'pathology of cultural communities,' the sickness of society. For the effect of disease on a victim is both the realistic subject of the book and the symbol of moral, social or political pathology; the illness of the hero, who is both an individual and a representative of his epoch, is analogous to the sickness of the State.[23]

In the battle of wills between the Bishop and the Reverend Kingston both men exhibit a strength of will that transcends physical sickness or pain. McNab observes and notes the peculiar strength of will each character possesses. On his first visit to Elysium House, as he witnesses an arm-wrestling contest between the Bishop and a young contender, McNab wonders 'how ... do I know as surely as the night follows day that the Bishop will prevail though he is the weaker?' (80). His answer is that

> physical strength is in some way connected with moral strength or strength of personality ... or can it be that physical strength may in some way be tapped and channelled from a position of authority, such as the Bishop's vis-à-vis this athletic young man? To McNab it seemed that this small piece of evidence linking the moral to the physical was another indication that there could very well exist 'a moral dimension' to a physical illness ... (80)

The Bishop wins his contest because of his superior strength (moral rather than physical), though as the novel progresses we are left to wonder at the morality of the Bishop's strength (which is one of the many ironies of the novel). That there will be a contest for much higher stakes between the Bishop and Kingston is evident from the scene which follows, where McNab is present in the Bishop's study during an interview between the two men at which time their 'private difficulties' (88) are aired.[24] It is clear from this meeting that the Bishop wants Kingston to 'submit to [his] authority' (88), while Kingston is respectfully adamant that he will submit only to a higher authority. Kington's strength of will is demonstrated in the way he conducts himself during this interview. His ability to transcend physical pain and sickness is also amply demonstrated in the sermon he delivers at St Saviour's. Again McNab is a witness:

> Despite himself McNab found that he was captivated by what he knew to be a trick of oratory. That Kingston should display a gift as a speaker was unexpected; that he should use it with such power in his present circumstances was altogether remarkable, at least to McNab who had listened to his lungs. (144)

And, of course, the reader is reminded of the Reverend Kingston's condition when he is forced to spit (presumably the tell-tale blood-specked sputum that Emily observes on the train journey to Kalka [29]) into his handkerchief after climbing the steps to the pulpit.

The rabies plot signalled in Chapter 18 would apparently have involved Mrs Forester's little boy catching the disease. While rabies may not have been developed as fully as the interest in tuberculosis (which itself has a considerable literary pedigree, as Meyers outlines[25]), it may be instructive to remember that the name of the disease means angry, and perhaps offers another link between the mind and the body which Farrell was exploring in *The Hill Station*.

Dr McNab's role is a particularly important one in *The Hill Station*. He acts as our guide to the themes of sickness and religion, and it is through his belief in something beyond the physical dimension of sickness that the two are linked. His is a role which recalls those of the central male characters in *The Lung* and *A Girl in the Head* particularly, rather than those of the trilogy where a variety of characters share a central position and the sympathies of the author are not invested in one character alone. Significantly, McNab is the latest in a line of doctors that extends right through Farrell's fiction: the doctor who attends Regan in *A Man from Elsewhere*, Dr Baker in *The Lung*, the rather cynical Dr Cohen in *A Girl in the Head*, Dr Ryan in *Troubles*, Dr McNab and Dr Dunstaple in *The Siege of Krishnapur*, and the comic Dr Brownley in *The Singapore Grip*. Of these Dr Baker, Dr Cohen, Dr Ryan, and Dr McNab can be classed as 'wise doctors'. This is of importance because it demonstrates a clear line of interest and development that began with the early novels. It is particularly interesting that in *The Hill Station* McNab is developed in such a way that he most resembles Dr Baker through whom an interest in the psychological dimensions of sickness was earlier raised in *The Lung*. This represents a significant shift away from the character of Dr Brownley in *The Singapore Grip*, who is the most comic of all Farrell's doctor figures (and almost Shakespearian in his comic dimensions), back to the type of doctor figures found in the early novels.

Just as the theme of sickness is signposted at the outset of the novel, so the religious theme is foregrounded as soon as the Reverend Kingston boards the train and begins to read a copy of Keble's *The Christian Year* (18) – sales of which were phenomenal during the middle of the nineteenth century. Spurling believes that 'religion was to have been the main burden of *The Hill Station*'.[26] And Binns, while arguing that the main theme of the novel would have been sickness, accepts that '[t]he plot of *The Hill Station* centres on a doctrinal row about ritualism'.[27] The battle ground for this row is also set out early in the novel, before any of the characters actually reach Simla, by Mr Lowrie, who tells McNab:

> that there have been certain ... ah ... difficulties at Saint Saviour's in the past few weeks. The parishioners have been upset by certain rituals of what one would have to call ... ah ... a Puseyite cast, quite unknown to our Protestant traditions. Kingston is thought to be ... ah ... going 'over the Tiber' ... (45)

Lowrie's gossip, in particular his mention of Pusey, who, like Keble, was one of the founders of the Oxford Movement, brings the doctrinal disputes of the time to the reader's attention. (The third leader of the Oxford Movement, Newman, is introduced later in Bo'sun Smith's lecture.)

The third major concern of *The Hill Station* is ritual, one of the set of structures by which human life appears to gain meaning. The nature of the ritualism that disturbs Mr Lowrie so much is explained early on when the Bishop, interviewing the Reverend Kingston in the presence of McNab, outlines the complaints made about the services at St Saviour's: lighted candles on the altar, choirboys dressed in surplices trained to sing the Psalms and responses, processions with a crucifix, kissing the prayer book, using wafer bread, and making the sign of the cross (84–87). This ritualism and the opposition to it are played out in the church service that the McNabs and their niece attend at St Saviour's – the great set piece of the unfinished novel. Farrell's notes suggest that there would have been a second church service which would have ended with a pitched battle at the chancel gates.[28] Remarkable though these scenes are, they are actually based on what took place in London, at St George's-in-the-East, Stepney, in 1859. As Spurling explains,

> Farrell simply shipped it to Simla together with Bo'sun Smith (a real person), elements of Bishop Tait, Bishop of London and later Archbishop

of Canterbury during the heyday of anti-Ritualism, and much curious material from Michael Reynolds's biography (*Martyr of Ritualism*) of the Rev. A.H. Mackonochie, Vicar of St Alban's, Holborn.[29]

The lecture Bo'sun Smith delivers at Lowrie's Hotel is used to outline in broader terms the 'dangers threatening the Church' which 'arose from the publication of *The Tracts for the Times* and the ritualistic movement which it spawned' (115–16).[30] Thus while St Saviour's is used to play out the contoversy in all its glorious comic and tragic detail, Smith's lecture, and that of Dr Bateman which follows, is used to set the wider context of the controversy.

Although the predictions of the various critics noted above are made confidently, it is important to remember that this is an unfinished draft of a novel. In it Farrell employs direct allusions and references – to Austen, Keble's *The Christian Year* (first published in 1827), *Tracts for the Times*, Marx – which stretch the time-frame well beyond the action of the novel. Such elasticity is not evident in the published versions of his earlier historical fictions. It is worth noting that manuscript evidence shows that Farrell frequently substantially revised his completed drafts, cutting or adding entire scenes, excising characters or introducing new ones, conflating two characters or dividing a single one.

Just as there is a long line of medical men in Farrell's fiction, so too clergymen feature frequently in his work. Usually in Farrell's novels, and particularly in the first two volumes of the trilogy, religion and clergymen provide a rich source of comedy. This is true of the Padre's many exchanges with Fleury, or when he and Father O'Hara compete over bodies for Protestant or Catholic burial in *The Siege of Krishnapur*. At other times there is a darker vein to Farrell's treatment of religion as in *Troubles* where at one point, as Spurling notes, Farrell's 'ridicule turns to disgust' during an exchange between the Major and Father O'Byrne.[31] In *The Hill Station* Farrell's treatment of the Reverend Kingston, while still providing the opportunity for comedy, is largely sympathetic, and in many ways Kingston is a developed version of the eccentric (possibly mad) ex-clergyman Exmoore that Martin Sands meets in *The Lung*. Both are ritualists, and both are sick, Exmoore in mind and Kingston in body – though in both instances the connection between the mind and the body is explored. Similarly, in considering the struggle between the Bishop and Kingston Spurling notes an important connection between *The Hill Station* and *A Man from Elsewhere*:

> In *A Man from Elsewhere* a 'Bishop' (Gerhardt the Communist) and an apostate (Regan) wrestle for mastery, compete for no good reason except competition's sake and in doing so are meant to stand for the greater, equally purposeless, competition between the Soviet bloc and the West. Once one has spotted the theme one can see it lurking in all Farrell's work.[32]

It is evident that in *The Hill Station* Farrell was again exploring some of the concerns and developing some of the ideas that had first occupied him in the early novels, which must call into question the conviction behind Farrell's reported desire to dismiss or disown *A Man From Elsewhere* and *The Lung*.

Farrell's interest in language games, evident in those two early novels, is continued and developed in this novel; indeed, games occupy a significant place in *The Hill Station*. When the Bishop is seen for the first time, for example, he is observed '[p]laying croquet with his Chaplain and Secretary and the handful of young curates he liked to assemble around him' (75). When Farrell adds in parentheses '(the Bishop believed there was no game like croquet for revealing what a man was made of)' (75) we are obliged to consider the relationship between games and life. And the significance of this relationship is attested to shortly afterwards when the Bishop greets McNab for the first time, apologising for his delay in doing so by explaining that 'I had to show these young men of mine how they should play the game ...' (78) – which sees Farrell taking up once more the metaphor of life as a game which he first explored in *A Girl in the Head*. The game the Bishop refers to is both croquet and life. The phrase 'play the game' suggests the Bishop wishes to teach his young curates how to observe the rules, or more colloquially, how to behave honourably (in life) – yet in his own dealings with Kingston the Bishop chooses to ignore the rules and his behaviour is anything but honourable.

The word 'game' is used in another context when the narrator explains how Emily came to enjoy a somewhat higher social standing than her uncle:

> The fact was that Emily's mother had married a little above her rank in society when she had become the wife of Sir Hector Anderson from being plain Miss McNab (not plain in appearance, though, for she was a great beauty). It had not been a difficult feat for her to adapt herself, intelligent and cultured as she was, to her improved circumstances, particularly since she had no family of her own except her brother in India. It's the family which gives the game away in such a situation ... (91)

(Farrell cannot resist the aside in parentheses which provides another opportunity to play with language.) At the end of this short extract the phrase 'give the game away' suggests a revelation of something that was hidden – in this instance Emily's family background that on one side betrays less fortunate circumstances. Beyond the linguistic games, this is perhaps another tilt in the direction of Jane Austen. Early in *Pride and Prejudice* (1813), for example, Darcy is painfully aware of the fact that he will never be able to forget Elizabeth Bennet's family circumstances.

Emily's desire to play the games played by others in Simla is evident in her attitude towards fashion: 'If she saw people being fashionable she wanted to join in, learn the rules and, if possible, be more so' (94). Emily's desire to learn the rules suggests a desire to behave honourably, but ironically, fashion has no honour to it, and as Emily soon learns, neither does 'fashionable' Simla society.

Farrell's linguistic play with the word 'game' continues much as it did with the word 'grip' in *The Singapore Grip*. When the old gentlemen who escort Mrs Forester and Emily back to the former's bungalow are referred to as 'gamey' (97) the adjective could suggest gallant, spirited, valiant gentlemen, but is more likely to mean high or past its best. Indeed, Farrell's greatest game in this novel is with language. On one level simple punning games, which littered *The Singapore Grip*, persist in this novel. The name of the Reverend Kingston's parish, St Saviour's, is clearly intended to echo St Xavier's, the school Kim reluctantly attends in Kipling's novel. And it is in relation to *Kim* that Farrell's play with the word 'game' reaches its zenith.

Farrell frequently uses the language of nineteenth-century adventure fiction in scenes which focus on Teddy Potter, Emily's apparent admirer, and the other young officers of her acquaintance. One particularly significant scene involving the young officers and the somewhat taciturn Captain Hogan (a group of military men who bear a passing resemblance to Captain Bolton and his cohorts in *Troubles*) unfolds as the various parties – the Reverend Kingston and his Indian bearer, Mrs Forester, her son Jack, and Emily, Captain Hagan and the Lieutenants Woodleigh, Arkwright, and Potter, and Dr McNab and his wife – come together for an unplanned picnic during their respective journeys from Kalka to Simla. This scene, which includes many of the important characters of the novel, does much to establish the future direction of our sympathies even before the protagonists reach Simla and the themes of sickness and religion are fully taken up or the sub-plot is developed.

Farrell's parody of the language of adventure fiction, already noted in our discussion of *The Siege of Krishnapur*, is evident early in this scene from *The Hill Station*:

> Teddy Potter, meanwhile, was explaining to the ladies and especially to Emily that the road to Simla was positively infested with hostile tribesmen, with thugs and dacoits of every shape and description who were, moreover, particularly interested in making away with fair young English damsels … yes, it was jolly lucky that he and Woodleigh and Arkwright, under the 'awe-inspiring command' of the 'universally dreaded' Captain Hagan, should be on hand 'in the nick of time' to prevent Miss Anderson being carried off to become the unwilling bride of a hook-nosed Pathan chieftain with a dagger in his belt. Why, most likely the rascal was already watching them from behind those very trees! (55)[33]

Teddy's conscious parody – complete with clichés in quotation marks – does indeed spell out a stock-in-trade storyline that was typical of the romantic adventure fiction which Britain's imperial position in India spawned in the second half of the nineteenth century. It is significant that in Teddy's story an Englishwoman is in danger of being carried off by a Pathan, which raises the spectre of miscegenation that pervaded so much nineteenth-century adventure fiction set in India, and was only later, in novels like E.M. Forster's *A Passage to India* and Paul Scott's *The Jewel in the Crown*, subjected to serious scrutiny. Such stories were particularly common in magazines like *Blackwood's Edinburgh Magazine*, which is specifically named as Teddy's story (which now includes roaming tigers) reaches its climax a few lines on:

> 'But why are you fighting them with your bare hands?'
> 'Because our guns have missed fire, of course, as they always do according to *Blackwood's*.' (56)

This '*Boy's Own*'-style parody (which has been present in all Farrell's fiction since the naming of the invisible Wilson and Hurricane Harris in *The Lung*) – complete with markers of colonial India: dashing young officers, hook-nosed Pathans, fair young English damsels, tigers – is obviously designed to show that the popular image of this period is a distorted one. And this is reinforced by the way Teddy's performance is regularly interrupted by Captain Hagan's apparent interest in Kingston's bearer, which clearly emphasises the 'fictionality' of Teddy's story. And by so doing Farrell is questioning other colonial constructions of India as misleading or inappropriate too.

Lieutenant Potter's performance, which has the appearance of a light-hearted parody of colonial constructions of identity gives way to a much darker attack on colonial attitudes, played out in the confrontation between Captain Hagan, who wishes to feed Kingston's bearer, a Hindu, a beef sandwich, and McNab, who stops him out of respect for the bearer's religion:

> 'Here, Woodleigh, let us give the fellow a sandwich,' said Hagan, folding the slice of spiced beef into a chapati and handing it to Woodleigh.
> ...
> 'No, wait a moment, please,' said Dr McNab, rising to his feet to detain Woodleigh. 'He must not eat that.'
> 'Ah? And why not, pray?' asked Hagan.
> 'The man is a Hindu and must not eat beef.'
> 'Still ... let us see whether he will eat it.'
> 'That wouldna be right,' said McNab calmly but in a firm tone. ...
> 'He is an imbecile and will not notice,' pursued Hagan pleasantly.
> 'Nevertheless, it shouldna be done.' (56)

In this extract Hagan puts forward a colonial view common in the late nine-teenth century (which still persists today) that refuses to recognise any value in Hindu culture, and seeks to override Hindu beliefs and customs as a means of demonstrating the superiority of the colonising (or dominant) culture. In particular, the attempt to disguise the beef in a chapati (to disguise it as Indian food in a gesture which suggests that the emptiness of Hindu culture can be filled by British culture) in order to persuade the bearer to unknowingly break religious taboos recalls one of the immediate causes of the 1857 Sepoy Revolt or so-called Indian Mutiny. (And this is one of the causes of the Sepoy Revolt that Farrell draws attention to in *The Siege of Krishnapur* [31–32], along with details of an ominous distribution of chapatis). It was widely believed at the time (and most historians now accept) that cartridges (which had to have the end bitten off) had been greased with a mixture of cow's and pig's fat, which would defile both Hindu and Muslim sepoys alike. As Philip Woodruff graphically explains:

> On the lips of a Hindu cow's fat would be an abomination for which there is no parallel in European ways of thinking; it was not merely disgusting, as excrement would be; it damned him as well; it was as bad as killing a cow or a Brahman. To a Muslim pig's fat was almost as horrible.[34]

Through McNab, on the other hand, an enlightened view of culture is presented, which accepts difference. This brief but immensely important episode also paves the way for some of the later doctrinal debates of the novel. Here, through Hagan, the missionary zeal of Christianity is raised, though not supported by Kingston (which early sets him at odds with the thinking of many in his church). It also epitomises certain common, arrogant, nineteenth-century colonial views of native others. Here the bearer, an imbecile, can be seen as a metaphor for the primitive or uncivilized Hindu nation which the British colonisers must provide for by destroying (in this instance polluting). Indeed, Hagan effectively voices another nineteenth-century belief, that 'the only good native is a dead one', when, in response to Potter's suggestion that the bearer could eat a melon left behind by some other traveller, he says 'Certainly, let him eat that and infect himself with cholera ... and that will put him swiftly out of his misery, which is the best solution of all' (57).

The chapter ends with one more sally from Hagan and a final response from McNab:

> 'Doctor, I'm surprised that you should want to defend these Hindu superstitions. The natives would do a damn sight better in my opinion if they ate some of these filthy cows that roam about everywhere.'

'It's a matter of common humanity,' replied McNab testily, 'that one shouldna impose upon an idiot that which he wouldna agree to if he were in his right mind. And that's all there is to be said about it.' (59)

Again Hagan's colonial arrogance is evident as he voices another common misconception about India, based entirely on ignorance. McNab, conversely, speaks as a liberal humanist, placing him in a long line of such characters in Farrell's fiction.

In an early draft of *Troubles* there is another doctor who does not appear in the published version; he is Dr Snipe, who is looking after the Major's elderly aunt in London while she is dying. He and the Major have a long conversation (in this version) about the cycles of civilization, during the long days while they tend the dying old lady. At one point Snipe says that essentially

> success [in setting up an Empire] inevitably brings security, security brings leisure, leisure brings flabbinesss and equivocation. Poets and moralists take over from soldiers. Barbarians on the frontiers [of the Roman Empire] are no longer put down so swiftly, there are long debates about the rights and wrongs of the matter. Do barbarians have the right to live also? ...

He continues,

> For an empire to last forever it would have to remain always in the primitive state of ruthless and unspiritual self-interest. This is as impossible, my dear good Major, as for a human being always to remain young and vigorous.[35]

Dr Snipe's words are interesting in relation to the concern in *The Hill Station* with religion and the rise in interest in the spiritual in late-nineteenth century civilizations. Dr Snipe is also reiterating the idea that youth and health is to individuals what early energy is to civilization, and talking about the moral relativism which makes governing so difficult in late civilizations, and leads in two directions, to tolerance and to decadence.

McNab's investigation of the unforseen inner element of healing in *The Hill Station*, his belief 'not in religion as such but in something that lies behind the observable facts of medicine',[36] would probably have been related by Farrell to humanity's recent tendency to put too much emphasis on the seen. The text leaves open the possibility that the apparently naïve signifier of the bird for the Holy Spirit (an intertextual reference to Gustave Flaubert's 'A Simple Heart', published in *Three Tales* [1877]) may actually conceal a real signified.

According to Spurling the novel would have ended with the death of Kingston and the ensuing recovery of the Bishop:

Finally Kingston, having taken refuge in the McNabs' new bungalow, was to renounce his living [providing the opportunity for further word games?] at the earnest request of the apparently dying Bishop and leave Simla, only to die himself; whereupon

> The Bishop, recovered, is playing croquet again. Another curate-challenger. McNab does not wait, he knows how it will end.[37]

But there could, too, have been some sort of miraculous healing, if not of Kingston then of Emily's withered hand. It is possible, too, that most of the others, McNab apart, would have either not noticed the healing or discounted it because they refuse to believe the non-scientific or non-rational. It could be argued that Farrell has sown the seeds for such an event in his first mention of Emily's withered hand. As Emily's hand is evidently not obvious to many, and as little mention is made of her deformity elsewhere in the novel, it would have been easy for people to refuse to recognise the healing of something few had been aware of in the first place.

8 / Coda
'Becoming-animal'; 'the body without organs': 'The Pussycat Who Fell in Love with the Suitcase'

There remains one published work of Farrell's to consider, one which is never usually discussed. The shortest, the least-known, and in many ways the most curious of all, 'The Pussycat Who Fell in Love with the Suitcase', a four and a half page story, was ostensibly written for children. It was published in the winter of 1973–74 in *Atlantis*, a magazine co-edited by Farrell's good friend, the poet and journalist Derek Mahon. The provenance of the story is uncertain. Farrell's brother Robert had thought it was written at Derek Mahon's suggestion.[1] Mahon in turn believed it had been written for the artist Patricia Moynagh, mentioned at the end of *The Singapore Grip* (566).[2] Moynagh has no knowledge of the story, but recalls an unpublished children's book called *Pussymodo*, about a hunchback cat, which was illustrated by Monika Beisner, another artist-friend of Farrell's.[3]

The first interesting feature of 'The Pussycat Who Fell in Love with the Suitcase' is its genre. Children make only rare appearances in Farrell's work, the world of his novels is a place of essentially adult thinking about the experiences of culture, politics, war, sexual matters, disease, and death. *Atlantis* was not a publication for children, and therefore Farrell's contribution of this kind of story is not easy to explain except in so far as it might be a vehicle allowing for a free kind of satirical 'double entendre'. It can be read simply as the ubiquitous kind of comic fantasy for children that uses animals in place of humans,[4] but at another level it looks almost Swiftian or Orwellian in its sexual/political satire, and proves to contain a complex degree of compression and manipulation, or perhaps one could say 'condensation' and 'displacement', of many elements deeply characteristic of Farrell's longer fictions.

There are well-placed signals in this work which direct the reader towards each of the two different ways of reading it suggested above, children's fantasy or satire. But there is also the possibility of an extended reading, an interpretation of the satire through Deleuze and Guattari's *Capitalism and Schizophrenia* which would invoke the whole trajectory of Farrell's fictional attempts to relate Empire, capitalism, historiography, and the Britain of his own generation.

Here we need a cautionary pause, largely self-admonitory. After several years immersed in Farrell's entertaining textual company, we are very well aware that the sardonic shadow of Farrell may be murmuring with amusement over our shoulders about 'a serious gathering of academic vultures'[5] around a simple short story, perhaps highly tickled that we have fallen into a teasingly prepared trap for vulgar Freudians and Marxists manqué. If ever there was a time, though, for us to take the license to play a little, to speculate, it is probably at the end of a serious attempt to do justice to Farrell. It may be productive to use this short story as a way of re-examining some aspects of his work which will probably always be elusive, and drawing attention to some manuscript and unused draft material which offers tantalising hints of his working methods and aesthetic choices.

An attempt to summarise 'The Pussycat Who Fell in Love with the Suitcase' gives an immediate idea of its suggestive details. It concerns a beautiful black tomcat called Rameses who finds in his bedroom one day a mysteriously-arrived suitcase. This suitcase, evidently one of the typical productions of the nineteen-sixties so satirically treated by Farrell in *A Girl in the Head* (it could belong to Maurice the seducer), is covered in a golden-coloured nylon plush which looks like fur. Rameses immediately falls in love with the suitcase, who refuses to speak to him. Rameses's unrequited love becomes a sickness that keeps him away from his vital job as shop-steward in the town's factory, producer of almost the only food eaten here – peppermints. His job is to settle disputes amicably, to keep 'the workers whistling while they worked and the managers in their offices with their feet on their desks puffing cigars and counting their profits' (!).[6] But Rameses isolates himself in his room and becomes thin and weak. His disintegration is observed with concern by his friend the Mayor (Major?), especially when, without Rameses, disputes close the factory, and the animals begin to have to eat their peppermints raw rather than cooked into all the delicious forms they are used to: 'peppermint cornflakes, or shredded peppermints, or tinned pepper-mints in syrup which you could eat with cream or custard. And sometimes the peppermints were minced and turned into peppermint-burgers' (6).[7] After a time the Mayor discovers what the problem is, and with the help of the town coun-cillors secretly introduces a tape-recorder into the suitcase, which now repeats a short message of love and admiration every five minutes. The difficulty is solved. Economic production is resumed and the narrator predicts that even when the battery of the tape-recorder runs out, Rameses and his suitcase will continue to live happily ever after.

Here, at even the most cursory glance, is a familiar Farrellian narrative structure with an equally familiar cast of characters and a typically surreal use of images. The dark male who would like to think of himself as a hero falls in love with a blonde he has only just met, and whose real nature he severely misunderstands. Like most of Farrell's central male characters he then demonstrates a humorous degree of 'sexual ineptness' in pursuit of his desire.[8] The female is represented here by a fur-covered space, an emptiness which is made to talk, an image which surely reopens Margaret Drabble's reassuring discussion of the strangeness of many of Farrell's representations of women and sexuality.[9] (The 'Singapore Grip' may be a suitcase, a sexual hold, a symbol of both capitalist economic control and of patriarchal-imperialist psychological baggage.) The advent of the mysterious elusive female (Gretchen, Sands's wife, Flower, Inez, Angela, Sarah, Louise, Vera) into the previously self-contained life of the hero is a regrettable contingency; love is simply a cosmic blight that interferes with male friendship and work. It arrives with the sudden and devastating effects of an unexpected illness. The best thing to do is for the hero's friends, different kinds of males (the Mayor is a large spaniel), to arrange things somehow to keep the hero operating satisfactorily in a community in which he is an agent for some kind of socialism, however diluted, in a system which depends heavily on production and consumption.

The strong directive within this work towards a reading as 'mere' children's story comes essentially through the tone and positioning of the narrator in the first lines. The friendly confiding voice addresses the reader directly in the second person:

> Did you know that in our town there was once a pussycat who fell in love with a suitcase? If you sit up straight, and don't bite your nails, and listen carefully, I shall tell you about it. (6)

This is, of course, highly characteristic of a long tradition of British writing; it could have come straight out of Kipling's *Just So Stories* (1902) or any of Beatrix Potter's tales. In a story genuinely intended for children it is unexceptionable, if somewhat old-fashioned and patronising, the voice of the nanny, the parent, the trusted adult. It is an exaggeration of the tone taken by the narrator in the Empire trilogy and which John Spurling describes from those novels as 'slightly old-world, fireside, nannyish cosiness'.[10] Spurling associates it with 'tricks of storytelling' borrowed by Farrell from Richard Hughes and Thomas Mann. Yet in Farrell's work particularly, it is always far less candid than it appears. It allows the narrator to tell a story for which he evasively implies that he both is and is not responsible: the story itself pre-dates the present situation of the telling, and by implication, both narrator and listener. The narrator therefore has responsibility only for the present reporting; not for the truth of the events themselves, since he, too, is only passing on a textualised account previously passed to him ('so I've been told' [6], says the narrator in 'The Pussycat Who Fell in Love with the Suitcase' at one point).

The initial time placement of the narrated events supports the narrator's refusal of responsibility: 'there was once' a pussycat is the traditional formula of legend-time; the narrated events took place in 'those days', a phrase repeated twice in the second paragraph of this story, recalling similar phrases in *Troubles*, *The Siege of Krishnapur*, *The Singapore Grip*, and *The Hill Station*. The exaggeration of this narrative method here is a reminder of how carefully this device is used throughout Farrell's work to obtain a kind of 'uncertainty gap' between the actuality of past events and the mythical accretions of their continual retelling as 'history'. It has been pointed out that this manner is used by E.M. Forster and Henry James in their novels of the early twentieth century, symptom of a modern anxiety about historical truth and judgement and about 'the condition of England'.[11] Farrell puts a postmodern metafictional twist on this by adopting their method itself as parody. The recognisably pseudo-Edwardian pose becomes an intertextual 'pointing' to the difficulty of finding a place for the narrator to stand in retelling history, the slipperiness involved in the complex illusion of re-presenting the world.

Having trustingly accepted the foregoing set-up, the adult reader comes to the end of 'The Pussycat Who Fell in Love with the Suitcase' only to confront an implicit demand that they rapidly revise all their earlier estimates of the narrator, the genre, and the meaning of the story. This shock begins in the second last paragraph which departs from the romance conventions of the fairytale ending. It becomes acute when the narrator suddenly returns as an intrusive first-person voice in the last paragraph. The conventional happy ending is now offered, belatedly, sardonically:

> One of these days I expect the Mayor will forget to change the batteries and the suitcase will stop telling Rameses that it loves him. But I doubt if Rameses will even notice. He's quite affectionate towards the suitcase, however, and I'm quite sure they will both live happily ever after, the way people do. (10)

Gone is the invitation to fantasy, replaced by a brisk practical cynicism; the time has changed swiftly to bring the past into the present and future, and the very last phrase deliberately invites a retrospective correlation between people and animals which wrenches the work towards satire. (Recall Martin Sands imagining his own marriage at the end of *The Lung*: 'I marrried my ex-step-daughter and we had ten children and lived happily ever after. It was just terrible' [207].)

The meaning of 'The Pussycat Who Fell in Love with the Suitcase' is thus changed from something like 'people often make idiots of themselves, especially over love, but friends will rally round and everything will be all right in the end', to something much bleaker and more socially incisive. One could put it as follows: this is a society in which socialist ideals have become complicit with capitalist organisation. The bourgeois story of love and marriage is simply a way of ensuring that personal desire serves the needs of a capitalist ideology which continually reproduces itself. Rameses is 'Oedipalised, conjugalised' by a capitalist society which recaptures him to its service. Capitalism needs not just love and marriage as practices, but the Oedipal story of love and marriage, no matter how bizarre and unlikely it is shown to be. Love, like Fleury's 'civilization', becomes 'a great, beneficial disease' (*The Siege of Krishnapur* 38).

This reading borrows Deleuze and Guattari's 'anti-oedipal' arguments about capitalism. For them, 'becoming-animal' and 'the body without organs' are two ways of using ideas developed from schizophrenic rather than psychoanalytic experience to effect an escape from the closed circuit of the 'four dense points' of capitalism, 'commodity/consumer, worker/capitalist'.[12] Deleuze and Guattari see psychoanalysis as deeply complicit with capitalism, while other models may offer release. The insistence of psychoanalysis on Oedipal explanations continually returns all symptoms of discontent to the family, the bourgeois triangle which capitalism needs for the reproduction of labour, the security of property, the capital-serving round of production-consumption. 'Becoming-animal' is not, they emphasise, merely using animals as metaphor; nor is it the 'playing' animal of the 'old man playing horse or dog on an erotic postcard from 1900', though at times it may appear to have elements of both of these.[13] 'Becoming-animal' is in some respects totemic, it leads to an awareness of other modes of possible operation in the world.

The BwO, 'body without organs', is a more difficult and much-debated phrase which Deleuze and Guattari take from the schizophrenic playwright and poet Antonin Artaud:

> The BwO is the *field of immanence* of desire, the *plane of consistency* specific to desire (with desire defined as a process of production without reference to any exterior agency, whether it be a lack that hollows it out or a pleasure that fills it).[14]

The Body without Organs is inseparable from 'a becoming-woman',[15] but it also seems to be a body made up of a kind of 'abstract machine' or 'group subject', which can work against the entrapment of the capitalist 'subject (subjected) group'. Ronald Bogue emphasises that Deleuze and Guattari are full of 'machines', but that theirs is not a mechanistic view of the universe as this might suggest. It is instead an attempt to show that the mind operates 'less as a theatre than as a factory'.[16] Is it far-fetched to suggest that in the case of Farrell's story, the suitcase together with the Mayor, the town councillors, and Rameses could act as a 'deleuzoguattarian'[17] 'group subject', a BwO?

> During desiring-production, a moment comes when the desiring machines congeal and form 'an enormous undifferentiated object. Everything stops dead for a moment, everything freezes in place' (AO 7, *13*). That undifferentiated object is the body without organs, the desiring machines at zero-degree of intensity, a moment of antiproduction constantly fed back into the process of production (hence Deleuze and Guattari's statement that desiring-machines only function by breaking down).[18]

The suitcase becomes a 'line of flight', a possibility of escape from the all-consuming logic and necessity of production, but only if it could be recognised as a suitcase, and not mis-recognised as the object/commodity of desire which returns one to the Oedipal net. For Rameses the story of bourgeois love and marriage performs the ideological work of 'naturalising' his relations with the production network. (Result: 'Happy Families' – Mr Bun the Baker, Mrs Bun the Baker's Wife, Billy and Betty Bun.) For the reader, Farrell's story itself operates in the same way if it is read as a children's story; but if its signals are respected and it is read differently, it reveals exactly how capitalism depends on certain kinds of blindness and certain kinds of 'story' to produce the ideology which conceals actual lived relations with capital and commodity.

It is possible that Farrell might have read *Anti-Oedipus* soon after it was published in French in 1972, or have heard some of the intellectual brouhaha which greeted its publication. It is even more likely, given the tenor of his progressive exploration of the politics and persons of Empire in the trilogy, that he arrived at the same sort of answers about the contemporary state of capitalism by an independent and poetic means rather than by a theoretical and philosophical one.

In one sense none of this is new in Farrell. As most critics have noted, he makes recurrent use of animals in frequently comic/satiric/symbolic relation to humans, beginning with two dogs in *A Man from Elsewhere*, continuing with the black cat in *The Lung* and the dog Bonzo in *A Girl in the Head*, and per-sisting in a profusion of subtle and significant manifestations throughout the Empire trilogy. The disease-ridden dog in *The Singapore Grip*, nicknamed 'The Human Condition', is only the most obvious and farcical of these. Humans show their best and worst sides through their dealings with and resemblances to animals; animals betray both affection and a vulnerability which is shockingly human.

Lieutenant Cutter, riding his reluctant horse into the house in *The Siege of Krishnapur*, ordering champagne to drink, and calling his Indian servants Ant, Ram, and Monkey, is 'deterratorializing' both horse and house: his actions can again be 'read' in two ways. To Cutter's like-minded friends, his behaviour reads as the epitome of the dare-devil heroic; to the reader and at least partly to Fleury, it reveals that the heroic Empire story to which these men subscribe has gone beyond the point of recognising distinctions between animal and human, between public and private spaces; that the fictions of all-power are now mistaken for reality, and that the consequences are likely to be a sharp fall which involves more than one horse and rider.

Similarly, when Fleury sees the dog Chloë eating the face of the dead sepoy in *The Siege of Krishnapur* and orders her to be shot, the horror of the moment cannot be reduced to simply the sight of a starving dog eating a dead human. Fleury would certainly not have bothered in any such way about the pariah dogs who continually haunt the corpses. Chloë is different. She has a strong resemblance to a woman since she is a golden spaniel with long ears like curls framing each side of her face. She is Fleury's gift to, and in some ways, substitute for, Louise. When Fleury is travelling with Chloë in the closed carriage some passing sepoys salute 'the pallor of the faces they glimpsed in the dim interior of the carriage (not to mention Chloë's gilt curls)' (42–43). A domesticated lapdog, she understands perfectly that eating people is wrong, but in breaking the cannibalism taboo she indicates to Fleury the imminent descent of all the besieged humans to a position outside culture and civilization. Most horrifyingly, this includes the women, who, like Chloë, resemble lapdogs in their real existence, and at the other end of the scale are the protected species 'angel-in-the-house' in their idealised/ideologised roles. The fiction of the latter helps to conceal the former. Fleury responds to Chloë's action by ordering for her the traitor's and deserter's execution: he has her shot.

It is significant that Chloë is eating the face, the point where, Deleuze and Guattari argue, citing both Sartre and Lacan, the white wall of signification and the black holes of subjectification coincide to produce a particular machine of power. Again, it reveals the ugly rapacity which Empire and capitalism may find it necessary to resort to in defence of their powers.

In *Troubles*, after Edward has shot the young Sinn Feiner, there is a moment when the face of the enemy comes close to being the animal-face:

> Edward sighed faintly and his uptilted gaze wandered around the panelled walls at the various antlers, at the winter forest of stags, at the ibex and antelope and zebra ... For an instant the dreadful thought occurred to the Major that Edward had now gone completely insane and was looking for a place on the wall to mount the Sinn Feiner. (416)

Here the moment when the defence of property and power has brought the humanist to the edge of the civilized is offered by Farrell in terms of an insanity which cannot recognise true relations between human and animal, nor the differences betweeen them. This is nothing so simple as Edward's or potentially Fleury's retrograde descent along a chain of being, or a putative evolutionary line, into animal, as in William Golding's *Lord of the Flies* (1954). It is a radical political statement of the deformative power of certain global metanarratives.[19]

Similar study of Farrell's use of the fox in the snow in *The Lung*, Lady Jane and her lion in *A Girl in the Head*, the bullet-riddled pet rabbit and Edward's three piglets, Mooney, Johnston and O'Brien, in *Troubles*, the orang-utan who places a hand on Vera Chiang's naked bottom in *The Singapore Grip*, and many other such scenes, would show his varied and subtle examination of the point where the interface between animal and human is always a reminder of the limits of the human and of the extent of the universe which continually evades human control. By placing themselves centrally and exclusively, and regarding civilization and capital as co-terminous, Western Europeans distort their relations with the rest of the universe. In a book which Farrell could not have read, Deleuze and Guattari say that

> the relationships between animals are the object not only of science but of dreams, symbolism, art and poetry, practice and use. And on the other hand, the relationships between animals are bound up with the relation between man and animal, man and woman, man and child, man and the elements, man and the physical and microphysical universe.[20]

Farrell seems everywhere to affirm the modern/postmodern insight that the human impulse to see its own condition as heroic, epic, must be mediated by the view of it as tragi-comic, absurd, pitiable. '[C]rawling between Heaven and earth', in Hamlet's words,[21] humankind is too like the animal to be fully tragic, and on occasions, too like a god to be really absurd. But most of all humanity is social, and the price for the comforts of a neo-Romantic individualist ego may be the manifestations of late capitalism.

The writing of 'The Pussycat Who Fell in Love with the Suitcase' probably occurred between the end of *The Siege of Krishnapur* and alongside the beginning of work on *The Singapore Grip*, at a time when Farrell had been writing about the failure of communist anti-capitalist ideals in the former, and was researching economics for the latter. One of the titles included in a page of titles proposed by Farrell for *The Siege of Krishnapur* is 'The Dogs', but this has a line through it.[22] One of the several tentative openings of *The Singapore Grip* which were later abandoned contains a typically light thrust at half-hearted socialists:

In order for someone to be invited to dine at 'The Larches' it was necessary that he should possess certain qualities, not the least surprising of which was that he should be a socialist. If 'socialist' is putting it too strongly, it was at least necessary that he should harbour egalitarian notions of the kind that, Lady Curtis believed, are held by every cultured and enlightened person. But if the 'socialist' in question, quailing before life's difficulties, was unable ever to put them into practice, he could be confident that neither Lady Curtis nor her husband would hold it against him.[23]

Farrell seems to have even had such a satirical function in mind in several references in the working notes for *Troubles* about 'the socialist's cat':

A socialist in Killnalough who takes in the Colonel's cat when he goes to America. Then after it has got fatter and fatter finally ejects it ... [24]

In another draft fragment of *The Siege of Krishnapur* there appear two items among the Collector's prized possessions which have nothing to do with either Progress or Art, and probably for that reason do not survive into the published version. They are two glass cases, one containing a group of stuffed cats and one a group of stuffed frogs, from Wurtemberg. The cats are having a tea-party. One of the frogs is being shaved by another.[25] The final version of *The Siege of Krishnapur* includes a Magistrate with long cat-like ginger whiskers, and the members of the siege community indulge in a continuing round of progressively bizarre tea-parties very similar to the Mad Hatter's Tea Party in Lewis Carroll's *Alice's Adventures in Wonderland* (1865) as Ronald Binns has shown.[26] Finally, only the barest elements of the tea-party ritual survive, there being no tea, sugar, milk, or food.

Deleuze uses Lewis Carroll's works as an example of the way in which nonsense can break through inbuilt discursive and linguistic restraints on meaning to cover a wide metaphysical field of signification:

As Deleuze shows throughout *The Logic of Meaning*, the nonsense works of Lewis Carroll provide numerous examples of ... pre-logical meaning, of shifting identities and reversible relations of causality and temporality, of contradictory realms in which real and imaginary, material and conceptual, possible and impossible objects coexist and interact. Carroll's works are usually characterized as nonsense works, but they are not devoid of meaning; they have a sense, simply not good sense, and hence they delineate an extended meaning that embraces both the logical and the illogical.[27]

What is really new in 'The Pussycat Who Fell in Love with the Suitcase' is the overdetermined nature of its impact, so adroitly combining late Marxist implications with Freudian symbols, and yet arriving at a fable which transcends this conjunction. The conjunction of Marxism with psychoanalysis and the revision of both is Deleuze and Guattari's theme. One of the problems of classical Marxism for later commentators had been that it was a theory of historical process without a theory of the subject. The difficulty seemed to have been resolved in one way, and at least for one kind of academic discourse, when Lacan joined Marxism to a revision of Freud's psychoanalytical theory, a theory of the subject with no real theory of social or political process.

In another way though, fiction, a form which is intensely concerned with character and subjectivity, is always at work on a theory (through poetics) of the subject. A body of fiction like Farrell's, which is grappling at the same time with making sense of the individual's location in the historical process seen from a Marxist view, is a strong discursive site for the working out of a combined theory/poetics of history and the subject.

There is evidence from both drafts and published versions of the second and third volumes of the trilogy that Farrell was considering the problem of fictionally representing sexuality, especially 'authentic' historical accounts of sexuality, and particularly scenes in which sex appears manically and absurdly funny, as it had in his earlier novels. In the published version of *The Siege of Krishnapur* these cluster around Lucy, the 'fallen woman' at the dak bungalow, and include Harry's and Fleury's several encounters with her. Farrell based one of these on evidence given in the legal case brought against John Ruskin, influential Victorian writer and art critic, by his wife Effie, for non-consummation of their marriage.[28] In several drafts for this novel though, there is far more about Fleury's sexual problems. He is worried about 'secret disorders' and 'solitary habits' which

> ... exhaust the vital energies of manhood, and all the diseases and derangements resulting from indiscretion ... whereby the pleasures of life are marred, the objects of marriage frustrated and the existence itself rendered a term of unceasing misery and regret.[29]

This sounds like either a quotation from one of 'the bound nineteenth-century volumes of the *British Medical Journal* which [Farrell] picked up from a barrow'[30] and which he was reading for their accounts of cholera, or a clever pastiche of one. It is followed in the draft by a splendid scene of misunderstanding and confusion in which the Collector, who is ill, replies 'I am a tiger',[31] and Fleury tries to ask the Collector whether it is possible for men to get married without knowing that they have 'destroyed their physical and mental powers and frustrated the objects of marriage'.[32] The Collector may be delirious at this stage but his remark is deliberately ambiguous. (Consider June Furlough's remark to Boris after their scene of sexual blundering in *A Girl in the Head*: 'You look like a tiger' (96) and in *The Singapore Grip*: '[Matthew's] *yang* spirit, which had been dozing like a tiger in its cave, was abruptly awoken by that lithe yet slippery arm which had encircled his waist ...' [392].) In the draft version of *The Siege of Krishnapur* the Collector's comment is succeeded by a long passage in which the Collector dreams that he sees plump white rabbits ('the ladies') being pursued about the room by Rayne, the Opium Agent.[33] But this is not a dream – he wakes to find that he's been sleeping through an alcoholic orgy. All this was cut at some point.

The many dreams in *The Singapore Grip* and quite a number of the scenes with either direct sexual point or sexual overtones suggest that Farrell with his usual thoroughness may have been researching Freud's influence in the late 1930s as a source for comic possibilities. ('As for Monty, in his dreams you might expect to find naked women jostling each other for the best position under the eye of his subconsciousness; surprisingly this was not the case. ... Monty, fated to toil in sexual salt-mines throughout his waking hours, now faintly heard from an unexpected direction' [215].) Ideas arising from *The Singapore Grip* may have flowed over into the short story (or vice versa). Walter Blackett cogitates about the marriage of his daughter Joan: 'A great deal of thought must be given to your daughter's marriage. Otherwise she will simply slink off like a cat on a dark night and get herself fertilized under a bush by God knows whom!' (421). Joan's father must convert her 'natural' sexuality into woman-as-commodity for the better preservation of capital and property.

Matthew too understands woman-as-commodity, but in a modern/postmodern concentration on the visual, gets it all mixed up with aesthetics, epistemology and metaphysics:

> Was there any point in possessing a beautiful woman all to oneself? The answer was: no, not really. ... For, unless you are the sort of Mohammedan who keeps his wife heavily veiled, her beauty is scarcely less available to casual passers-by in the street than it is to *you*, whose job it is to foot the bill for her food, lodging and general maintenance. ... The effect produced by a beautiful woman is *visual* ... touching her does not bring you any closer to her beauty than touching the paint of a Botticelli brings you closer to the beauty of his painting. ... In the most intimate position of all, with your eyeball, so to speak, resting against the paint itself you would be hard put to tell any difference at all between this one and another. What had happened in the case of beautiful women, Matthew

reflected, was that lust and aesthetic pleasure had got hopelessly mixed up. As a result, men felt obliged to marry beautiful women when in many cases they would have been better advised to marry a plain woman with a pleasant disposition and acquire, perhaps, some compensatingly beautiful object such as a piece of T'ang porcelain. (302–03)

Or a beautiful suitcase.

Matthew's relationship with Vera Chiang proposes the possibility of re-textualising the conjugal relation into something non-Western, non-Freudian. Vera is a Eurasian girl whose presence in Singapore is largely unexplained, and who has the ability to slide between different worlds, evading entrapment by any particular one. In another of Farrell's light touches the Chinese treatise on sexual techniques beside her bed sits easily beside Waley's translation of *170 Chinese Poems* (1918), but uneasily with Samuel Smiles's *Self Help* (1859), an evangelical tract of nineteenth-century capitalism, and Percy F. Westerman's *To the Fore with the Tanks* (1918). In their first scene of sexual intent, the comic emphasis is on a very deleuzoguattarian 'naming of parts' of the body, in which the object seems to be to produce a 'desiring machine' made up of two heads, four legs, four arms, and sundry other useful members. The aim is to arrive successfully at such 'manoeuvres' as 'Butterfly Hovering over Snow White Peony', and even 'Goldfish Mouthing in Crystal Tank', which requires the addition of a third party to the 'group subject'.

This manic comedy is both Beckett-with-sex, and taken together with Matthew's long discussions of the immorality of capitalism and the difficulties of opposing it, it is an acknowledgement that none of the metanarratives of the late-twentieth-century are satisfactory to explain the human condition; not humanism, nor Marxism, nor Freud. Matthew's bumbling willingness to cooperate with Vera indicates that his re-education is possible. But this voluntary change is too late, Singapore is already overtaken by another of Deleuze and Guattari's accessories to capitalism, the 'war machine'. Vera Chiang disappears, the new capitalists, Joan and Nigel, get dangerously away, as does playboy Monty with his three blood-nailed 'harpies', the Da Sousa sisters. The badly embalmed body of old capital, Solomon Langfield, is carted about, disintegrating, subjected to indignities it would never have foreseen.

By the end of the Empire trilogy we cannot ignore Farrell's rueful demonstrations that whatever the spiritual or mental or intellectual side of humankind, it is linked, as Yeats said, to a dying animal.[34] Farrell draws comic and exasperated attention to the enduring demands of the body, the appetites and sensations which refuse to allow the theorising mind to float too high off the ground, and yet he shows clearly too, that one of the unexplainable assets of humanity is its tendency to go on asking, like Matthew, through failure, war, apocalypse:

'What is the best way in which to live one's life?' (476) and to be able to believe that 'a vast, universal change of heart' (429) is possible.

In his last, unfinished novel, *The Hill Station*, there are many signs that he reserved the right to speculate about spiritual qualities in humanity. The most strenuous of the contemporary pragmatist philosophers, Richard Rorty, has claimed that 'the real issue [for postmodern thinkers] ... is between people who think our culture, our purpose or institutions cannot be supported except conversationally and people who still hope for other sorts of support [i.e. metaphysical foundations]'.[35] It is fortunate that Farrell's works are among those that will remain to show that such a choice may not be necessary. The conversation about 'our culture, our purpose and institutions' runs high in Farrell's novels, but so too does meditation about the extraordinary metaphysical persistence of the comic and the virtuous in humanity.

At the end of *The Singapore Grip* Matthew is in a Japanese prison camp without a forseeable future:

> Accustomed to speculate grandly about the state and fate of nations he now found that his thoughts were limited to the smallest of matters ... a glass of water, a pencil, a handful of rice. Hope had deserted him completely. It came as a surprise to him to realize how much he had depended on it before. (565)

Into this hopeless life there comes a symbol of the troubled pleasures of Empire, the difficulties of understanding those of other cultures and gender, and yet the hint that attempts at communication will survive this violent rending of an old regime. A cigarette packet is surreptitiously passed to Matthew. It contains an enigmatic sign of Vera, a lump of sugar and two cooked white mice.

Notes

p.11 Ms. 9155/69, Papers of James Gordon Farrell (1935–79), Trinity College Dublin.

INTRODUCTION

1 Francis King, 'The Loner Who Loved Company', *Sunday Telegraph*, 19 Aug. 1979: 14.

2 Derek Mahon, 'J.G. Farrell 1935–1979', *New Statesman*, 31 Aug. 1979: 313.

3 John Spurling, 'Jim Farrell: A Memoir', *The Times*, 11 Apr. 1981:6.

4 This essay – which treats Farrell alongside David Caute, John Berger, B.S. Johnson, and with reference, too, to Angus Wilson, Malcolm Bradbury, Margaret Drabble, and John Fowles – is reproduced as a chapter entitled 'Fictions of History' in the second edition of his excellent study of postwar British fiction, *The Situation of the Novel*, 2nd ed. (London: Macmillan, 1979) 214–37.

5 Swinden writes, 'The younger novelist who had learned most from Hughes, J.G. Farrell, died the following year, but not before completing his trilogy on colonial themes, *Troubles* (1970), *The Siege of Krishnapur* (1973) and *The Singapore Grip* (1979). All three of these novels owe to Hughes something of their relaxed unfolding of historical events; local shocks administered by the timing and grouping of events; and, above all, an intense, often bizarre representation of visual detail'. Patrick Swinden, *The English Novel of History and Society, 1940–80* (London and Basingstoke: Macmillan, 1984) 11–12.

6 Malcolm Bradbury, *The Modern British Novel* (1993; London: Penguin, 1994) 382.

7 Linda Hutcheon, *A Poetics of Postmodernism: History, Theory, Fiction* (New York and London: Routledge, 1988) 113–14.

8 See John McLeod, 'Exhibiting Empire in J.G. Farrell's *The Siege of Krishnapur*', *Journal of Commonwealth Literature* 29.2 (1994): 117–32, and Lars Hartveit, 'The Carnivalistic Impulse in J.G. Farrell's *Troubles*', *English Studies* 73.5 (1992): 444–57.

9 Malcolm Dean, 'Grip of Empire', *Guardian*, 13 Sept. 1978: 10.

10 Mss. 9128–60, Papers of James Gordon Farrell.

11 See Lars Hartveit, 'The Art of Emplotment: the Mechanism of Amalgamating Fact and Fiction in J.G. Farrell's *The Singapore Grip*', *Studies in Modern Fiction: Presented to Bent Nordhjem on His 70th Birthday 31 May 1990*, ed. Eric Jacobsen, Jorgen Eric Nielsen, Bruce Clunies Ross, and James Stewart (Copenhagen: Faculty of Humanities, U of Copenhagen, 1990) 79–100, and Lars Hartveit, 'The Imprint of Recorded Events in the Narrative Form of J.G. Farrell's *The Siege of Krishnapur*', *English Studies* 74.5 (1993): 451–69.

12 Dean 10.

13 Hutcheon 114.

14 Hutcheon 101.

15 Mikhail Bakhtin, *The Dialogic Imagination: Four Essays*, ed. Michael Holquist, trans. Caryl Emerson and Michael Holquist (Austin: U of Texas P, 1981).

16 McLeod 125.

17 Malcolm Bradbury, *No, Not Bloomsbury* (London: Arena, 1989) 101. Cited in McLeod 131n.

18 Hutcheon 141.

19 Donna Landry and Gerald MacLean, *Materialist Feminisms* (Cambridge, MA: Blackwell, 1993) 128–9.

20 'J.G. Farrell Comments', *Contemporary Novelists*, ed. James Vinson (London: St James Press, 1970) 399.

21 Hutcheon 213.

22 Cited in Randall Stevenson, *The British Novel since the Thirties: An Introduction* (London: Batsford, 1986) 123.

23 Mary Sullivan, 'And now Unlucky Jake', *Sunday Telegraph*, 17 Sept. 1978: 12.

24 Cited in Ronald Binns, *J.G. Farrell* (London: Methuen, 1986) 27(Binns's emphasis removed).

25 Cited in Hutcheon 113.

26 Walter Jackson Bate, *The Burden of the Past and the English Poet* (Cambridge: Harvard UP, 1970).

27 See Susan Stanford Friedman, 'Weavings: Intertextuality and the (Re)Birth of the Author', *Influence and Intertextuality in Literary History*, ed. Jay Clayton and Eric Rothstein (Madison and London: U of Wisconsin P, 1991) 146–80. See also Tilottama Rajan, 'Intertextuality and the Subject of Reading/Writing', *Influence and Intertextuality in Literary History* 61–74.

28 Thomas Schaub, 'Allusion and Intertext: History in *The End of the Road*', *Influence and Intertextuality in Literary History* 185.

29 Schaub 191.

30 Nancy K. Miller, 'The Text's Heroine: A Feminist Critic and Her Fictions', *Diacritics* 12 (1982): 52. Cited in Friedman 158.

31 Roland Barthes, 'The Death of the Author', *Modern Criticism and Theory: A Reader*, ed. David Lodge (London and New York: Longman, 1988) 171.

32 Farrell reviewed two versions of Kipling's life. See J.G. Farrell, 'Complicated Tales', rev. of *Rudyard Kipling*, by Lord Birkenhead, and *Rudyard Kipling: His Life and Work*, by Charles Carrington, *Guardian*, 5 Oct. 1978: 14.

33 Cited in Raman Selden and Peter Widdowson, *A Reader's Guide to Contemporary Literary Theory*, 3rd ed. (New York and London: Harvester Wheatsheaf, 1993) 162.

34 J.G. Farrell, *The Hill Station* (1981; London: Flamingo, 1987) 92. All subsequent page references are to this edition.

35 Julian Barnes, *Flaubert's Parrot* (1984; London: Picador, 1985) 14.

CHAPTER 1 / A SKETCH FROM LIFE

1 J.G. Farrell, 'Under the Seat', rev. of *Jack B. Yeats*, by Hilary Pyle, *Spectator* 6 June 1970: 748.

2 J.G. Farrell, 'Miller's Tale', rev. of *Witchcraft at Salem*, by Chadwick Hansen, *Spectator* 7 Mar. 1970: 310.

3 J.G. Farrell, *Troubles* (1970; London: Flamingo, 1984) 102. All subsequent page references are to this edition.

4 See Brigid Allen, 'A Feline Friend: Memories of J.G. Farrell (1935–1979)', *London Magazine* 32.1 and 2 (1992): 69, 67.

5 Caroline Moorehead, 'Writing in the Dark, and Not a Detail Missed', *The Times* 9 Sept. 1978: 12.

6 Benny Green, 'J.G. Farrell', *Spectator* 25 Aug. 1979: 20.

7 R.P.J. Williams, 'Presenting the Raj: The Politics of Representation in Recent Fiction on the British Empire', diss. U of Nottingham, 1988, 61.

8 In *Troubles* this tendency to use names from his own life sees guests at the ball bearing names of some of Farrell's friends and family – 'the Russells from Maryborough', for example, are relatives on his mother's side of the family, and Miss Bridget O'Toole (327) is a friend who was to review the novel.

9 Dean 10.

10 Dean 10.

11 J.G. Farrell, *The Lung* (London: Hutchinson, 1965) 95. All subsequent page references are to this edition.

12 As well as Dylan Thomas, Farrell was enthusiastically reading A.E. Housman's poetry at this time. 'On Bredon Hill' was a particular favourite according to his brother Robert (conversation with Ralph Crane, 28 May 1996).

13 Binns 38.

14 Unsigned, 'Mr J.G. Farrell', *The Times* 16 Nov. 1979: iv.

15 Spurling 6.

16 Gordon Brock, 'Epitaph for Empire', *Observer Magazine* 24 Sept. 1973: 11.

17 Spurling 6.

18 Binns 31.

19 Binns 31.

20 Allen 70.

21 Brock 73, contd 75.

22 Moorehead 12.

23 Brock 75.

24 Allen 66.

25 J.G. Farrell, *A Girl in the Head* (1967; London: Fontana, 1981) 62–6 and 104–6.

All subsequent page references are to this edition.

26 Bernard Bergonzi, *The Situation of the Novel*, 2nd ed. (London: Macmillan, 1979) 86.

27 Quoted in the note to the Penguin edition of *Troubles* (London: Penguin, 1975).

28 The connection between Farrell and Scott is explored in detail by R.P.J. Williams, 'Presenting the Raj: The Politics of Representation in Recent Fiction on the British Empire'.

29 J.G. Farrell, 'Indian Identities', rev. of *A Division of the Spoils*, by Paul Scott, *Times Literary Supplement* 23 May 1975: 555.

30 Dean 10.

31 Spurling 6.

32 Dean 10.

33 Green 20.

CHAPTER 2 / A SOFT-SPOKEN ANARCHY

1 J.G Farrell, *A Man from Elsewhere* (London: New Authors, 1963) 18. All subsequent page references are to this edition.

2 Interestingly in *The Lung*, while trying to convince Martin Sands to take communion, Exmoore tells him 'you've nothing to lose' (80), a phrase which recalls Pascal's famous premise for accepting the existence of God.

3 Farrell's second published novel is probably a substantial revision of a novel he wrote in the late 1950s entitled *Lung*. This first novel was rejected by a number of publishers and no manuscript appears to have survived.

4 Günter Anders, 'Being without Time: On Beckett's Play *Waiting for Godot*', *Samuel Beckett: A Collection of Critical Essays*, ed. Martin Esslin (Englewood Cliffs, NJ: Prentice-Hall, 1965) 140.

5 Binns 37.

6 In *Troubles* the letter M falls from the wall of the Majestic Hotel and crashes on to the tea table. In *The Singapore Grip* there are characters named Matthew and Monty. The Major appears in both novels.

7 Frank Kermode, *The Sense of an Ending: Studies in the Theory of Fiction* (1967; Oxford: Oxford UP, 1968) 142–43.

8 Samuel Beckett, *Three Novels by Samuel Beckett: Molloy, Malone Dies, The*

Unnamable (1955, 1956, 1958; New York: Grove Press, 1981) 414.

9 Salman Rushdie, introduction, *On Writing and Politics, 1967–1983*, by Günter Grass, trans. Ralph Manheim (1985; Harmondsworth: Penguin, 1987) x.

10 *The Boyhood of Raleigh*, which hangs on the wall of the young Saleem's bedroom, is both a literal and metaphorical presence in Salman Rushdie's *Midnight's Children* (1981).

11 See Frank Kermode's discussion of Sartre in *The Sense of an Ending* 145.

12 Hugh Kenner, 'The Cartesian Centaur', *Samuel Beckett: A Critical Study* (1961; Berkeley and Los Angeles: U of California P, 1973) 117–32.

13 William Golding, 'Fable', *The Hot Gates and other occasional pieces* (London: Faber, 1965) 87.

14 Georg Lukács, *The Historical Novel*, trans. Hannah and Stanley Mitchell (London: Merlin Press, 1962) 53.

15 There is also a veiled reference to Hughes's *A High Wind in Jamaica* (1929) in *The Singapore Grip* (1978; London: Flamingo, 1984) where Farrell writes 'A high wind in Jamaica and it's goodbye to bananas' (61). All subsequent page references are to this edition.

16 *A Man from Elsewhere* has never been re-issued; a paperback edition of *The Lung* appeared in 1967. On the printer's copy (in two volumes) of *The Singapore Grip* Farrell erased the title of *A Man from Elsewhere* from the list of earlier novels 'By the same author'. Significantly, perhaps, he left *The Lung* there. It appears then that it is only his first novel that Farrell disowned. (See ms. 9143/ii, Papers of James Gordon Farrell.

CHAPTER 3 / THE HERO AS TEXT

1 Ms. 9131/1, Papers of James Gordon Farrell.

2 John Spurling describes Maidenhair Bay as 'an English south-coast resort' ('As Does the Bishop', *The Hill Station* [1981; London: Flamingo, 1987] 160). However, the imaginary resort is more likely to be situated on the Lancashire coast.

Southport, a Victorian seaside resort on the Lancashire coast has the wide beach and dunes described in the novel, and racehorses are regularly exercised there. That Farrell names the Dongeon family home 'Boscobel' after his own family's home in Southport is another indication that aspects of that resort are borrowed for Maidenhair Bay.

3 Bergonzi 81. It may be more than coincidence that Farrell chooses to name a dog in *The Singapore Grip* the Human Condition.

4 Robert Farrell, who sent his brother a copy of *Lolita* when it was first published, believes that Nabokov's novel influenced the writing of *A Girl in the Head* (conversation with Ralph Crane, May 1990).

5 Binns 41–42. Boris's dark glasses, his alcoholic unsteadiness, and his perambulations are also remininiscent of Martin Sands, the hero of Farrell's previous novel, *The Lung*.

6 Note that this passage (and others), indented in the Pan edition, appears in italics in the first edition.

7 W.H. Auden, 'Musée des Beaux Arts', lines 4 and 12–13, *W.H. Auden: Selected Poems*, ed. Edward Mendelson (London: Faber, 1979) 79–80. Auden, a cardholding Communist, had, like Regan in *A Man From Elsewhere*, left the Party. 'Museé des Beaux Arts', written in 1938, was first published in 1940.

8 Norman K. Denzin, *Images of Postmodern Society: Social Theory and Contemporary Cinema* (London: Thousand Oaks, and New Delhi: Sage Publications, 1994) vii.

9 Pynchon imports a whole revenge tragedy into the centre of this novel in order to demonstrate the connections between the American society of the 1960s and the amoral, violent, and intensely political world of Jacobean tragedy.

10 In 'Girls and Boys', rev. of *Hind's Kidnap*, by Joseph McElroy, *The Rape of Tamar*, by Dan Jacobson, *Godded and Codded*, by Julia O'Faolain, and *A Start in Life*, by Alan Sillitoe, *Spectator* 10 Oct. 1970: 407, Farrell describes the manner of Joseph McElroy's *Hind's Kidnap* as 'strangely reminiscent of Thomas Pynchon's *The Crying of Lot 49*'.

11 Marguerite Alexander, *Flights from Realism: Themes and Strategies in Postmodern British and American Fiction* (London: Edward Arnold, 1990), 19.

12 From Webster's *The White Devil*. These are almost the last words Vittoria speaks before she dies. The full speech reads 'My soul, like to a ship in a black storm, / Is driven I know not wither' (5.6.246–47).

13 See Laurence Bristow-Smith, '"Tomorrow is Another Day": the Essential J.G. Farrell', *Critical Quarterly* 25.2 (1983): 47.

14 Denzin vii.

15 There is a human pyramid in Richard Hughes's *The Fox in the Attic* (London: Chatto and Windus, 1961) 74–75, a novel which Farrell admired greatly.

16 Elizabeth Grosz, *Sexual Subversions: Three French Feminists* (Sydney: Allen & Unwin, 1989) 9–10.

17 David Lodge, 'The Novelist at the Crossroads', *The Novelist at the Crossroads and other Essays on Fiction and Criticism* (London: Routledge, 1971) 3–34, esp. 19ff.

18 For further discussion of this period see Randall Stevenson, *The British Novel since the Thirties* (London: Batsford, 1986), and Lodge 19ff.

19 The animal imagery which occurs throughout the novel is also reminiscent of Lowry and Bellow.

20 There may also be a reference to Blake's 'Ah! Sunflower' in 'T'neige', the virgin white as snow (and Inez seems always to be dressed in white), and Alessandro, the pining youth. Blake's poem is associated with a longing for both love and death, implying further connections with Boris's mood. The complete poem reads:

Ah Sunflower! weary of time.
Who countest the steps of the Sun:
Seeking after that sweet golden clime
Where the travellers journey is done.

Where the Youth pined away with desire,
And the pale Virgin shrouded in snow:
Arise from their graves and aspire,
Where my Sun-flower wishes to go.

William Blake, *The Complete Poems*, ed. Alicia Ostriker (Harmondsworth: Penguin, 1987) 126.

21 Webster, *The White Devil*, 4.2.151–52.

22 T. Winnifrith, 'J.G. Farrell', *Dictionary of Literary Biography*, vol. 14, 289.

23 The cover of the 1981 Pan paperback features a studio photograph of a beach scene with a young woman friend of Farrell's sitting cross-legged and clad in a bikini while Farrell himself crouched out of sight beneath the artificial shore with just his head showing through the sand. Binns suggests that this bizarre photograph inspired the scene at the end of *Troubles* (Farrell's next novel, which he was writing when this paperback imprint of *A Girl in the Head* appeared) where the Major is buried up to his neck in the sand and left to drown (26). But it is also an unusually pertinent cover illustration which amplifies the title.

24 From Shakespeare's *Romeo and Juliet*, 2.2.63–65. The full lines read:

> The orchard walls are high and hard to climb,
> And the place death, considering who thou art,
> If any of my kinsmen find thee here.

25 Jay Clayton and Eric Rothstein, 'Figures in the Corpus: Theories of Influence and Intertextuality', *Influence and Intertextuality in Literary History* 22.

26 Thomas Docherty, introduction, *Postmodernism: A Reader*, ed. and introd. Thomas Docherty (London and New York: Harvester Wheatsheaf, 1992) 21.

27 Bergonzi 86.

28 Brock 73.

29 Binns 43.

30 History in this novel is a series of snapshots or fragmented memories around which stories are woven (as in some postmodern works like Timothy Findley's *Famous Last Words* [1981] and Michael Ondaatje's *Running in the Family* [1982]).

CHAPTER 4 /
NEWSPAPERS, WAR, AND GAMES:

1 Binns 26. This chapter develops ideas first presented in Jennifer Livett, 'Newspapers, War, and Games: History in J.G. Farrell's *Troubles*', *Irish-Australian Studies: Papers Delivered at the Eighth Irish Australian Conference, Hobart July 1995*, ed. Richard Davis, Jennifer Livett, Anne-Maree Whitaker, and Peter Moore (Sydney: Crossing Press, 1996) 103–12.

2 Brock 75.

3 Margaret Scanlan, 'Rumours of War: Elizabeth Bowen's *Last September* and J.G. Farrell's *Troubles*', *Éire-Ireland* 20.2 (1985):71.

4 See in particular mss. 9136/406–414, Papers of James Gordon Farrell.

5 Binns 47.

6 Binns suggests the location is County Wexford (45).

7 Fifteen leaders of the Easter rebellion were executed, including the leader of the Irish Volunteers, Patrick Pearse, who was shot three days after the surrender. James Connolly, leader of the Irish Citizen's Army, was shot nine days later (in a chair because he could not stand on a gangrenous ankle).

8 Lawrence Bristow-Smith in his article 'Expandable Architecture', *Peake Studies* 1.1 (1988): 27–30, draws attention to this similarity and also proposes Michael Moorcock's Palace of Albion in *Gloriana* and J.P. Donleavy's Charnel Castle in *The Onion Eaters* as related fantasy architecture.

9 See Binns 47.

10 Bergonzi 232.

11 Homi Bhabha, *The Location of Culture* (London: Routledge, 1994) 145.

12 Hutcheon 89.

13 J.G. Farrell, 'The Army Game', rev. of *The I.R.A.*, by Tim Pat Coogan, *Spectator* 18 July 1970: 44.

14 Binns 60–61.

15 Lars Hartveit, 'The Carnivalistic Impulse in J.G. Farrell's *Troubles*' 456.

16 Bill Ashcroft, Gareth Griffiths, and Helen Tiffin, *The Empire Writes Back: Theory and Practice in Post-Colonial Literatures* (London and New York: Routledge, 1989) 12.

17 Elizabeth Bowen, 'Ireland Agonistes', *Europa* 1 (1971): 59. Farrell himself referred to Bowen's review of *Troubles* in an interview with Malcolm Dean:

> in her review of 'Troubles' Elizabeth Bowen made a remark that pleased

me very much. She said that it was not a 'period piece' but 'yesterday reflected in today's conciousness'. I should like people to think of 'The Siege of Krishnapur' in the same way. ('An Insight Job', *Guardian* 1 Sept. 1973: 11.)

CHAPTER 5 /
CULTURE AND COMMODITY

1 Allen 75.

2 Barnes 136.

3 McLeod 119.

4 Sara Suleri, *The Rhetoric of English India* (Chicago: U of Chicago P, 1992) does not mention Farrell but deals with Forster's *A Passage to India*, to which Farrell makes a variety of implicit references in *The Siege of Krishnapur*.

5 Unsigned, 'The Indian Mutiny in Fiction', *Blackwood's Edinburgh Magazine* Feb. 1897: 218.

6 Shailendra Dhari Singh, *Novels on the Indian Mutiny* (New Delhi: Arnold-Heinemann, 1973) 230–32.

7 Dean, 'An Insight Job' 11.

8 Dean, 'An Insight Job' 11.

9 J.G. Farrell, *The Siege of Krishnapur* (1973; London: Flamingo, 1985) 225–26. All subsequent page references are to this edition.

10 Lars Hartveit, 'The Imprint of Recorded Events in the Narrative Form of J.G. Farrell's *The Siege of Krishnapur*' 451–69.

11 Karl Marx, 'The Future Results of the British Rule in India'. Cited in Binns 64.

12 Terry Eagleton, *Marxism and Literary Criticism* (London: Methuen, 1976) 24.

13 McLeod 120.

14 Bristow-Smith, '"Tomorrow is Another Day": the Essential J.G. Farrell' 46.

15 P.N. Furbank, 'Between Past and Present', rev. of *The Hill Station*, by J.G. Farrell, *Times Literary Supplement* 22 May 1981: 563.

16 Gilles Deleuze and Félix Guattari, *Capitalism and Schizophrenia*, vol. 2, *A Thousand Plateaus*, trans. Brian Massumi (Minneapolis and London: U of Minnesota P, 1987) 143ff.

17 Louis Althusser, 'Ideology and Ideological State Apparatuses' in *Lenin and Philosophy, and Other Essays*, trans. Ben Brewster (London: New Left Books, 1971) 123–73.

18 Paul de Man, *The Resistance to Theory* (Manchester: Manchester UP, 1986) 11.

19 Alfred Lord Tennyson, 'The Charge of the Light Brigade', lines 1–3, *Poems and Plays*, ed. T. Herbert Warren, rev. Frederick Page (1953; Oxford: Oxford UP, 1971) 206–07.

20 Alfred Lord Tennyson, 'The Defence of Lucknow', lines 1–6, *Poems and Plays* 482–84.

21 William Shakespeare, *Henry V*, 4.3.63–64. Shakespeare's lines read: 'And gentleman in England now abed / Shall think themselves accursed they were not here'.

22 See Binns 74. He cites Maeve Kennedy, 'Farrell's Unfinished', rev. of *The Hill Station*, by J.G. Farrell, *Irish Times*, 16 May 1981:14; Paul Theroux, 'An Interrupted Journey', rev. of *The Hill Station*, by J.G. Farrell, *Sunday Times* 26 Apr. 1981: 42; and John Spurling, 'As Does the Bishop', 164.

23 Evidence that this is the way Farrell himself may have thought about marriage is found in his statement that Jack B. Yeats 'married soon and happily ... and as far as the mating urge is concerned that appears to have been the end of the matter'. J.G. Farrell, 'Under the Seat' 748–49.

24 The manuscript appears to have been submitted to Weidenfeld and Nicolson under the title 'Siege or The Spirit of Science Conquers Ignorance and Prejudice'. See ms. 9142/231, Papers of James Gordon Farrell.

25 Fredric Jameson, 'Periodizing the 60s', *The 60s without Apology*, ed. Sohnya Sayres, Anders Stephanson, Stanley Aronowitz, and Fredric Jameson (Minneapolis: *Social Text* and U of Minnesota P, 1984) 180. Cited in Hutcheon 112.

26 Bristow-Smith, '"Tomorrow is Another Day": the Essential J.G. Farrell' 49.

27 Frances B. Singh, 'Progress and History in J.G. Farrell's *The Seige of Krishnapur*', *Chandrabhaga* 2 (1979): 29.

28 Malcolm Dean records Farrell's 'discovery of a self-taught Marxist doctor at the home of a mutual friend' and 'their hour-long dialogue over the meaning of surplus labour'. 'A Personal Memoir', *The Hill Station* 199.

29 Binns 68.
30 Gayatri Chakravorty Spivak, 'Three Women's Texts and a Critique of Imperialism', *'Race', Writing, and Difference*, ed. Henry Louis Gates, Jr. (Chicago and London: U of Chicago P, 1986) 262.
31 See ms. 9141/320, Papers of James Gordon Farrell.
32 See Binns 75.
33 Karl Marx, preface, *Critique of Political Economy*. Cited in Raymond Williams, *Culture and Society 1780–1950* (1958; Harmondsworth: Penguin, 1971) 259.
34 Raymond Williams, *The Long Revolution* (1961; Harmondsworth: Penguin, 1980) 325–331.

CHAPTER 6 / THE THEATRE OF EMPIRE

1 J.G. Farrell, 'Indian Identities'. In Scott's novel Guy Perron and the Indian editor of a popular English-language newspaper, whose office he is visiting, look at a series of cartoons dated between August 1945 and 5 June 1947, the period covered by this volume of *The Raj Quartet*. Each cartoon depicts a significant event in the movement towards Independence. It is also worth noting that Farrell has regularly used paintings as metaphors in his fiction since his second novel, *The Lung*; and Caroline Moorehead quotes him as dreaming that he might become a painter (12).
2 See ms. 9142/85, Papers of James Gordon Farrell. Thirty-one possible titles, thirteen of them crossed out but still legible, are listed on an index card. 'The Siege of Krishnapur' is not one of them.
3 See Lars Hartveit, 'The Art of Emplotment: the Mechanism of Amalgamating Fact and Fiction in J.G. Farrell's *The Singapore Grip*' 79–100. Hartveit explains that '[t]he Grip phrase is part of the language of social comedy in the novel' (98).
4 Binns 90. Binns believes that Farrell 'intended the reader to have *War and Peace* in mind when reading *The Singapore Grip*' (89), and explains that Matthew Webb and his father are deliberately modelled on Tolstoy's Pierre Bezuhov and his father Count Bezuhov (89–90).
5 Jeffrey Meyers, *Disease and the Novel, 1880–1960* (New York: St Martin's Press, 1985).
6 These two references to Shanghai, along with the list of trading centres in the Far East – 'Shanghai, Hong Kong, Bombay, Colombo, Rangoon, Saigon and Batavia' (250) – are clear indicators that on one level *The Singapore Grip* is intended as a serious critique of colonialism, or perhaps more specifically (as these are all trading centres and the novel focusses on the economic angle of Empire) colonial capitalism.
7 Binns 95.
8 Commenting on the manuscript of the novel for Weidenfeld and Nicolson, Nigel Nicolson has this to say of Farrell's title:

> The only real quarrel I have with the book is its title. Eventually, on p. 837 [of the typescript submitted to the publisher], one reaches an explanation of it, but it is a let-down, and irrelevant, and rather nasty – and if there is some deep symbolic meaning, it missed me, for the whole point of the book is not a grip, but a loosening of the grip.

See ms. 9150/569, Papers of James Gordon Farrell.
9 The breadth of Farrell's intertextual allusions is highlighted by this phrase which echoes nineteenth century comedies of manners. Together with phrases like 'the marriage of a daughter is something to which a great deal of attention must be given' (39) it also calls to mind Restoration marriage comedies.
10 Brock 73. A copy of the *Saigon Post* 10 Feb. 1975 which carries the front-page headline 'Defence Bolstered Saigon Awaits Red Offensive', presumably bought by Farrell during his visit there, is catalogued as ms. 9160/130, Papers of James Gordon Farrell.
11 Denzin 3. Denzin's citation is to Ihab Hassan, 'The Culture of Postmodernism', *Theory, Culture & Society* 2 (1985): 119–32.
12 Ronald Binns, 'The Novelist as Historian', *Critical Quarterly* 21.2 (1979): 70.

13 There is an irony in Farrell's French phrase. Literally 'that *grand emmerdeur,* Charles Dickens' translates as that 'great bore', Charles Dickens – but it can also mean one who 'annoys' or 'bothers'.

14 Lukács 243.

15 Iris Murdoch, *The Red and the Green* (1965; Harmondsworth: Penguin, 1988) 274.

16 Murdoch 275.

17 See Bristow-Smith, '"Tomorrow is Another Day": the Essential J.G. Farrell' 51.

18 The AFS units are presented as an example of the co-operation that Matthew's idealism envisages, and are a marked contrast to the colonial exploitation that has been the example of Blackett and Webb Ltd and other businesses in the rubber trade.

19 Bristow-Smith, '"Tomorrow is Another Day": the Essential J.G. Farrell' 51.

20 J.M. Rignall, 'Walter Scott, J.G. Farrell, and Fictions of Empire', *Essays in Criticism* 41 (1991): 25.

CHAPTER 7 / 'FINALE IN A MINOR KEY'

1 Yasmine Gooneratne, 'Paul Scott's *Staying On*: Finale in a Minor Key', *Journal of Indian Writing in English* 9.2 (1982): 1–12.

2 It may be that Farrell's literary reputation has suffered from comparisons with Paul Scott, whose own literary reputation has in turn suffered because of his popularity (in the pejorative sense) and perceived commonality with so-called 'Raj writers' like John Masters and M.M. Kaye. (In particular Scott has been criticised for his recommendation of M.M. Kaye's *The Far Pavilions* [1978], which, as a publisher's reader, he correctly forecast would be a bestseller.)

3 Binns, *J.G. Farrell* 82.

4 There is an apparent inconsistency late in the novel when Farrell refers to McNab as 'a physician who had exercised his profession throughout the third quarter of the nineteenth century and a little beyond' (110) which suggests that the novel would perhaps have extended over a time period of five or six years.

5 Barthes 170.

6 T.S. Eliot, *The Waste Land and Other Poems* (1940; London: Faber, 1972) 32–33.

7 Kermode 47.

8 Theroux 42.

9 Binns, *J.G. Farrell* 83.

10 Binns, *J.G. Farrell* 83.

11 Binns, *J.G. Farrell* 84.

12 Spurling, 'As Does the Bishop' 167.

13 Theroux 42.

14 See Meyers, *Disease and the Novel*. In his opening chapter Meyers discusses broadly the position that disease has occupied in literature over the centuries before concentrating on eight significant works published between 1880 and 1960, including Thomas Mann's *The Magic Mountain*, in which he believes the theme of disease 'achieves its finest literary expression' (14).

15 Theroux 42.

16 Spurling, 'As Does the Bishop' 169–70.

17 See Ralph J. Crane, *Inventing India: A History of India in English-Language Fiction* (London: Macmillan, 1992) 69–70.

18 The published work is about fifty thousand words. Farrell had written to Rosemary Legge, his editor at Weidenfeld, the day before his death suggesting the completed novel would be between eighty and a hundred thousand words. See John Spurling, foreword, *The Hill Station* 7.

19 Binns, *J.G. Farrell* 83.

20 Binns, *J.G. Farrell* 83.

21 Spurling, 'As Does the Bishop' 175.

22 Binns, *J.G. Farrell* 83.

23 Meyers 1.

24 When the Bishop explains that he values McNab's presence as 'an outside intelligence on hand to prevent us from becoming turned in on ourselves' (88) Farrell is reinforcing McNab's position as an 'objective' outsider and our guide through the novel.

25 See Meyers 4ff.

26 Spurling, 'As Does the Bishop' 170.

27 Binns, *J.G. Farrell* 82.

28 See Spurling, 'As Does the Bishop' 172–73.

29 Spurling, 'As Does the Bishop' 173. The 'curious material' Farrell borrowed from Reynold's biography suggests that as in his previous two novels an Afterword acknowl-

edging his sources may have been included at the end of the novel, perhaps even, as in *The Singapore Grip*, a bibliography.

30 *Tracts for the Times* were a series of ninety position papers published by the leaders of the Oxford Movement between 1833 and 1841.

31 Spurling, 'As Does the Bishop' 170.

32 Spurling, 'As Does the Bishop' 176.

33 Here, too, Farrell appears to be indulging his penchant for wordplay. The word 'thug' in our current usage tends to mean someone who is brutal, a ruffian of some sort. In the late-nineteenth century its original (Indian) meaning would have still been current. Thugs were members of a religious cult of robbers (or dacoits) and assassins that were suppressed by the British about fifty years prior to the setting of *The Hill Station*.

34 Philip Woodruff, *The Men Who Ruled India*, vol. 1, *The Founders* (London: Jonathan Cape, 1953) 353.

35 Ms. 9136/39–40, Papers of James Gordon Farrell.

36 Spurling, 'As Does the Bishop' 172.

37 Spurling, 'As Does the Bishop' 175.

CHAPTER 8 / CODA

1 Conversation with Ralph Crane, 28 May 1997.

2 Letter to Ralph Crane, 21 Dec. 1996.

3 Letter to Ralph Crane, 19 Feb. 1997.

4 Robert Farrell explains that 'Jim's use of animals in his books was something he inherited from his father – in part at least His father imputed motives and character. to domestic animals to amuse his children' (letter to Ralph Crane, 17 Mar. 1997).

5 J.G. Farrell, 'Late Lowry', rev. of *Malcolm Lowry: His Art and Early Life*, by M.C. Bradbrook, *New Statesman* 19 July 1974: 87.

6 J.G. Farrell, 'The Pussycat Who Fell in Love with the Suitcase', *Atlantis* 6 (1973–74): 8. All subsequent page references are included in the text.

7 A tempting digression offers itself here via 'food in Farrell' read through Claude Lévi Strauss and 'the raw and the cooked' as manifestations of difference between 'primitive' and 'civilized' societies.

Peppermints are always 'cooked' but in this story are able to manifest rawness during the turmoil of desire.

8 Chris Ferns, 'Building a Country; Losing an Empire: The Historical Fiction of Thomas H. Raddall and J.G. Farrell', *Time and Place: The Life and Works of Thomas Raddall*, ed. Alan R. Young (Fredericton, NB: Acadiensis, 1991) 162.

9 Margaret Drabble, 'Things Fall Apart', *The Hill Station* 184–88.

10 Spurling, 'As Does the Bishop' 168.

11 Clea Burrell, 'The Condition of England Novel – "Between Journalism and Literature"?' unpublished.

12 Brian Massumi, *A User's Guide to Capitalism and Schizophrenia: Deviations from Deleuze and Guattari* (Cambridge, MA and London: MIT Press, 1992) 132.

13 Deleuze and Guattari, *A Thousand Plateaus* 260.

14 Deleuze and Guattari, *A Thousand Plateaus* 154.

15 Deleuze and Guattari, *A Thousand Plateaus* 276.

16 Ronald Bogue, *Deleuze and Guattari* (London and New York: Routledge, 1989) 91.

17 A neologism coined by Bogue 'to refer to their collaboratively developed ideas' (9).

18 Bogue 93. They are quoting Deleuze and Guattari's *Anti-Oedipus*.

19 Another digression would trace the presence in Farrell's work of elements relating to Virilio's three phases of civilization, the hunt for the animal, the hunt for the woman, followed by the domestication of the woman which leads to the homosexual hunt of war. See the discussion of Virilio by Thomas Docherty in the introduction to *Postmodernism: A Reader* 20.

20 Deleuze and Guattari, *A Thousand Plateaus* 123.

21 William Shakespeare, *Hamlet*, 3.1.128.

22 Ms. 9142/85, Papers of James Gordon Farrell.

23 Ms. 9147/1, Papers of James Gordon Farrell.

24 Ms. 9136/409, Papers of James Gordon Farrell.

25 Ms. 9140/150–51, Papers of James Gordon Farrell.

26 Binns, *J.G. Farrell*, 78.
27 Bogue 71.
28 Drabble 186–87.
29 Ms. 9140/389, Papers of James Gordon Farrell.
30 Dean, 'A Personal Memoir' 197.
31 Ms. 9140/389, Papers of James Gordon Farrell.
32 Ms. 9140/390, Papers of James Gordon Farrell.
33 Ms. 9140/465–66, Papers of James Gordon Farrell.
34 See W.B. Yeats, 'Sailing to Byzantium' (first published in 1928), lines 21–24:

> Consume my heart away; sick with desire
> And fastened to a dying animal
> It knows not what it is; and gather me
> Into the artifice of eternity.

The Collected Poems of W.B. Yeats, def. ed. (New York: Macmillan, 1956) 191–92.
35 Cited in Chantal Mouffe, 'Radical Democracy: Modern or Postmodern?', *Universal Abandon? The Politics of Postmodernism*, ed Andrew Ross (Minneapolis: U of Minnesota P, 198) 37.

Bibliography

This bibliography is divided into three section. It includes only those works which have either been mentioned in the book, or were essential to its composition. The first section lists works by J.G. Farrell; the second lists biographical and critical works on Farrell; and the third collects all other material not directly related to Farrell. A full bibliography has not been attempted here. For a more comprehensive bibliography of Farrell's work see Ralph J. Crane, 'J.G. Farrell: An Annotated Bibliography', *Éire-Ireland* 28.1 (1993): 132–48.

WORKS BY J.G. FARRELL

Novels

A Man from Elsewhere. London: New Authors, 1963.
The Lung. London: Hutchinson, 1965.
A Girl in the Head. London: Jonathan Cape, 1967.
Troubles. 1970; London: Flamingo, 1984.
The Siege of Krishnapur. 1973; London: Flamingo, 1985.
The Singapore Grip. 1978; London: Flamingo, 1984.
The Hill Station: an unfinished novel and an Indian Diary. 1981; London: Flamingo, 1987.

Short Story

'The Pussycat Who Fell in Love with the Suitcase'. *Atlantis* 6 (1973–74): 6–10.

Non-Fiction

'J. G. Farrell Comments'. *Contemporary Novelists*. Ed. James Vinson. 1st ed. London: St James Press, 1970. 399.
'Miller's Tale'. Rev. of *Witchcraft at Salem*, by Chadwick Hansen. *Spectator* 7 Mar. 1970: 310.
'Under the Seat'. Rev. of *Jack B. Yeats*, by Hilary Pyle. *Spectator* 6 June 1970: 748–9.
'The Army Game'. Rev. of *The I.R.A.*, by Tim Pat Coogan. *Spectator* 18 July 1970: 44–5.
'Girls and Boys'. Rev. of *Hind's Kidnap*, by Joseph McElroy, *The Rape of Tamar*, by Dan Jacobson, *Godded and Codded*, by Julia O'Faolain, and *A Start in Life*, by Alan Sillitoe. *Spectator* 10 Oct. 1970: 407.
'Late Lowry'. Rev. of *Malcolm Lowry: His Art and Early Life*, by M.C. Bradbrook. *New Statesman* 19 July 1974: 87–8.
'Indian Identities'. Rev. of *A Division of the Spoils* by Paul Scott. *Times Literary Supplement* 23 May 1975: 555.

'Complicated Tales'. Rev. of *Rudyard Kipling*, by Lord Birkenhead, and *Rudyard Kipling: His Life and Work*, by Charles Carrington. *Guardian* 5 Oct. 1978: 14.

Manuscript Material

Papers of James Gordon Farrell (1935–1979). Mss. 9128–60. Trinity College Dublin.

BIOGRAPHICAL AND CRITICAL WORKS ON J.G. FARRELL

Allen, Brigid. 'A Feline Friend: Memories of J.G. Farrell (1935–1979)'. *London Magazine* Apr.-May 1992: 64–75.

Bergonzi, Bernard. 'Fictions of History'. *The Situation of the Novel*. 2nd ed. London: Macmillan, 1979. 214–37.

Binns, Ronald. 'The Novelist as Historian'. *Critical Quarterly* 21.2 (1979): 70–72.

————— *J. G. Farrell*. London: Methuen, 1986.

Bowen, Elizabeth. 'Ireland Agonistes'. Rev. of *Troubles*, by J.G. Farrell. *Europa* 1 (1971): 58–9.

Bristow-Smith, Laurence. '"Tomorrow is Another Day": The Essential J. G. Farrell'. *Critical Quarterly* 25.2 (1983): 45–52.

————— 'Expandable Architecture'. *Peake Studies* 1.1 (1988): 27–30.

Brock, Gordon. 'Epitaph for Empire'. *Observer Magazine* 24 Sept. 1978: 73+.

Dean, Malcolm. 'An Insight Job'. *Guardian* 1 Sept. 1973: 11.

————— 'Grip of Empire'. *Guardian* 13 Sept. 1978: 10.

————— 'A Personal Memoir'. *The Hill Station*. By J.G. Farrell. 1981. London: Flamingo, 1987. 192–205.

Drabble, Margaret. 'Things Fall Apart'. *The Hill Station*. By J.G. Farrell. 1981. London: Flamingo, 1987. 178–91.

Ferns, Chris. 'Building a Country; Losing an Empire: The Historical Fiction of Thomas Raddall and J.G. Farrell'. *Time and Place: The Life and Works of Thomas Raddall*. Ed. Alan R. Young. Fredericton, NB: Acadiensis, 1991. 154–64.

Furbank, P. N. 'Between Past and Present'. Rev. of *The Hill Station*, by J.G. Farrell. *Times Literary Supplement* 22 May 1981: 563.

Green, Benny. 'J. G. Farrell'. *Spectator* 25 Aug. 1979: 20.

Hartveit, Lars. 'The Art of Emplotment: the Mechanism of Amalgamating Fact and Fiction in J.G. Farrell's *The Singapore Grip*'. *Studies in Modern Fiction: Presented to Bent Nordhjem on His 70th Birthday 31 May 1990*. Ed. Eric Jacobsen, Jorgen Eric Nielsen, Bruce Clunies Ross, and James Stewart. Copenhagen: Faculty of Humanities, U of Copenhagen, 1990. 79–100.

————— 'The Carnivalistic Impulse in J.G. Farrell's *Troubles*'. *English Studies* 73.5 (1992): 444–57.

————— 'The Imprint of Recorded Events in the Narrative Form of J.G. Farrell's *The Siege of Krishnapur*'. *English Studies* 74.5 (1993): 451–69.

Kennedy, Maeve. 'Farrell's Unfinished'. Rev. of *The Hill Station*, by J.G. Farrell. *Irish Times* 16 May 1981: 14.

King, Francis. 'The Loner Who Loved Company'. *Sunday Telegraph* 19 Aug. 1979: 14.

Livett, Jennifer. 'Newspapers, War, and Games: History in J.G. Farrell's *Troubles*'. *Irish-Australian Studies: Papers Delivered at the Eighth Irish Australian Conference, Hobart July 1995*. Ed. Richard Davis, Jennifer Livett, Anne-Maree Whitaker, and Peter Moore. Sydney: Crossing Press, 1996. 103–12.

McEwan, Neil. 'J.G. Farrell: Empire Trilogy'. *Perspective in British Historical Fiction Today*. Wolfeboro, NH: Longwood Academic, 1987. 124–58.

McLeod, John. 'Exhibiting Empire in J.G. Farrell's *The Siege of Krishnapur*'. *Journal of Commonwealth Literature* 29.2 (1994): 117–32.

Mahon, Derek. 'J. G. Farrell 1935–1979'. *New Statesman* 31 Aug. 1979: 313.

Moorehead, Caroline. 'Writing in the Dark, and Not a Detail Missed'. *The Times* 9 Sept. 1978: 12.

Rignall, J.M. 'Walter Scott, J.G. Farrell, and Fictions of Empire'. *Essays in Criticism* 41 (1991): 11–27.

Scanlan, Margaret. 'Rumours of War: Elizabeth Bowen's *Last September* and J.G. Farrell's *Troubles*'. *Éire-Ireland* 20.2 (1985): 70–89.

Singh, Frances B. 'Progress and History in J.G. Farrell's *The Siege of Krishnapur*'. *Chandrabhaga* 2 (1979): 23–29.

Spurling, John. 'Jim Farrell: A Memoir'. *The Times* 11 Apr. 1981: 6.

——— 'As Does the Bishop'. *The Hill Station*. By J.G. Farrell. 1981. London: Flamingo, 1987. 155–77.

Sullivan, Mary. 'And Now Unlucky Jake'. Rev. of *The Singapore Grip*, by J.G. Farrell. *Sunday Telegraph* 17 Sept. 1978: 12.

Theroux, Paul. 'An Interrupted Journey'. Rev. of *The Hill Station*, by J.G. Farrell. *Sunday Times* 26 Apr. 1981: 42.

Unsigned. 'Mr J.G. Farrell', *The Times* 16 Nov. 1979: iv.

Williams, R.J.P. 'Presenting the Raj: The Politics of Representation in Recent Fiction on the British Empire'. Diss. U of Nottingham, 1988.

Winnifrith, T. 'J.G. Farrell'. *Dictionary of Literary Biography*. Vol. 14. 288–91.

WORKS NOT DIRECTLY RELATED TO J.G. FARRELL

Alexander, Marguerite. *Flights from Realism: Themes and Strategies in Postmodern British and American Fiction*. London: Edward Arnold, 1990.

Althusser, Louis. 'Ideology and Ideological State Apparatuses (Notes towards an Investigation)'. *Lenin and Philosophy, and Other Essays*. Trans. Ben Brewster. London: New Left Books, 1971. 123–73.

Anders, Günter. 'Being without Time: On Beckett's Play *Waiting for Godot*'. *Samuel Beckett: A Collection of Critical Essays*. Ed. Martin Esslin. Englewood Cliffs, NJ: Prentice-Hall, 1965. 140–51.

Arnold, Matthew. *A French Eton*. 1864. London: Macmillan, 1892.

Ashcroft, Bill, Gareth Griffiths, and Helen Tiffin. *The Empire Writes Back: Theory and Practice in Post-Colonial Literatures*. London and New York: Routledge, 1989.

Auden, W.H. *Selected Poems*. Ed. Edward Mendelson. London: Faber, 1979.

Austen, Jane. *Pride and Prejudice*. 1813. London: Penguin, 1981.

―――― *Mansfield Park*. 1814. London: Penguin, 1977.

Bakhtin, Mikhail. *The Dialogic Imagination: Four Essays*. Ed. Michael Holquist. Trans. Caryl Emerson and Michael Holquist. Austin: U of Texas P, 1981.

Barnes, Julian. *Flaubert's Parrot*. 1984. London: Picador, 1985.

Barthes, Roland. 'The Death of the Author'. 1968. Trans. Stephen Heath. *Modern Criticism and Theory: A Reader*. Ed. David Lodge. London and New York: Longman, 1988. 167–72.

Bate, Walter Jackson. *The Burden of the Past and the English Poet*. Cambridge: Harvard UP, 1970.

Baum, Frank L. *The Wizard of Oz*. 1900. New York: Tom Doherty Associates, 1993.

Beckett, Samuel. *Three Novels by Samuel Beckett: Molloy, Malone Dies, The Unnamable*. 1955–58. New York: Grove Press, 1981.

―――― *Happy Days*. 1961. London: Faber, 1966.

Bellow, Saul. *Seize the Day*. London: Weidenfeld and Nicolson, 1957.

―――― *Henderson the Rain King*. 1959. London: Penguin, 1966.

―――― *Herzog*. 1964. London: Penguin, 1965.

Bennett, Tony. *Formalism and Marxism*. London and New York: Routledge, 1979.

Bergonzi, Bernard. *The Situation of the Novel*. 2nd ed. London: Macmillan, 1979.

Bhabha, Homi. *The Location of Culture*. London: Routledge, 1994.

Bloom, Harold. *The Anxiety of Influence: A Theory of Poetry*. New York: Oxford UP, 1973.

―――― *A Map of Misreading*. New York: Oxford UP, 1975.

Bogue, Ronald. *Deleuze and Guattari*. London and New York: Routledge, 1989.

Bowen, Elizabeth. *The Last September*. 1929. London: Jonathan Cape, 1948.

Bradbury, Malcolm, and David Palmer, eds. *The Contemporary English Novel*. Stratford-upon-Avon Studies 18. London: Edward Arnold, 1979.

Bradbury, Malcolm. *No, Not Bloomsbury*. London: Arena, 1989.

―――― *The Modern British Novel*. 1993. London: Penguin, 1994.

Burgess, Anthony. *The Long Day Wanes: A Malayan Trilogy*. 1956–59. London: Penguin, 1987.

Burrell, Clea. 'The Condition of England Novel – "Between Journalism and Literature"?' Unpublished.

Camus, Albert. *The Outsider*. 1942. London: Penguin, 1983.

―――― *The Plague*. 1947. London: Hamish Hamilton, 1948.

Carroll, Lewis. *Alice's Adventures in Wonderland*. 1865. London: Macmillan, 1929.

―――― *Through the Looking Glass*. 1871. London: Macmillan, 1929.

Cervantes, Miguel de. *Don Quixote*. 1605 and 1615. London: Penguin, 1950.

Clayton, Jay, and Eric Rothstein. 'Figures in the Corpus: Theories of Influence and Intertextuality'. *Influence and Intertextuality in Literary History*. Ed. Jay Clayton and Eric Rothstein. Madison and London: U of Wisconsin P, 1991. 3–36.

Conrad, Joseph. *Heart of Darkness*. 1899. London: Penguin, 1984.

Crane, Ralph J. *Inventing India: A History of India in English-Language Fiction*. London: Macmillan, 1992.

Darville [Demidenko], Helen. *The Hand That Signed the Paper*. St Leonards, NSW: Allen and Unwin, 1994.

Deleuze, Gilles, and Félix Guattari. *Capitalism and Schizophrenia*. Vol. 1. *Anti-Oedipus*. Trans. Robert Hurley, Mark Seem, and Helen R. Lane. New York: Viking, 1977.
—— *Capitalism and Schizophrenia*. Vol. 2. *A Thousand Plateaus*. Trans. Brian Massumi. Minneapolis and London: U of Minnesota P, 1987.
de Man, Paul. *The Resistance to Theory*. Manchester: Manchester UP. 1986.
Denzin, Norman K. *Images of Postmodern Society: Social Theory and Contemporary Cinema*. London: Thousand Oaks, and New Delhi: Sage Publications, 1994.
Dickens, Charles. *Hard Times*. 1854. London: Penguin, 1977.
—— *A Tale of Two Cities*. 1859. London: Oxford UP, 1949.
—— *The Mystery of Edwin Drood*. 1870. Oxford: Oxford UP, 1982.
Docherty, Thomas, ed. and introd. *Postmodernism: A Reader*. London and New York: Harvester Wheatsheaf, 1992.
Dos Passos, John. *U.S.A.* 1930–36. London, Penguin, 1978.
Drabble, Margaret. *The Millstone*. London: Weidenfeld and Nicolson, 1965.
Durrell, Lawrence. *The Alexandria Quartet*. 1957–60. London: Faber, 1986.
Eagleton, Terry. *Marxism and Literary Criticism*. London: Methuen, 1976.
Eliot, T.S. *The Waste Land and Other Poems* 1940. London: Faber, 1972.
Findley, Timothy. *Famous Last Words*. 1981. London: Penguin, 1982.
Flaubert, Gustave. *Three Tales*. 1877. London: Penguin, 1961.
Forster, E.M. *Howard's End*. 1910. London; Arnold, 1947.
—— *A Passage to India*. 1924. London: Penguin, 1979.
—— *Aspects of the Novel*. 1927. London: Pelican, 1966.
Fowles, John. *The Magus*. 1966. Rev. ed. 1977. London: Granada, 1983.
—— *The French Lieutenant's Woman*. 1969. London: Granada, 1979.
Friedman, Susan Stanford. 'Weavings: Intertextuality and the (Re)Birth of the Author'. *Influence and Intertextuality in Literary History*. Ed. Jay Clayton and Eric Rothstein. Madison and London: U of Wisconsin P, 1991. 146–80.
Golding, William. *Lord of the Flies*. London: Faber, 1954.
—— *The Hot Gates and other occasional pieces*. London: Faber, 1965.
Gooneratne, Yasmine. 'Paul Scott's *Staying On*: Finale in a Minor Key'. *Journal of Indian Writing in English* 9.2 (1982): 1–12.
Green, Martin. *Dreams of Adventure, Deeds of Empire*. New York: Basic Books, 1979.
—— *The English Novel in the Twentieth Century: The Doom of Empire*. London: Routledge and Kegan Paul, 1984.
Grosz, Elizabeth. *Sexual Subversions: Three French Feminists*. Sydney: Allen & Unwin, 1989.
Hardy, Thomas. *Far from the Madding Crowd*. 1874. London: Macmillan, 1974.
Hughes, Richard. *A High Wind in Jamaica*. London: Chatto and Windus, 1929.
—— *In Hazard*. London: Chatto and Windus, 1938.
—— *The Fox in the Attic*. London: Chatto and Windus, 1961.
Hutcheon, Linda. *A Poetics of Postmodernism: History, Theory, Fiction*. New York and London: Routledge, 1988.
—— *The Politics of Postmodernism*. London and New York Routledge, 1989.
Jameson, Fredric. 'Periodizing the 60s'. *The 60s without Apology*. Ed. Sohnya Sayres, Anders Stephanson, Stanley Aronowitz, and Fredric Jameson. Minneapolis: *Social Text* and U of Minnesota P, 1984.

Jameson, Fredric. 'Postmodernism or the Cultural Logic of Late Capitalism'. *New Left Review* 146 (1884): 53–92.

——— 'Third-World Literature in the Era of Multinational Capitalism'. *Social Text* 15 (1986): 65–88.

Kenner, Hugh. 'The Cartesian Centaur'. *Samuel Beckett: A Critical Study*. 1961. New ed. 1968. Berkeley and Los Angeles: U of California P, 1973. 117–32.

Kermode, Frank. *The Sense of an Ending: Studies in the Theory of Fiction*. 1967. Oxford: Oxford UP, 1968.

Kipling, Rudyard. *Kim*. 1901. London: Macmillan, 1985.

——— *Just So Stories: for little children*. 1902. London: Pan, 1975.

Landry, Donna, and Gerald MacLean. *Materialist Feminisms*. Cambridge, MA: Blackwell, 1993.

Lodge, David. *The British Museum is Falling Down*. 1965. London: Penguin, 1983.

——— *The Novelist at the Crossroads and other Essays on Fiction and Criticism*. London: Routledge, 1971.

Lowry, Malcolm. *Under the Volcano*. 1947. London: Penguin, 1984.

Lukács, Georg. *The Historical Novel*. Trans. Hannah and Stanley Mitchell. London: Merlin Press, 1962.

McHale, Brian. *Postmodernist Fiction*. New York and London: Methuen, 1987.

Mann, Thomas. *The Magic Mountain*. 1924. London: Secker and Warburg, 1945.

Massumi, Brian. *A User's Guide to* Capitalism and Schizophrenia: *Deviations from Deleuze and Gauttari*. Cambridge, MA and London: MIT Press, 1992.

Meyers, Jeffrey. *Disease and the Novel*, 1880–1960. New York: St Martin's Press, 1985.

Mitchell, Margaret. *Gone with the Wind*. New York: Macmillan, 1936.

Morris, James. *Pax Britannica; The Climax of an Empire*. London: Faber, 1968.

Mouffe, Chantal. 'Radical Democracy: Modern or Postmodern?' *Universal Abandon? The Politics of Postmodernism*. Ed. Andrew Ross. Minneapolis: U of Minnesota P, 1988. 31–45.

Murdoch, Iris. *The Red and the Green*. 1965. London: Penguin, 1988.

Musil, Robert. *The Man without Qualities*. 1930–32. London: Secker and Warburg, 1979.

Myers, L.H. *The Near and the Far*. 1929–40. London: Cape, 1943.

Nabokov, Vladamir. *Lolita*. 1955. London: Penguin, 1983.

O'Casey, Sean. *The Plough and the Stars*. 1926. London: Macmillan, 1957.

Ondaatje, Michael. *Running in the Family*. 1982. London: Picador, 1984.

Osborne, John. *Look Back in Anger*. 1957. London: Faber, 1973.

Peake, Mervyn. *Titus Groan*. 1946. London: Penguin, 1975.

——— *Gormenghast*. 1950. London: Penguin, 1974.

——— *Titus Alone*. 1950. Rev. ed. 1970. London: Penguin, 1974.

Pynchon, Thomas. *The Crying of Lot* 49. Philadelphia: Lippincott, 1966.

Rajan, Tilottama. 'Intertextuality and the Subject of Reading/Writing'. *Influence and Intertextuality in Literary History*. Ed. Jay Clayton and Eric Rothstein. Madison and London: U of Wisconsin P, 1991. 61–74.

Robbe-Grillet. *Jealousy*. 1957. London: John Calder, 1977.

Rushdie, Salman. *Midnight's Children*. 1981. London: Picador, 1982.

Rushdie, Salman. Introduction. *On Writing and Politics, 1967–1983*. By Günter Grass. Trans. Ralph Manheim. 1985. London: Penguin, 1987.

Schaub, Thomas. 'Allusion and Intertext: History in *The End of the Road*'. *Influence and Intertextuality in Literary History*. Ed. Jay Clayton and Eric Rothstein. Madison and London: U of Wisconsin P, 1991. 181–203.

Scott, Paul. *The Jewel in the Crown*. 1966. London: Granada, 1980.

—— *The Day of the Scorpion*. 1968. London: Granada, 1979.

—— *The Towers of Silence*. 1971. London: Granada, 1979.

—— *A Division of the Spoils*. 1975. London: Granada, 1979.

—— *Staying On*. 1977. London: Granada, 1978.

Scott, Sir Walter. *Waverley*. 1814. Oxford: Oxford UP, 1986.

Selden, Raman, and Peter Widdowson. *A Reader's Guide to Contemporary Literary Theory*. 3rd ed. New York and London: Harvester Wheatsheaf, 1993.

Shakespeare, William. *Hamlet*. London: Penguin, 1980.

—— *Henry V*. London: Penguin, 1968.

—— *Romeo and Juliet*. London: Penguin, 1977.

Somerville, E.OE, and Martin Ross. *The Irish R.M. Complete*. 1928. London: Faber, 1968.

Singh, Shailendra Dhari. *Novels on the Indian Mutiny*. New Delhi: Arnold-Heinemann, 1973.

Spark, Muriel, *The Prime of Miss Jean Brodie*. 1961. London: Penguin, 1978.

Spivak, Gayatri Chakravorty. 'Three Women's Texts and a Critique of Imperialism'. *'Race', Writing, and Difference*. Ed. Henry Louis Gates, Jr. Chicago and London: U of Chicago P, 1986. 262–80.

Stevenson, Randall. *The British Novel since the Thirties*. London: Batsford, 1986.

Suleri, Sara. *The Rhetoric of English India*. Chicago: U of Chicago P, 1992.

Swinden, Patrick. *The English Novel of History and Society, 1940–80*. London and Basingstoke: Macmillan, 1984.

Tennyson, Alfred Lord. *Poems and Plays*. Ed. T. Herbert Warren. Rev. Frederick Page. 1953. Oxford: Oxford UP, 1971.

Thackeray, William. *Vanity Fair*. 1848. London: Penguin, 1980.

Thomas, Dylan. *Under Milk Wood*. 1954. London: Everyman, 1977.

Unsigned. 'The Indian Mutiny in Fiction'. *Blackwood's Edinburgh Magazine* Feb. 1897: 218–31.

Williams, Raymond. *Culture and Society 1780–1950*. 1958. London: Penguin, 1971.

—— *The Long Revolution*. 1961. London: Penguin, 1980.

Webster, John. *The White Devil*. London: A & C Black, 1983.

Wilson, Colin. *The Outsider*. 1956. London: Pan, 1963.

Woodruff, Philip. *The Men Who Ruled India*. Vol. 1. *The Founders*. London: Jonathan Cape, 1953.

Yeats, W.B. *The Collected Poems of W.B. Yeats*. Def. ed. New York: Macmillan, 1956.

Index